QUEEN
ALBUM BY ALBUM

QUEEN
ALBUM BY ALBUM

MARTIN POPOFF

WITH CHRIS CAFFERY, RALPH CHAPMAN

STEPHEN DALTON, DAVE ELLEFSON, JIM JENKINS

HANSI KÜRSCH, REINHOLD MACK

ROGER MANNING JR., SIR PAUL MCCARTNEY

IAN MOSLEY, PATRICK MYERS

DANIEL NESTER, NINA NOIR

JOHN NORUM, DARIUS RUCKER

DEREK SHULMAN, DEE SNIDER

RICHIE UNTERBERGER, AND JEB WRIGHT

VOYAGEUR
PRESS

CONTENTS

INTRODUCTION

Queen. The greatest band to ever walk the earth.

In more than twenty years of having a blast talking and writing about this stuff on radio, magazines, and the internet, I'm pretty sure I've made that argument repeatedly. It's crazy, I know, picking just one band, and someone invariably challenges the claim with the idea that the band that can win an accolade like this must be great start to finish, and that Queen might get knocked down a peg on this point.

Fair enough. But as soon as that happens, I fall back to the following position: Queen is absolutely the greatest band to ever walk this earth, based on a specific and substantial run of albums. Judas Priest, to my mind, comes close with their 1976 to 1979 output, but Queen is clearly the victor. Their remarkable run of seven albums between 1973 and 1978 just might be the greatest hot streak of pure genius in all recorded music. No one in the '60s (let's not have the Beatles talk right now, please), not Led Zeppelin in the '70s, not U2 or R.E.M. in the '80s, not whatever run you might cite from the '90s—none of them can touch the royal hem of Queen as they set about crafting their first seven albums. Bloody 'ell . . . I get heart palpitations just thinking about it.

And then Queen provoked and challenged that legacy, like true fearless artists, challenging their millions of fans to follow them into the unknown. Which we did, with mixed results—delight, revulsion, every emotion on the rainbow—as Queen concluded a catalog of incredible range.

Which is the perfect setup for the explosion in the fireworks factory you're about to read, as an army of dedicated Queen fans and I hack our way through the good, the bad, and the ugly on our way to myriad new ways of understanding what it was Queen was after at the various phases of their career. Together, I think we've created an amusing celebration of all things Queen, couched in a cacophony of enthusiasm that evokes you and your smartest music-fan buddies standing around the kitchen, slowly depleting the fridge of its brews.

Here's hoping that you get out of this book what I most certainly did: a pile of new ways to look at Queen's bewildering bees' nest of styles and songs. What I further appreciate is the way our panel of experts paints pictures of the larger milieu in which Queen was operating at any given time. I find helpful and endearing the personal stories about initial reactions to the records, as well as the many ways our speakers compare Queen to other bands. These personal anecdotes helped me feel closer to the albums and the larger Queen community. I took great comfort in the fact that the impact of these songs was being felt simultaneously around the world by millions of passionate music fans like me. My communion with many of those fans was the greatest joy in compiling this book.

So, without further ado, let's hack into the thick of *Queen: Album by Album* and the intense, sometimes controversial, opinions of a cast of Queen fans from many walks of life. I hope the Queen album that is the love of your life emerges unscathed—and that if it doesn't, you are good-humored and open-minded enough to accept into your heart the judgements of our cast. Like you, they are here because they care so damn much.

DISCOGRAPHIC NOTES
A FEW NOTES ON THE PRESENTATION OF THE ALBUM CREDITS:

Credits and citations of all types, where available, are reproduced in the spirit of the first UK issue of each album.

Song times are cited per the earliest issue of the album. If not available on UK issue, as was the standard, I went next to the US and then the Canadian issue from the same year. Failing that, I went with either the German, Japanese, or CD issue.

Performance credits are presented as close to the spirit of the first issue as possible, rationalizing scattered locations of credits and stripping out redundancies and jokes. And so they are slightly edited, perhaps simplified (for example, leaving out designations pointing to performances on specific tracks).

Writing credits cited on record center labels take precedence over back cover credits (to add a level of detail beyond the curious full-band credit on the packaging from time to time).

Side 1/Side 2 designations are used for vinyl-era releases; straight-through track-sequence numbers are used for the two CD-era albums, *Innuendo* and *Made in Heaven*.

In the interest of neatness, song titles are not in double quotes in the chapter-opening sidebars (as they are in the interviews).

Obvious typos in album credits have been fixed without the use of "[*sic*]." Other liberties were made, decisions taken, when the situation required.

RELEASED JULY 13, 1973

1 QUEEN
WITH DEREK SHULMAN, DEE SNIDER, AND RICHIE UNTERBERGER

SIDE 1

1. **Keep Yourself Alive** 3:42
(MAY)

2. **Doing All Right** 4:11
(MAY, TIM STAFFELL)

3. **Great King Rat** 5:42
(MERCURY)

4. **My Fairy King** 4:06
(MERCURY)

SIDE 2

1. **Liar** 6:25
(MERCURY)

2. **The Night Comes Down** 4:24
(MAY)

3. **Modern Times Rock 'n' Roll** 1:49
(TAYLOR)

4. **Son and Daughter** 3:22
(MAY)

5. **Jesus** 3:45
(MERCURY)

6. **Seven Seas of Rhye** 1:15
(MERCURY)

PERSONNEL:

FREDDIE MERCURY – *vocals, piano;*
BRIAN MAY – *guitars, piano, vocals;*
JOHN DEACON – *bass guitar;*
ROGER MEDDOWS-TAYLOR
– *percussion, vocals*
Recorded at TRIDENT STUDIOS *and*
DE LANE LEA STUDIOS, *London*
Produced by JOHN ANTHONY,
ROY BAKER, *and* QUEEN

OPPOSITE: Queen rehearses for their first major tour, opening for Mott the Hoople.

The path to Queen's monumental first album was traveled swiftly and with flair. A brief review of the facts is in order.

In 1968, with their eyes on promising futures, Brian May had completed an honors-level Bachelor of Science in Physics, and Roger Taylor had switched from dentistry to biology, also completing a BSc.

Meanwhile, Farrokh "Freddie Mercury" Bulsara's pathway to rock 'n' roll royalty was a bit more colorful. Born in present-day Tanzania, Freddie spent much of his childhood in India before the family returned to Africa. Eventually, however, the family fled the Zanzibar Revolution to Britain, where Freddie obtained an art and graphic design diploma and set about making a go of it in music, singing with the likes of Wreckage and the unfortunately named Sour Milk Tea.

Around the same time, Brian, Roger, and a bassist/vocalist named Tim Staffell saw some promise as Smile, recording a couple of demos before Staffell was off to join folkies Humpy Bong. Freddie convinced Brian and Roger not to give up, and the three convened as Queen, with Bulsara (soon to become Freddie Mercury) inspired by a line from the band's soon-to-be-classic "My

Fairy King." After running through several bassists, the band played their first gig on July 18, 1970, before John Deacon (with a degree in electronics) auditioned for the band at a lecture room at Imperial College. He entered the Queen fold in February 1971, cementing the band's classic lineup, which played their first show on July 2, 1971.

While on the path to their remarkable first album, Queen served as somewhat of a test band for London's De Lane Lea Studios, an arrangement that benefited them in the form of an uncommonly professional demo session. Signing on with Norman Sheffield and his brother Barry, who ran Trident Studios, boosted the band's reputation as studio specialists and essentially provided free hours of otherwise expensive studio time. Although the band had to toil during off-hours, the arrangement resulted in the *Queen* record, issued on Trident-associated EMI in summer 1973 after months of shopping it.

Labels that passed missed out on what is considered one of the great debut records of all time. At the ballad end of the spectrum, "Doing All Right" had roots in Smile, and a '60s psychedelic, folk, and even blues vibe was apparent. But "The Night Comes Down" proved Queen's ability to write rich and unusual melodies and turn on a dime into prog and nascent heavy metal. What's more, demonstrating the strength of the De Lane Lea sessions, the band opted for that earlier version of this classic for the final record.

But more than anything, *Queen* is an album of flash, thespian, prog metal before the term "heavy metal" was even in play. Throughout, Queen touched upon various tropes, tendencies, and tempos of early metal, applying a sense of gravitas consistent with the band members' and the regal air of their band name.

But the rich banquet of dishes the band brought to their first feast would shortly prove too varied for a society in love with fast food, and *Queen* would be passed over, as, indeed, would the band's even fussier follow-up.

But years on, "Liar" and "Keep Yourself Alive," nowhere near hits in their day, would become, arguably, two of the top dozen most beloved chestnuts of the band's extensive oeuvre, go-to classic-rock radio staples whenever a bracing blast of Brian May is needed to wake up those stuck in rush hour traffic.

Despite its monumental significance, *Queen* has so far only been certified gold in both the US and UK, demonstrating the almighty importance of a hit single to the success of an album. Still, the band's debut lives on in the hearts and minds of Queen fans who revel in the record's exploration of plush dynamics, from classical and folk flights of fancy to the most crushing of power-chorded heavy metal.

In its sense of purpose, *Queen* is representative of any act's first record—a canvas on which the paint is applied feverishly and thickly. As the band evolved, they learned where to let in more light; but as a first statement, *Queen* remains a bold demonstration of density, almost unparalleled among debut records.

POPOFF: To kick things off, take me back to 1973. This band Queen shows up. What kind of impression did they make?

SNIDER: Well, okay, here's a day-one Queen fan story for you [*laughs*]. I majored in communications and was on college break and got a job wiring computers. Back then it wasn't some sort of brilliant thing; you actually wrapped copper wire around coils in a pattern and you would sit there listening to the radio all day, passing boring time, because I'm gonna be a rock star and I don't know what I'm doing in college anyway. I dropped out shortly after.

And on the radio—Jonathan Schwartz, WNEW—each Friday they'd do "Things from England." And this song comes on, and it's "Liar." I can't identify the band. I'm a Zeppelin

TREGYE FESTIVAL OF CONTEMPORARY MUSIC
UNDERCOVER TREGYE COUNTRY CLUB CARNON DOWNS, TRURO. UNDERCOVER
MID-DAY — MIDNIGHT
21st AUGUST 1971
WITH
• ARTHUR BROWN'S KINGDOM COME
• HAWKWIND
• DUSTER BENNETT BAND
• Tea & Symphony
• BREWER'S DROOP
• Indian Summer
• GRAPHITE
• QUEEN
• Barracuda
SOUNDS BY GERRY GILL — LIGHTS BY JOHN LUMLEY-SAVILE
£1·00 in advance from
MOJO MANAGEMENT 37 HARCOURT ST NEWARK· NOTTS
£1·25 on the day
FOOD·FREAKS·LICENSED BAR · LOVELY THINGS

ABOVE: First reported flyer for a Queen gig, Carnon Downs Festival, Truro, UK, August 21, 1971. OPPOSITE: The classic Queen lineup was codified when bassist John Deacon (center) entered the fold in February 1971.

fan, I'm a Yes fan. I had a very pure clean voice and those were the inspirations, until I burned it out singing Alice Cooper songs. And I'm just sitting there—I literally stopped working—going, "This is incredible, who's this band?! Who is singing? Is this Jon Anderson, Robert Plant?"

And when it's over Jonathan Schwartz goes, "Things from England, that's a new band called Queen." That's when I start becoming a Queen freak. As a huge Sabbath fan, I loved it. This was one of the things that people didn't realize for years—in the earliest interviews, Brian May talked about being a Black Sabbath fan, and the album connected with me because they ripped off so much from Sabbath, especially on something like "Son and Daughter."

I was a classically trained counter tenor as well as a rock singer, so my respect for tenor voices, and pure tenor voices like Freddie's, with that clarity and that purity on top of that heavy music was just amazing. Like I say, when I joined Twisted Sister, I got in the band because I did a perfect Robert Plant impersonation, which was gold in the bar days. But after six months of singing in bars, I burned my voice out and I got a career. I got this husky voice and could no longer sing that stuff, but I could still appreciate it.

Which brings us to seeing them live. This is May '74, so *Queen II* had just come out. They are opening for Mott the Hoople, and I'm a big Mott the Hoople fan. Mott was doing five nights at the Uris Theatre on Broadway. And nobody knew Queen. I knew Queen. And I remember sitting in the balcony, Queen comes out, dressed all in white with their choir robe tops, and you know, Freddie with the chain mail glovelet on his hand and the half mic stand, long hair, buckteeth you can see from the back of the room, no moustache. And they open with "Procession," the intro music to "Father to Son."

I am losing my mind. I'm the only person in the theater screaming. I mean, the *only* person. I am on my feet from song one and I am just losing it. I'm wearing platform shoes, with this big brown afro. I'm skinny as a toothpick. I hadn't discovered bodybuilding. I'm just this rail-thin, glittered-out monstrosity in the balcony. The only thing worse than nobody

reacting when you go to a show is one person reacting. It's like, if you get no tip, it's like, well, maybe they forgot. But if they put a penny on the table, there's no way they forgot, they're saying "Fuck you."

So, I'm just screaming so loud, my friends are begging me to please stop. It's embarrassing. Brian May looks up at one point to see what the commotion is. He looks right at me, one tall moustachioed afro, parted in the middle, pencil-thin lunatic Queen freak in the balcony screaming with every song. It was incredible. And I'll tell you, if you ever hear any of those early Queen tapes of some of those early concerts—and they are out there, these great radio bootlegs—their vocals were on, they were on, it was just amazing. And nobody appreciated it at that point.

POPOFF: Love it. Derek, you were introduced to Queen in a completely different way.

SHULMAN: Yes, our band, Gentle Giant, were in the same studio at the very same time when we were doing our first record, with Tony Visconti. And we were taking three-hour turns, and I'm not sure who was producing Queen at the time. This might have been their first demo session. Roy Baker was maybe the engineer, I'm not sure. But he was our tape op at that time, so we would see them coming in and out, in Wardour Street, and we kind of got friendly with them. But funny enough, in all the years that followed, we never played with Queen, as a group.

POPOFF: What were your first impressions? Did it look like they had something special?

SHULMAN: Actually, yes. They were very different from what we had, of course. But there was something about them that intrigued us. They were fairly . . . I hate to use the word, *intelligent* [*laughs*], but they had sort of an education that was slightly above the regular, rather than "We're gonna rock 'n' roll and take drugs et cetera." They seemed a little more articulate, quite smart, and they were adept and appeared to know where they were going. And obviously they did, because, as we all know, they became massive.

POPOFF: Did you consider them part of the prog or glam scene?

SHULMAN: That's the interesting part about this band. They were kind of prog, but they were also very pop, and of course with Freddie, they had an incredible front man. So, they crossed all sorts of borders. The glam scene was happening, the Bowie thing. At the very same time we were recording our first record, Tony was producing *The Man Who Sold the World*. But Queen were able to transcend glam, prog, rock—they took in everything. They were very different in the way they presented themselves. They made simple songs sound—how can I put this?— very complicated, and complicated songs sound simple.

POPOFF: Richie, for you, where does the *Queen* album fit within the tenor of the times?

UNTERBERGER: It's a strange record because there are a lot of collisions of influences. For starters, Queen seem to be lumped in somewhat with glam, in the United States, anyway. There were rough similarities to some of the other groups that were getting attention in the US, like David Bowie and T. Rex, or even some of the more singles-oriented bands like Sweet and really obscure ones to Americans like Hello and Mud.

But clearly there was more sophistication—not more than Bowie, but more than the average glam act. There are elements of real hard rock and there's also classical music influence,

OPPOSITE: Backstage with Ian Hunter of Mott the Hoople (rear center), Hunter's wife Trudi (front center), and producer Roy Thomas Baker (far right).

which is maybe secondhand as filtered through art rock. But like later Queen albums, there is some sense that from track to track you're getting almost a different band. There are also elements that can be traced to the late 1960s, with the really dense vocal harmonies, similar to *Abbey Road* but given, like, this helium sheen.

At the hard rock end, some of the guitars are crunching, but some have a real sustained, soaring sound. There were comparisons to Led Zeppelin when Queen were circulating their De Lane Lea tape to companies. Like, "We don't want another Led Zeppelin." Sure, there's a bit of that heavy metal crunch and a histrionic quality to the lead vocals, but I never thought, "Oh, this is another one of those groups trying to sound like Zeppelin."

POPOFF: What else do you know about this ramp-up period to getting the debut record on the shelves?

UNTERBERGER: Like a lot of early '70s groups, they had roots in 1960s British rock and had been in some bands. Where they really started to get something together was getting this demo session in late 1971 at De Lane Lea, where Jimi Hendrix had recorded. They were very fortunate to get studio time at a very good studio. It wasn't Abbey Road or Olympic, but it was pretty good, and they got a bunch of time to work out a very professional recording.

When they came out of the studio, they almost had an album-quality, or half an album-quality release. Most of their peers or managers or agents were shopping around demo tapes that were relatively crude, not exactly homemade but maybe a live-in-the-studio tape that was recorded in a cheap facility. And they had more of a state-of-the-art tape that they could shop around, even though they didn't own a tape player where they could play the tape themselves, which is kind of a funny trivia note.

But the record companies could almost hear the album as it would sound in its finished product. The demo tracks, which are now available as bonus tracks on the deluxe edition, don't sound that different from the final recordings. The guy who signed them for the States, Jac Holzman of Elektra Records, said it was like a diamond landing on his desk. It seemed that refined. He was probably used to getting pitched, even by high-powered managers, demos that sounded kind of unfinished or like they needed more time to write better songs. That really helped them get a deal in the United States with Elektra.

POPOFF: The final product turned out that much better because they essentially signed with a studio, or with the co-owners of a studio.

BELOW: Brian's unusual and superb style could be categorized as "progressive" because it wasn't the norm at the time. Here he performs in the UK in November 1973.

New single 'Keep yourself alive'
EMI 2036

Queen A beautiful first album on
EMC 3006

UNTERBERGER: Yes, and the situation at Trident was such-and-such doesn't need the studio now, come on over. It was like being on pins and needles: "Whenever the studio's available, we gotta get in there and do what we can." But it would've been unaffordable to have a comparable facility otherwise. Also, since you brought up that Trident deal, it was beneficial to them, I think, in the long run, to not sign directly with a label. Other bands have done that, like the Stones in the early years, who were signed to Andrew Loog Oldham. That could make them a little more particular about the record deal that they wanted, because they had the backing of somebody already.

POPOFF: At the heart of this band is this guitarist who, on this record, has a sort of violent, choppy sound, yet it's not exactly heavy metal. How would you articulate who Brian is as a guitarist?

SHULMAN: You're right, Brian's style is very unusual. He's not a whammy bar, power chord kind of guy, and he's not a guitar hero sort of person, playing a million miles an hour on top of an E or B or writing these three-chord riffs, and he's not poppy. He picks at his notes superbly well and very differently. It was progressive because it wasn't the norm.

SNIDER: One aspect is that you have Brian May coming in as a Tony Iommi freak. People don't realize just how significant that is, and I've communicated with Brian but have yet to sit down with him and discuss this, but it's even in his vibrato. Tony Iommi has a weird vibrato because of his plastic fingertips. Brian May's vibrato is imitating Tony Iommi. He's a Sabbath fan. I remember, he stopped saying it after early interviews. And then one day, lo and behold, who's on stage at Wembley Stadium for the Freddie Mercury tribute concert? Tony Iommi playing rhythm guitar with Queen.

POPOFF: When the full Queen album became available, Dee, what did you think of it?

TOP: UK print advert for "Keep Yourself Alive."
ABOVE: US promo copy of "Keep Yourself Alive." Like "Liar," it still stands out for a memorable chorus that serves as a hook.

SNIDER: Well, like I said, it had the influences of so many bands that I loved. And I was a choir geek, and not only did you have this pure, brilliant, almost operatic voice, but he was a rocker, Freddie. There was a range and a sweetness plus the harmonies, but he could really lay into it too when he wanted to be aggressive, all of which you get in that [*sings*] "I want you to be a woman."

And then being a day-one Black Sabbath fan—I was in a Sabbath cover band in high school—hearing that influence mixed with the melodic . . . Brian was bringing it, and being a Zeppelin fan, Roger Meddows-Taylor was very Bonham-esque in his drumming, and on top of everything else, he was beautiful with that incredibly high voice. I was also fan of glitter rock and they were somewhat connected to that as well.

As for the songs, well, "Liar" and "Keep Yourself Alive" are fresh, original, powerful, and they make a left turn where others would make a right. When you think you know where they're going to go, they go someplace else. I was just more drawn to heaviness early on, tracks like "Good King Rat" and "Son and Daughter," which were just metal songs. That really had broad appeal to me. And "Jesus" certainly.

UNTERBERGER: This isn't going to be a surprise or be in opposition to what most of the public would vote for, but the songs that really stand out on the record are the ones that are the most well-known, and certainly the ones that got the most airplay, in the States at least, when I was growing up: "Keep Yourself Alive" and "Liar." And they stand out because they have memorable choruses, which serve as the hooks.

Though Mercury possessed a pure, almost operatic voice, he could really lay into it too when he wanted to be aggressive.

Portuguese, Japanese, and Dutch (opposite) pressings of "Keep Yourself Alive" b/w "Son and Daughter." Written by Brian May before John Deacon joined, the single is in keeping with many anthemic songs that would become Queen trademarks.

The other songs have scope and ambition, but those songs have the input that would attract airplay and keep them remembered for the band's whole career. It took quite a while, up until "Killer Queen," for them to become stars on any level in the US. By '76, '77, a lot of fans went back to the albums they'd missed, and "Keep Yourself Alive" and "Liar," especially, got airplay beyond 1973 and have become perennials.

"Keep Yourself Alive," written by Brian even before John Deacon joined, is in keeping with a lot of the anthemic songs that would become Queen trademarks. You might even draw a link to "We Are the Champions." You know, we will prevail.

"Liar" is a little different, although it's typical of other songs on the first album because it, as I say, shows a collision of influences. A lot of their songs seem to be collations, or maybe some people would prefer the term "suites," where different elements could be entire songs on their own. It's not a really long song, but at six and a half minutes, it's certainly something that wouldn't get played on AM radio. But FM picked up on it. They had the format, at least back then, where they could play some long tracks and that was a good song for the playlist.

POPOFF: At the other end of the spectrum, there's "The Night Comes Down," a lighter track but also one of sophistication.

UNTERBERGER: I have Jac Holzman's book, *Follow the Music*, his autobiography, and before he kind of stepped down from Elektra, which he had founded, Queen was really about the last major act that he signed. And he specifically remembers "Keep Yourself Alive," "Liar," and "The Night Comes Down." Those got his attention when he heard the tapes.

But as far as the song itself, they didn't have the term "power ballad" yet. That's something that really came into vogue, at least among rock critics, in the 1980s. But Queen were kind of an originator of that style where you have a ballad with hard rock elements and not a singer-songwriter type ballad like Harry Chapin or Barry Manilow, in terms of it being a pop ballad. And there's an operatic quality, certainly, to Freddie Mercury's vocals, but also to the construction of a song like this itself. Even if there might not be elements of opera in the lyrics, the structure might suggest opera.

POPOFF: And to swing wildly again, in the spirit of Queen I suppose, there's "Modern Times Rock 'n' Roll." Hard to ignore!

SNIDER: Of course. My post–high school band, the one I was in at the time called Harlequin, three-piece power trio with vocals, we would do a lot of Zeppelin and Montrose. We also did "Modern Times Rock 'n' Roll." It's just such a blazing rocker, and that's Roger Taylor on vocals. But Freddie sang it live. It became a popular song for them. I remember seeing them do it while opening up for Mott, and going, "Freddie's singing?!" It was as if Freddie didn't want any part of that trashy little thing, and then suddenly everyone wanted to hear "Modern Times Rock 'n' Roll" and he was like, "I'll take it from here, Roger" [*laughs*].

POPOFF: A cool thing with Roger, you get the biggest distinction in terms of subject matter when he writes lyrics. Lyrically, Brian, Freddie, and John can be similar, but Roger stands out in this regard.

SNIDER: Yes, and not to mention he's a great singer and the most beautiful guy in the band [*laughs*]. At a time when you're talking about Sweet and Bowie and androgyny, he was the most androgynous-looking in the band, yet he was the most "guy's guy" if you look at his lyrics. Because it's about a car, growing up in the East End, just rockin' in the modern world and dealing with the business of being a rock 'n' roll star. So yeah, he's as legit as it comes.

POPOFF: Plus he's got the Rod Stewart voice.

SNIDER: Yes, and when he's not doing that, he's the guy holding down the fort on all those super-high parts. Roger brings a lot to the table and I don't think the band have ever disregarded him. Whereas John Deacon, I never really was sure of his place in the band [*laughs*]. I remember seeing them live and his big solo spot was that descending line in "Liar." They would put the spotlight on him for that bass run. That's his moment [*sings the bass part*] "All day long, all day long." I was like, really?! That's the best we can come up with? For this poor bastard? He's the Bill Wyman of Queen.

POPOFF: Richie, can you go deep with a couple of lesser-sungs on the album?

UNTERBERGER: Well, "Jesus," even though it's not going to stick in someone's memory as well as "Liar" and "Keep Yourself Alive," is still an important song because it has the most pronounced operatic quality of any track on the record. In fact, you could imagine it as part of a rock opera, but it just doesn't happen to connect with other songs on the record. It seems like it should be part of a story, like maybe it's the gutsy rock version of *Jesus Christ Superstar.*

Some people might see that as a fault of Queen, like maybe they could come up with something like a *Dark Side of the Moon* or *Quadrophenia*, a record where the songs had a connective thread. Nonetheless, the song on its own has an epic, biblical feel. What bigger topic can you choose in the western world than Jesus? When you look

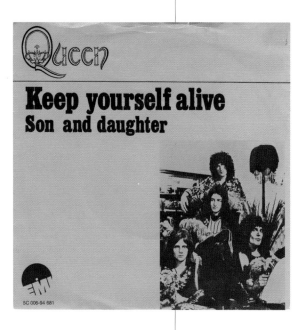

at the lyrics, it's not especially controversial, but a lot of people in the United States would consider it controversial to have any rock song about Jesus that's not like a Christian or gospel rock song.

In songs like "My Fairy King" and "Great King Rat," it sounds like it's part of a story, but you're only getting a small portion of it. As well, the intro to "My Fairy King," that's where some of that classic art rock thing comes in, primarily with the piano-dominated intro and the falsetto vocal.

POPOFF: Once the fairy dust has settled, what kind of messaging falls out of Queen? With that band name, that record cover, this music, do they establish themselves as the quintessential British band? Sort of spokesmen for Britishness? Or is the messaging one gets from the glam look of the band and the name of the band one of homosexuality?

SNIDER: Freddie's homosexuality, not that it's an issue, was not something anybody really knew about, so for a few years that was never part of the discussion. Geoff Workman, who engineered our *Stay Hungry* album, was Roy Thomas Baker's right-hand man later on; he told us so many stories, and he figured as Freddie came out, around *A Night at the Opera*, that's when his sexual orientation started to affect the music. So, it became a thing and actually affected the music after a while.

But in the beginning, Queen, even though that was a word for being gay, you didn't get his gayness. To me, it was purely regal. They were presenting themselves as being regal, almost above the fray. We're this talented, we're this good, and we're this classy. And, you know, one of my favorite moments—this is much later, going to see them during *A Night at the Opera*—this is a gag he would do all the time, where Freddie would drink a glass of champagne and then offer it to the crowd, "Share this amongst yourselves," and he'd drop the champagne glass [*laughs*]. It was beautiful. Yeah, they were glammy, but they were coming from a regal glam, the white satin, the black satin, classy. It was amazing.

SHULMAN: They were able to combine all sorts of ideas, all sorts of music, all sorts of influences, and I commend them. But they were incredibly unique. There was not another band like them, so when you asked me, were other bands jealous of them? They couldn't be, because they were their own entity. There was no other band that could do what they did.

They were—and wanted to be, considered themselves to be—a stadium and arena band, signified so strongly later, of course, by "We Are the Champions" and "We Will Rock You." I mean, think about how simple these songs were, those riffs, that banging rhythm to "We Will Rock You"—they were ready for stadiums. They weren't going to climb the ladder, which is what everybody else did back then except for maybe Zeppelin. They were a phenomenon and I think you hear that right from the first album.

POPOFF: You mention Zeppelin. How would you compare Queen to Zeppelin? Or to Sweet?

SHULMAN: Very different to both. Sweet were a purely glam, sort of a fun, silly band, whereas Queen were being silly in an ironic, satirical way. They rocked as hard as Led Zeppelin but weren't as overtly simple as Led Zeppelin. They combined rock, glam, pop, prog, everything, into one package. In that respect, they were very original. But again, back to that first impression, I saw these guys as very disciplined in what they were planning to do in the studio. I think they all were smart enough to realize that recording time took a lot of

US promo copy of "Liar." At six-and-a-half minutes long, this collision of influences wasn't going to get played on AM radio. Luckily, FM was able to pick up on it.

money, took a lot of energy, and they used it to their advantage. They weren't sloughing around, writing in the studio and doing massive amounts of chemically induced nonsense.

SNIDER: To that Zeppelin point, I certainly see the comparison, and as a Zeppelin freak, that appealed to me. They were drawing from Sabbath, Zeppelin, classical music. But Zeppelin is just one of those transcendent bands that even then, oh sure, you could *try* to shunt them aside [*laughs*]. A very famous rumor has it that at the Uris Theatre, on one of those five nights, John Bonham showed up and tried to go out onstage with Mott the Hoople—just crashed the stage, drunk—and there was literally a fistfight backstage. I don't think that was with Queen.

But, no, my take on it was Queen were not trying to be anybody but themselves. They were blazing their own trail.

UNTERBERGER: More than anything, I'd say *Queen* does a good job of introducing a variety of trademarks of the band's sound and one of those one is those choral harmonies. As a link back to the late '60s, if you listen to *Abbey Road*, there are some real dense, almost blockbuster harmonies in there. The Beatles always had great harmonies, but those qualities are more present on *Abbey Road* because the studio technologies that they could avail themselves of were getting more sophisticated. They had eight-tracks and various other advantages.

And Queen had that dense feel, but also an added bombastic flavor, almost like, it's going to wake you up if it's playing across the street. I've used the word operatic a few times, but there's that too. It's almost like the Greek chorus, or the chorus in an opera stage production is coming through to accentuate something. You hear that in "Liar," certainly, as well as others on the album.

They also establish here some of Brian May's trademarks: his sound, his sustain. Brian was able to achieve—with some production help—something that was very distinctive and symphonic. Of course, Queen were famous for putting on their records, almost as a badge of honor, that no synthesizers were used—on *Queen* it's " . . . and nobody played synthesizer."

And it doesn't sound like synthesizer now, maybe because we're so much more used to synthesizers since the '80s, but certainly at the time, some people in the industry thought they must be using synthesizers to create that really thick symphonic feel. But it wasn't. It was because of the way that Brian May played and overdubbed and how some songs were treated in the studio. It was something that—along with Freddie's very actorly lead vocals and the harmony vocals—conditioned you to realize instantly that even though this might be the first or second time you were hearing any specific song, that with the sonic palette being presented, it could be nobody but Queen.

OVERLEAF: The band poses in Tokyo with the gold disc for their first album.

2 II

WITH PATRICK MYERS, NINA NOIR, AND DEE SNIDER

SIDE 1

1. **Procession** 1:12
   (MAY)
2. **Father to Son** 6:14
   (MAY)
3. **White Queen (As It Began)** 4:34
   (MAY)
4. **Some Day One Day** 4:23
   (MAY)
5. **The Loser in the End** 4:02
   (TAYLOR)

SIDE 2

1. **Ogre Battle** 4:10
   (MERCURY)
2. **The Fairy Feller's Master-Stroke** 2:40
   (MERCURY)
3. **Nevermore** 1:15
   (MERCURY)
4. **The March of the Black Queen** 6:08
   (MERCURY)
5. **Funny How Love Is** 3:17
   (MERCURY)
6. **Seven Seas of Rhye** 2:50
   (MERCURY)

PERSONNEL:

FREDDIE MERCURY – *vocals, piano, harpsichord;*
BRIAN MAY – *guitars, piano, vocals, bells;*
JOHN DEACON – *bass, acoustic guitar;*
ROGER MEDDOWS-TAYLOR – *percussion, vocals*
Recorded at TRIDENT STUDIOS, *London*
Produced by ROY THOMAS BAKER *and* QUEEN; *additional production by* ROBIN GEOFFREY CABLE *and* QUEEN

Group photo, circa 1973. Their second album sunk the band, but also helped define them.

The album that almost sank Queen and yet still defined them, *II* is the band's *Caress of Steel* in some respects, their *Van Halen II* in others.

As with Rush and Caress, *II* finds Queen allowed to fulfill their vision for the first time. Essentially recorded twice, the band's debut had been quite conventionally recorded by a young, broke band stealing time when they could. For *II*, they were still young and broke, but intent on sculpting each song and thoughtfully locating it on the album, hence the unconventional "White Side" and "Black Side."

As with Rush, Queen followed up music that had established a firm base—and then asked too much of their audience too soon. Rush saved themselves by staying the course and making an even better album with *2112*; Queen, on the other hand, would combine what they learned about a mixing board on *II* with the immediacy of *Queen* to give us *Sheer Heart Attack*. But we're getting ahead of the story.

As for comparisons of Queen's *II* with *Van Halen II*, both bands made a darker, less accessible second album that was also a commercial stumble. Like Van Halen, Queen had written some of the material in advance. "Ogre Battle"

Brian on stage in London, 1974. The "Brian side" of *II* evoked the excitement and near divinity of Zeppelin and the Who. He's seen here on the *II* tour in Oklahoma City, April 19, 1974

was in the band's earliest sets, but they held it back until they could do it justice. The finished product became the most discussed song on *II*, largely for its studio trickery.

Another early composition, "Father to Son," was wisely held until Brian could fully explore what would become his trademark compressed and midrange-heavy sound. Not on the album but given the full studio monty (and used as the B-side to "Seven Seas of Rhye") was "See What a Fool I've Been," a Zeppelin-esque blues that reaches back to the Smile days.

At this point, again like Rush and Van Halen, Queen wanted to get onto their next thing. Van Halen would invent their "brown sound" on *Van Halen II* and Rush would shift even more prog metal on *Caress*, but Queen found themselves in the disconcerting conundrum of recording *II* while their debut, delayed while a deal got shopped, was just hitting store shelves. The situation cast a pall on the debut, for Queen was in love with their new direction and suddenly dismissive of their earlier material. Brian, an avowed Sabbath fan, viewed *II* through a lens that evoked the near divinity of Zeppelin and the Who, as well as the power trio excitement of those bands.

In truth, *II* is not particularly conceptual. Sure, Brian writes most of the first side and Freddie all of the second (and Freddie's Black Side is more fantastical). And indeed, "Father to Son," "Ogre Battle," and "The March of the Black Queen" are user-friendly to the likes of Genesis fans, and even more so "The Fairy Feller's Master-Stroke," basically the Hobbit version of "Bohemian Rhapsody" or "More of That Jazz." But storylines are multiple, and musical themes, although complex and numerous, recur only within the frameworks of the more art rock songs, not across the album.

Stepping away from the fanciful, "Some Day One Day" and "Funny How Love Is" demonstrate Queen's grasp of psychedelic folk on its way to wyrd folk, while Roger's lone writing credit (no John Deacon songs here) merges that same predilection with Led Zeppelin, a band adept at intellectualizing or at least art-rocking acoustic strummery. What further complicates the album (and confuses potential fans) are a couple of under-two-minute fragments and linked songs with transitions that are not much more than stylistic shifts.

Launching "Seven Seas of Rhye" as a single didn't do much to improve the prospects of *Queen II*, although touring the US on their first trip abroad surely represented a career milestone. The album eventually went gold despite itself, propelled by curiosity and completism following the success of "Bohemian Rhapsody."

That's *Queen II*. To conjure Van Halen once more, I paraphrase David Lee Roth, who once called Buffalo, New York, the glovebox of America: stick your hand in there—you never know what's gonna come out.

POPOFF: What are a few general characteristics of *II* as it exists between the debut and *Sheer Heart Attack*, which would somewhat save the band's bacon?

MYERS: Well, with their first album, they were living on borrowed time at Trident when David Bowie wasn't using it. They were crawling in there at eleven at night and staying until four in the morning when it was completely dead. So, they had to live with the drum sounds the kit was set up for, that close-mic'd sound prevalent at the time. They were basically getting used to the studio. With their second album, they got a drum sound that Roger was a lot happier with—a great, big, open, differently mic'd drum sound.

They also sort of introduced and refined their harmonies. You had harmonies on the first one, but they hadn't quite coalesced. They hadn't learned how to stack them in a way that became recognizable. They'd always had a refined ear, but by the time they got to *Sheer Heart Attack*, they learned how to keep an audience interested. They always had extraordinary

With their second album (and more time in the studio) the band achieved a drum sound that made Roger a lot happier.

arrangements. Brian's key changes and modulations were amazing and Freddie's harmonic constructions and melodies were always strong and caught the ear, on so many of the singles all the way through their career. So they had so much potential, but on *Queen II* they hadn't sharpened their focus so that it became radio-friendly and so that a wider audience could appreciate all those twists and changes.

POPOFF: What about the idea that, just as *A Day at the Races* is a deep-cuts album after *A Night at the Opera*, *II* serves that purpose against the debut?

NOIR: Sure, and it's interesting because I feel like *Queen* is the safer album. *II* has a lot of weird, interesting stuff and it's no surprise that they didn't get a lot of hits off it. There's a lot of material that people don't know well and it all starts fittingly with "Procession," this regal, inherently Queen-like processional music that sets up the theme of them being, you know, Queen [*laughs*].

SNIDER: To this day, it's one of my desert island albums . . . and their least popular record. It sort of made them reexamine themselves, regrouping for *Sheer Heart Attack*, because of the way *II* was poorly received worldwide. But *II* was just phenomenal! I literally carried a dictionary around just to look up the words Mercury was singing so I could understand what they were saying.

From the opening "Procession" into "Father to Son," there's a power, instantly, with the chords and [*sings*] "A word in your ear!" And then the concept that unfolds, everything about it, beginning to end, was just perfect. Other bands were doing stacked vocal harmonies, like Sweet

Glam rockers Sweet seemed to think that Queen's harmonies copped their style. Freddie belts out a tune in Oklahoma City, April 19, 1974.

with those early singles. I met Mick Tucker, the drummer from Sweet, now dead, and he claimed that Queen stole their vocal-layering style and it pissed off him and the band that Queen was getting all this recognition for these majestic, layered, choral vocals.

But back then, when these bands did it, it didn't really hit me. Queen does it and it's a statement. And the orchestration . . . Brian May and the "No synthesizers were used" thing, and you hear songs like "Procession" and it sounds like strings. How are they doing this? This is phenomenal. They're just commanding everything. But the public doesn't react—it does not go down.

But I remember circling my house because the album wasn't finished. I was listening in my car on eight-track, which used that horrible break in the middle of the song. But I was so fanatical that I couldn't get out of the car until the album finished. It would be disrespectful.

MYERS: As Dee says, there were comparisons to Sweet. It's difficult to say whether Queen were copying Sweet. Sweet seemed to think that was the case and they seemed to have their noses out of joint about it, from what I've read. But I think that's missing the point. Queen always cast their net wider in terms of musical influence. But if you've got those stacked harmonies, with that particularly piercing dog-whistle harmony just by having Roger Taylor in there, you could open yourself to accusations of that.

POPOFF: Okay, so those are the opening strains of the record. Let's move into the album a bit more. There's this White Side/Black Side dichotomy, with the first side, the White Side, being dominated by Brian in terms of songwriting.

NOIR: Yes, from "Procession" we're right into "Father to Son," which sounds like spacey Beatles but with heavy guitars—the vocals are very Beatles. And like you say, the first half of this album is all Brian May with one song by Roger. Freddie sings two of the four songs, "Father to Son" and "White Queen," but Brian sings "Some Day One Day" and Roger sings "The Loser in the End." The first three songs are written by Brian, so they have that Brian May feel with all the weird guitars. "White Queen" has kind of a Zeppelin feel to it, with all the medieval-sounding lyrics. And then "Some Day One Day," Brian wrote that about a crush he had on a girl in his biology class, which I thought was hilarious [*laughs*].

POPOFF: Before we leave Brian, what are the challenges of reproducing Brian's stuff live?

NOIR: Brian is fascinating because he works a lot in major keys, where a lot of other guitarists would do it in minor. So, it's challenging for the guitarists we've hired to play with us over the years. They have to rewire their minds. And then he has all this really cool vibrato on the strings. And yet it's somehow very "proper"-sounding guitar. He's a stoic gentleman and he dresses very much like a pirate sometimes on stage [*laughs*]. But he has that royal air about him.

And of course, he layers so much of his guitars that when we perform songs live, we have to go and look and see what he did live, to try figure it out. Otherwise it's like, which parts should I play? What's the most important part to play? If I take that part away, is it still going to come through as a song? Because we don't want to hire three guitar players to re-create this stuff. We just want it to be the five of us.

Also, at times, Brian will throw on some sort of an effects pedal and out comes that stacked round, that sort of echo. He creates interesting melodies and tones on his own. I've seen Queen multiple times, and there were a couple times where Brian got on stage by himself and created this intense landscape with one guitar.

MYERS: On *II*, they were still learning how to mix Brian in terms of panning his guitar. The panning gets a lot more sophisticated from *Sheer Heart Attack* on. A lot of the guitar work on the debut and *II*, this isn't a hard and fast rule, but a lot of it was guitar center, and then guitar left and right. And that's how you moved it through. There was a lot more variation later. And as a result, I think the guitar tends to sound bigger. They create a different space by not panning hard left and right on certain things and spread the guitar tracks in a slightly different way, and therefore, it sounds richer and fuller. Later, they'd taper back the echo and reverb you heard on the first album and quite a lot of on *II*, which dates the album a little bit. Not in a bad way. I love it, personally—I think it sounds great and open.

POPOFF: The writing on this album is very much down to Brian and Freddie. There's no John Deacon song and Roger only gets the one.

SNIDER: Yeah, it's so like George Harrison. He gets the one song. In the beginning, it was John and Paul, but suddenly George started to get his shit together and in Paul's words, come up with amazing songs. And his one song was always either fun and/or enjoyable and real. Ringo gets to sing one song per record. It was that way with John and Roger. Roger's just got a great take on things.

POPOFF: Forget the Beatles. An idea I formed when I was a kid was that Queen was Led Zeppelin on steroids—the new and improved version. Any validity to that?

SNIDER: You said on steroids—I think it was on fairy dust [*laughs*]. I don't know, I wouldn't say steroids, because it wasn't more muscular. It was fancier.

POPOFF: Could be. Back to the album. The Black Side kicks off with the album's most memorable track, "Ogre Battle."

NOIR: I really think that the saving graces of *II*, among diehard Queen fans, are "Ogre Battle," "Fairy Feller's Master-Stroke," and "Nevermore," which can be seen as a suite, almost a microcosm of the album as a whole. That middle part of the album that opens the Black Side really takes you on a journey into this epic, medieval soundscape. Certainly "Ogre Battle" would be great soundtrack music for an animated cartoon, some sort of sci-fi fantasy.

Then there are the heavy, thrashy guitars, which play with your mind because they are recorded backward. We've thought about doing "Ogre Battle" live, but the only way you can do that is if you have a backing track, because you can't create that whole opening live. Reverse recording is more common now, and the Beatles certainly did it, but Queen did it after this as well, for example in "Play the Game," where that sucking sound in the intro is a crash cymbal recorded in reverse.

SNIDER: Well, "Ogre Battle," of course, is very metallic, and part of that is based on a Sabbath riff. And the medieval imagery in it predates Ronnie James Dio, who wouldn't get to this place until 1975 with Rainbow. There was a little bit of this with Uriah Heep and even Sabbath, but

"Ogre Battle" is fully committed. It's almost silly in its medieval-ness, almost Spinal Tap. But at the same time, it was as metal as you can get. There's almost a "Whole Lotta Love"–esque breakdown, where they're screaming and fighting and there's actually a battle going on there. Of course, it's Roger Meddows-Taylor screaming his head off like a lunatic. It was *so* metal. It's funny now, but it wasn't funny at the time.

POPOFF: It gets even more insane for "The Fairy Feller's Master-Stroke," again medieval. This would soon be gone, one could argue replaced by a different kind of historical music.

SNIDER: Yes, and I wonder if the '20s and '30s music— "Bring Back That Leroy Brown" and such—did them better than the medieval stuff. You're right, the medieval material went away on the third record. I saw them on that tour and Freddie had lost the choir robe tops that he wore, although Brian hung on for a while. Lyrically, they left the *II* realm as well. Maybe they thought it was putting people off.

George Workman, who engineered with them and with Twisted Sister, told us *Sheer Heart Attack* was a reaction to the failure of *II*, that they were literally like, "All right, you want hit songs? We'll give you hit songs."

Of course, by the fourth record they're back to their old tricks with "Bohemian Rhapsody" and the medieval lyrics. So, in a way, *Sheer Heart Attack* was a departure, a reaction to getting slapped on the nose like a bad puppy over *II*. *Sheer Heart Attack* is the breakthrough. They get the attention and then go back to their old game and have the biggest hit ever.

POPOFF: But for the time being, we are still in the land of what is almost, or loosely, a concept album steeped in fantasy.

NOIR: Yes, and no more so than with "The Fairy Feller's Master-Stroke." That song was written about a painting by Richard Dadd, who painted it in the mid-1800s in a psychiatric facility where he was put after murdering his father. Freddie took some art history courses when he was in college and would drag the band out to see museums when they were on tour. "The Fairy Feller's Master-Stroke" is a painting that has so much going on in it, it's like a cluster of imagery.

Queen did a very good job of making the song sound very similar to that. It's got lots of layers, it takes you on a journey, and it's almost overwhelming. Roger Taylor said that was their biggest stereo experiment, with the layering and all the filters. People don't really view the band this way, but after perhaps the Beatles, Queen are one of the first overtly artist-type recording bands. They did a lot of stuff in the studio that they couldn't re-create live and that they had no intention of re-creating live. But nobody really considered them anything other than a rock 'n' roll band that was going to go out and do all this live.

MYERS: I think when any band starts, they have one eye on their agenda, but you can't help but show some of your influences, where you're coming from, who your heroes are. The choices that you make reveal who it is you like [*laughs*] or where you're coming from. Because everyone is borrowing from everyone when they start up.

So, a lot of the early lyrics were very fantastical. But there are also songs like "Father to Son" about tortured relationships with parents and trying to build your life from nothing with "Doing All Right." The lyrics are very much constructs of people who hadn't had much of a life yet. They're dealing with poverty, they want to create a fantastical landscape, but they haven't had the first-hand experience themselves, so they painted a picture. You can paint these elaborate pictures, and they were always narrators to the pictures that they were painting.

By the time you get to *Sheer Heart Attack*, they had real first-hand experiences. They've also a lot savvier about the industry. Suddenly, they had an agenda they could talk about. But what they did, which was so amazing and was going to appeal to such a wide audience, was take that cinematic lens they previously applied to a narrative-style song and apply it to touring and everyday life. And that's when Queen really started to discover just how powerful they were as songwriters.

SNIDER: "The Fairy Feller's Master-Stroke" is prog-rock genius, but it's still metallic. And now they're even going to the next level with the choral vocals; they're breaking new ground. Lyrically, this is the one where I was looking up every phrase, which are assembled poetically and completely accurately. It's drawing on a sensibility of minstrels and faerie folk, but from a medieval place. It's nuts from beginning to end, just a mad race, a mad dash. And the lyrics he is spitting out sound like nonsense, but I looked up everything. I needed an *Encyclopaedia Britannica* to look up that shit, because it wasn't words, it was phraseology. I found out that everything had meaning and was poetic. Just brilliant.

But I gotta tell you, that eight-track completely fucked me up when it came to which is the White Side and which is the Black Side. Because the Black Side is heavier and it's all Freddie, so how can we say that Freddie's nonmetallic? At that point, I wasn't as in tune with credits. Many years later, I'm assuming Brian wrote "Ogre Battle" because it's so heavy, right? But you've got "March of the Black Queen," the beauty of that song, and "The Fairy Feller's Master-Stroke," which is just insane. "Funny How Love Is," that's just a beautiful song that hints at some of the big, sing-songy things that you get later, melodic and not metallic in any way. It's funny, I've run into him and talked about it—Axl Rose is a big *II* fan; that's one of his favorite records.

POPOFF: *Queen II closes with "The Seven Seas of Rhye."*

SNIDER: Right, and that's a beautiful song, there's that little piano part at the end. They were hinting at things to come. And that was a moderate hit in England, which I didn't know at the time.

MYERS: Great having all the variety and the song development and the arrangements that move from one place to another, and quite breathtaking in unexpected ways, but you've got to harness that with arrangements that read quickly to someone who's never heard them before. With things like "Seven Seas of Rhye," they began to realize you've got to pack things in quickly. You've got to be economical. If you're going to have amazing, demonstrative, almost cinematic music, you need to hold the audience's attention. And I think that's what really came in with the next album, *Sheer Heart Attack*.

NOIR: "The Seven Seas of Rhye" is one of our favorite songs to perform. The second we go with that arpeggiated piano intro, the audience starts losing their mind. It's so iconic. We barely even have to announce what song it is. And it's fun to sing, because it's sort of pirate-themed. It's got this kind call-to-arms feel. And it's very demanding, right? "I stand before you, naked to the eyes/I will destroy any man who dares abuse my trust." It's fun because I'm a girl and I get to be a bit aggressive with the audience [*laughs*].

It's a complicated vocal, too, but that's Queen. They change lyrics constantly. There are songs like "Fat Bottomed Girls," the lyrics in the chorus, they don't repeat the way that you would expect a chorus to repeat. So, it takes a lot of memorization, and every once in a while, I'll be onstage rocking out and I'll get distracted by somebody jumping up and down or freaking out, and I'll be like, "Wait, which part of the song am I in? What's the lyric here?"

Also, I don't think a lot of people realize how proggy Queen can be. Along with Rush, there's no reason they can't be considered as the grandfathers of prog metal. There are odd time signatures, weird key changes, all the chromatic scales, the endings. It's not typical rock music, so the fact that they made it into pop history is somewhat shocking.

POPOFF: Dee, would you agree that Queen should be more recognized as integral to the birth of prog metal?

SNIDER: Well, let's not forget that heavy metal didn't exist then so maybe it's a bit of a moot point. Led Zeppelin called themselves a blues band. Black Sabbath viewed themselves as a jazz-blues fusion band! Are you kidding me?! Alice Cooper wanted to be a Doors-type psychedelic band. Bands try something and get a by-product they didn't intend. So when you've got Freddie's classical influences and his Liza Minnelli, and then Brian, Roger, and John, you can't predict what comes out.

AC/DC shows up and they don't consider themselves metal. So, some of the greatest metal bands of all time weren't metal or didn't consider themselves metal. But in the earliest days of Queen, up to *A Day at the Races*, they were a metallic, heavy power trio.

But then by the late '70s, when I'm discovering Judas Priest and AC/DC, and it's calling to me as a writer and I'm defining myself as metallic, Queen are going funkier and more esoteric and they're losing me. So, the Queen that exists for me, that band is forever a metal band, and I love them for being one of the great metal bands of all time. In my opinion [*laughs*].

The last thing I want to say about Queen—this is a diamond-in-the-pocket band, that band that you champion for so many years, and then when they get discovered, you feel you've lost something and they're taken from you and they're no longer your band. Even though in retrospect, you realize you were shouting from the hilltop. Like I say, I was the only guy screaming in the balcony at the Uris Theatre—once *everybody* was standing up, you'd start hearing, "Oh Queen, I love their first album, *A Night at the Opera*," and all you could do was call them a fucking idiot.

RELEASED NOVEMBER 8, 1974

3 SHEER HEART ATTACK

WITH PATRICK MYERS, JOHN NORUM, DEREK SHULMAN, AND JEB WRIGHT

SIDE 1

1. **Brighton Rock** 5:10
   (MAY)
2. **Killer Queen** 3:00
   (MERCURY)
3. **Tenement Funster** 2:48
   (TAYLOR)
4. **Flick of the Wrist** 3:18
   (MERCURY)
5. **Lily of the Valley** 1:41
   (MERCURY)
6. **Now I'm Here** 4:15
   (MAY)

SIDE 2

1. **In the Lap of the Gods** 3:23
   (MERCURY)
2. **Stone Cold Crazy** 2:14
   (MERCURY, MAY, TAYLOR, DEACON)
3. **Dear Friends** 1:07
   (MAY)
4. **Misfire** 1:49
   (DEACON)
5. **Bring Back That Leroy Brown** 2:15
   (MERCURY)
6. **She Makes Me (Stormtrooper in Stilettos)** 4:09
   (MAY)
7. **In the Lap of the Gods . . . Revisited** 3:44
   (MERCURY)

PERSONNEL:

FREDDIE MERCURY – *vocals, piano;*
BRIAN MAY – *guitars, vocals, piano, genuine Aloha ukelele;*
GEORGE FORMBY – *ukelele-banjo, guitar orchestrations;*
JOHN DEACON – *bass, double bass, guitars;*
ROGER TAYLOR – *drums, vocals, percussion*
Recorded at AIR STUDIOS, *London;*
ROCKFIELD STUDIOS, *Rockfield, Monmouthshire, Wales;* TRIDENT STUDIOS, *London; and* WESSEX SOUND, *London*
Produced by ROY THOMAS BAKER *and* QUEEN

OPPOSITE: Queen tasted just enough success with "Seven Seas of Rhye" and their first US tour dates to feel like a real band going places.

One step forward, two steps back. The Top 10 UK chart performance of "Seven Seas of Rhye," along with their first spate of US touring, gave Queen the feel of a real band going places. Brian put aside thoughts of finishing university for good, and John Deacon decided to knock his teaching job on the head. All four of the guys were now on the same page, dedicating all their faculties to Queen.

But then Brian, while on tour in the United States, came down with a serious case of hepatitis, followed by a duodenal ulcer, requiring months of recovery. Their third album was recorded sporadically at a series of studios, including the legendary Rockfield in Wales. Brian laid down parts when he could and even wrote in the hospital and at home rather than in the studio, as Queen tended to do. Doing the band full-time, the guys were more broke than they'd ever been, but in September 1974, as three months of recording neared completion, they were awarded a silver album for *II*, representing UK sales of over sixty thousand copies.

Things were about to get better. Brian was well into recovery as "Killer Queen" was issued as an advance single on October 11, 1974. When the album launched the following month, he was able to tour again. Both single and album would rise to No. 2 on the UK charts, even though the press was adversarial, shaking their pens at a band daring to do so much and with such bravado.

The *Sheer Heart Attack* narrative is that of an earthier, saltier record than *II* (only a little more so than *Queen*). It also rocks harder in more concentrated doses, none more concentrated than "Stone Cold Crazy." But the old prog tricks are still there. Two songs clock in under two minutes, one of them more of a segue, and side two includes two selections called "In the Lap of the Gods"; the first is more akin to "You Take My Breath Away," while the album closer (qualified with a "Revisited") is more like an early version of "We Are the Champions."

Elsewhere, there's some folk ("She Makes Me"), some folky pop ("Misfire"), a third look at what it's like to be Roger Taylor ("Tenement Funster"), and a pair of Brian May rockers ("Brighton Rock" and "Now I'm Here"), each Queen classics that would have sat well on the debut record but probably not *II*.

Sheer Heart Attack was saved in the marketplace by its hard rock and its ostentatious single, "Killer Queen." The rest of the record rolls and roils—lurches even—like Queen *II*, albeit with lyrics that feature real people just trying to get along. But that variety, including the old-timey "Bring Back That Leroy Brown," help create an album that feels like a step toward *A Night at the Opera* and *A Day at the Races*, even if the raw push-and-shove power exhibited here, creates a sense of immediacy found only on *Queen*, *II*, and arguably *News of the World*.

Sheer Heart Attack did brisk business in the UK, rising to platinum, but got stuck at gold in the United States. Queen would have to wait to garner widespread acceptance in the United States. Over time, however, the album would become a fan favorite and, for many, the last of a torrid trio, much more the rambunctious twin of the fiery debut than of said debut's fancy follow-up.

POPOFF: Patrick, set up the state of the band as they approached their third album.

MYERS: Well, their career wasn't going great. These days you have two albums, and if you haven't achieved the success you were looking for, you lose your deal. But they managed to get a big tour of America with Mott the Hoople that turned things around in a whole heap of ways. But a lot of problems arose from that. Brian got ill and Freddie had problems with his voice, so it wasn't plain sailing. But touring did open up their vistas and that really informed their songwriting. They started narrowing in on what became the Queen sound.

WRIGHT: I just saw it as an immature band becoming more mature. They were finding their sound. I like *II*, but it's not a great album. With *Sheer Heart Attack*, Queen becomes a band. The first two albums were raw and yet prog, art rock and they were trying to wed two things that didn't necessarily fit, or they weren't yet skilled enough to make them fit.

Kicking off the album, "Brighton Rock," even though that wasn't a big hit, that's the Queen sound. It's got the choppy, angular guitar stuff, the solos, it swoops up and down, the vocals, even though it's got kind of corny lyrics about the chick and the guy. But the music I liked, with the echo on the guitar, and Freddie's power in contrast to the falsetto. To me, with "Brighton Rock," Queen found their place.

NORUM: *Sheer Heart Attack* was the first Queen album I ever heard as well as bought. I didn't know anything about the band at all. A friend of

mine said, "You've got to check out this new band called Queen." So, I got the album and put it on at home and was totally blown away. Loved the guitar playing and the production and the songs were great. And I certainly don't hear a band that was being hit-conscious.

POPOFF: What statement does the band make with the opening track, "Brighton Rock"?

MYERS: You've got a narrative song, the context is less fantastical. It's more of a Victorian melodrama of tight sexual repression. Even the opening riff is packed with frustrated energy, this incredibly fast riff on the back of this cacophony of fairground noise. It's like a mission statement, they've arrived, they're grabbing your attention and painting a picture, but they're doing it much more quickly and economically. They break into this extraordinary multicharacter narrative of two lovers meeting. The working title of the track was actually "Brighton Fuck" [*laughs*].

It's quite an extraordinary song in terms of the different narrative voices Freddie employs as the female and the male. People have imagined them as a couple of mods, but I think, linguistically, it's much more Victorian. "No I must away" and "tarry with me pray." There's the arcane language that they used for the earlier albums, for the more fantastical and magical kind of lyrics. It seems to be a continuation of that but different, more satirical, with a knowing sense of humor.

But it's also incredibly theatrical. You open the curtain with this fun fair noise reminiscent of the *Sgt. Pepper* album, where they start with the orchestra tuning up and the band suddenly plowing in. It seems like "Here's our mission statement. You're going to sit down and take notice." They've always been theatrical, but now they're really taking a directorial eye. Every lighting switch happens at exactly the right moment without a second wasted so there's no danger of anyone settling in, because you don't know what's coming next with this album and that's its strength.

With "Brighton Rock," the melodrama descends into this seething battery of riffs, which is essentially a massive showcase for Brian's amazing guitar work and also introduces his multilayered harmony stuff, which would be a feature of the live shows later. But it's also a bridge that brings the fans from the first two albums. It's quite a prog track, "Brighton Rock," with the harmonies, the open solo, the little riffs, the movements, and changing sections. You

Japanese and French sleeves for "Killer Queen" b/w "Flick of the Wrist." The lead-off track was issued as an advance single a month ahead of the album.

could take a five-second blast of any of that and segue over B-roll of anything and it would all look amazing and all sound totally distinctive.

POPOFF: It's similar to "Keep Yourself Alive," right?

MYERS: It's a similar ethic, but tighter. They've gotten rid of a lot of extraneous drum stuff. If there's gonna be a drum roll or a fill, it's there for a reason. It's the difference between a band constructing a song because they need a set to play live, and the band constructing a song for an album and really honing in on what's going to attract radio. Still, that's not to say these twists and turns and this level of invention weren't on the earlier albums.

POPOFF: John, as a guitarist yourself, how about a little characterization of what makes Brian May's playing interesting?

NORUM: His sound is totally original and unique. He just needs to play one note and you know it's him. Part of that is that guitar as well as the Vox AC30 amps and the treble-booster thing. He found his own identity and tone early on.

He and his father built that guitar together, the Red Special. His father was a technician of some sort. And I've read that the wood is from an old mantelpiece that was a couple hundred years old or something. So yeah, the whole combination of that wood and those Burns pickups, which are unique-sounding, and the tremolo board together with the treble booster and the AC30s—that was it; he just plugs in and it's amazing.

He originally got that idea from Rory Gallagher. Because he went to see Gallagher live, and afterward he got to meet Rory and he asked him, "Oh, I love your guitar sound. What is it you're using?" And Rory said, "Well, you know, I'm using a Vox AC30 amp and a treble booster, that's it, and my Strat." So, he bought the same gear, but Rory used a Stratocaster, and so a lot of Brian's tone actually came from that guitar that they built, his dad and him, which has a lot of switches and selectors to get different combinations of sounds.

Plus, he's a very melodic player, and he's great with harmonies and vibrato, and he plays with a coin, a sixpence, which is very unusual [*laughs*], because usually you play with a pick or your fingers.

A couple of years ago we played a few songs at the Classic Rock Awards in London. We were sitting at the table with Motörhead having dinner. Anyway, to make a long story short, I saw Brian May from a distance, and my bandmates said, "Why don't you go up and talk to him?" I don't go up to people and shake their hands, like "Nice to meet you." I've never done that. Never asked for an autograph. Even when I met Gary Moore and Michael Schenker in 1984 when I was just a kid.

But Brian actually came up to our table and he said, "Are you John Norum? From the band Europe?" "Yes." "Oh, I finally get to meet you! I love your playing; you're great, man!" And I'm like, "What?!" Coming from Brian May, that is very exciting. You know, someone that I looked up to and idolized since I was a teenager and saw them live in Stockholm—I think I was fourteen years old the first time. And there he is—Brian May! Telling me that he likes my playing. Wonderful.

POPOFF: Very cool! We'd be remiss if we didn't discuss "Killer Queen," because in a sense, that's the song that allowed the band to continue.

SHULMAN: I was living in the UK at the time and I remember it coming on the radio and listening to the vocals and hearing this pop song but with so many layers. Again, they were able to make simple things sound complicated and complicated things sound simple. That song in particular—it was a simple pop song but with so many layers of vocals, led by a superb lead vocal and a sort of calmed-down, note-perfect solo from Brian that was not the usual frenetic avant-garde thing you were used to hearing.

POPOFF: How much weight would you put on any gay connotations to the song?

SHULMAN: Well, that was always there for those who wanted to see it. They used satire, they could be tongue-in-cheek. They have the famous video for "I Want to Break Free" where they are all in drag. That's a very British thing; in Britain to dress up in drag is funny, whether you're gay, straight, bi, or whatever. In North America, certainly in those days, any alternative sexuality, you better get out of here, especially in the South. Don't even think about it [*laughs*]. But, yeah, they played around with all these kinds of ideas, and the US was loath to embrace them in that respect. Maybe there's some of that in "Killer Queen" being big in the UK but not so much in America.

MYERS: *Sheer Heart Attack* is an album that wilfully serves up contrast. It's like a taster menu. They've got so much to offer and it's, well, mercurial [*laughs*]. They jump from thing to thing but not in a way that leaves you disoriented, but in a way that enthralls you.

So after "Brighton Rock," you're straight into the ultimate head-nodding groove of "Killer Queen." As soon as a song's currency expires, the next one's here and the segue becomes almost as important as the next song. The songs are so short and demonstrate so much so quickly, the linking part is almost as important as the song itself. It always sounds strange when they release compilations and you just suddenly hear the song in isolation, like "Lily of the Valley" away from "Flick of the Wrist."

"Killer Queen" is extraordinary, such a classy song and an easy, accessible lyric. Freddie seems to be talking very much in the present tense. It's not so retrospective and not so fantastical. It brings his wit to the fore as well as his amazing ear for melody. I think Brian was in hospital when most of the song was recorded. He came out of hospital and they played it to him and I think he went back in and said, "No, no, the harmonies aren't right on the chorus. We need to redo these and redo that." He redefined the song for them. It's such a well-written piece and so beautifully recorded.

POPOFF: Is this the start of Queen's flirtation with the vaudevillian?

MYERS: You've got a strong tradition of vaudevillian songwriting right through. The Beatles did the same thing. The Kinks. Ray Davies. The musical was very much a feature. "Killer Queen" is probably not exactly in the genre of vaudeville, but it's certainly got a Noel Coward feel to it, a wider musical palette. Queen were just drawing on a wider frame of reference obviously enjoying themselves in the process.

WRIGHT: "Killer Queen" represented the other side of Queen, the side that made them a lot of money, versus the heavy stuff. Would you ever think that the band that did "Great King Rat" would ever advance so quickly and create something as classic as "Killer Queen"? This one's all Freddie, where we see him sort of taking charge, becoming a front man versus just a vocalist. Plus, there's new sexuality aspect to the repertoire. You're talking about a high-class hooker in this song, so he's getting edgy, although that only goes so far with Queen—they're actually civilized, kind of prim and proper, just like this particular prostitute [*laughs*].

As for vaudeville, I'd say "Bring Back That Leroy Brown" is more that way and has even stronger gay touchstones. It's interesting, but gayness is perhaps signaled in Freddie's closeted years more through this '20s and '30s jazz thing; then when he's out, through disco and funk and synth-pop, right?

And it's fine, because Queen didn't subscribe to the idea of a cohesive style. You expected some weirdness, a silly little song like that. History never includes them in the box sets or the greatest hits. You've got to be a big fan or you had to be into them growing up. But this maybe was the start, to where they weren't afraid to be themselves or to be *more* than themselves.

MYERS: Jim Croce had "Bad, Bad Leroy Brown" the previous year, so it's kind of got that. There's double bass fills, jangle piano. I think the album's got a very fixed commercial eye on America. It references America like five or six times, like "America's new bride to be," "We want Leroy for President." It's very much trying to appeal to the American market with this Dixieland vibe. I think it would've worked great after "Dear Friends," but it's also nice to have a John Deacon song in there, so it doesn't feel too Friday showcase. That's the difficulty with an album like this: getting the balance exactly right so it doesn't become *The Gong Show* [*laughs*].

NORUM: "Killer Queen" is amazing, with the harmony vocals and those regal guitar arrangements. It still sounds fresh today. You know, having Roger and Brian sing as well, that was a match made in heaven. It was pure luck that those three guys' voices just fit so perfectly together. You have Roger, who can do this extremely high-pitched voice, and at the same time, he has this growl when he sings lead. Brian has a softer voice, and then of course Freddie, one of the greatest singers of all time. I imagine when they did it for the first time in the studio, they probably surprised themselves and recognized they had something special and decided to make heavy use of it moving forward.

POPOFF: Speaking of Roger and his manly howl, what do you make of "Tenement Funster"?

MYERS: A song like "Tenement Funster" represents that Beatle-esque dynamic. You knew that George would have the slightly disaffected song like "Don't Bother Me" or "You Like Me Too Much." Paul would either bring an out-and-out rocker or it's going to be more musical and John would have whatever John was doing at the time. You got personalities that you expected, that almost framed an album. You're beginning to really get that with Queen now, with John Deacon's first song, "Misfire," which almost jumps out of the album. It's a very bright pop song.

OPPOSITE: Roger at Freddie's flat on Holland Road in West Kensington, London, early 1974. The Beatle-esque "Tenement Funster" is the archetypal Roger song, presaging the boy racer thing he would take to a different level with "I'm in Love with My Car."

Getting ready to mime "Killer Queen" on *Top Pop* in Hilversum, Holland, November 1974. Interestingly, Brian is playing a Fender Stratocaster rather than the Red Special, perhaps to match John's Fender Jazz bass for the television cameras.

But "Tenement Funster" is the archetypal Roger song. It completely presages the whole boy racer thing that he is going to take to a whole different level through "I'm in Love with My Car." Production-wise, they've learned to record their voices higher in the mix. And it's such a funny lyric, witty, taking that same cinematic lens but applying it to something real. He's talking about a tenement block, a sort of dissolute teenage life, and getting out of there as fast as he can. "I'll make the speed of light out of this place." So, it's cosmic in its imagery, but it's set against an everyday backdrop.

POPOFF: "Flick of the Wrist" is one of the rare unsung doomy songs from the band.

MYERS: Sure, and in "Flick of the Wrist" you start to establish recurrent themes in Queen's music. "Flick of the Wrist" is very much the opening chapter to "Death on Two Legs" because it's all about signing the wrong deal. Freddie's lyrics now are about, you know, cross-collateralized deals [*laughs*]. Freddie's lyrics have really become a lot more grounded, and you can sense a genuine anger. I think any band is always at their strongest when there is that agenda, something they can unite behind. You could feel the anger simmering from one album to the next. They got a lawyer who became their manager, Jim Beach, to get them out of the contract they were in. Then the money started to roll in. Certainly, Freddie and Roger had done very well because Roger had sat in a cupboard while they were recording "Bohemian Rhapsody" and refused to come out and finish his drum parts until they promised that he could have the B-side [*laughs*]. But, yeah, the managers started turning up in nicer cars. That's when they knew there was trouble.

Vocally, Freddie very much jumps into different characters, with the exaggerated vocals and the exaggerated delivery. It's theatrical; you can feel it's a character portrait. It's not just drolly delivered satire.

WRIGHT: I almost view those three songs in a row there as a medley before the majesty of "Now I'm Here." Some Queen fans love the middle of that side, but to me it was like Jethro Tull, where I'm thinking, "Would you get onto the next song?" Because the next song is "Now I'm Here," which is one of Brian's greatest. That's where he became known, especially live, for his harmonizing and echo effects.

POPOFF: Switching gears, what did you think of the *Sheer Heart Attack* album cover?

NORUM: It was a typical '70s glam cover with the makeup job, Freddie Mercury's eyeliner [*laughs*]. There were a lot of glam bands going then and that look was popular.

WRIGHT: On *The Game*, they look uncomfortable dressed like that. *Sheer Heart Attack* is just the opposite. It looks like these guys are having fun, like they've been up all night. It looks like a photo you'd see of Led Zeppelin in a rock magazine. Especially Taylor, with the long hair. He's got the Plant thing going on and his shirt is wide open. But that is the perfect cover. Can you imagine that shot used on any other Queen album? It would not look right. But they look like rock stars, and in a way, this was the first album where they showed their potential to be rock stars.

POPOFF: Back to the record, things get out of control with "Stone Cold Crazy," don't they?

WRIGHT: Oh yeah, by some measures "Sheer Heart Attack" might be Queen's heaviest song, but this qualifies too. Maybe the song's influence wasn't much at first. Maybe it was more toward musicians than the band's fan base, because it's pretty much proto-thrash. I mean, Metallica covered it, right? I like bombastic heavy metal Queen. And although Queen definitely got more bombastic, I don't know if they ever got heavier.

NORUM: "Stone Cold Crazy" is my favorite song on the album because it was fast and aggressive and the riff was killer. But I wouldn't call Queen heavy metal. Metal might have been Sabbath and then Priest, but Queen was too varied, from pop to "Stone Cold Crazy," so many different styles and not just one thing over and over again.

POPOFF: Also in the heavy camp is "Now I'm Here." What role does that one play on the record?

MYERS: "Now I'm Here" is all about touring, born of experience, so it feeds that narrative of the band getting earthier. When you hear it on live recordings, it's quite fast and energetic and all about twists and turns and dynamics and pyrotechnics. On the record, it's quite laid-back but still ballsy. But still, there's a coalescing and sharpening of focus, from the lyrics to the music and even the production. It's so nice when you come back to the reassuring chug of Brian May's guitar, because he actually wasn't there for a lot of the recording, so the arrangements veered toward piano/bass/drums. So, when Brian May comes back in with "Now I'm Here," it just sounds such a delight.

POPOFF: What do you make of "In the Lap of the Gods"?

MYERS: "In the Lap of the Gods" is such an extraordinary opening. It's so Cecil B. DeMille, which apparently Freddie called Queen the Cecil B. DeMille of rock at some point. It's such a scene-setting song, with this extraordinary, broad, epic Roger Taylor intro with his incredibly high voice and great big chord changes. It's almost biblical. And then we get another of Freddie's different voices. It's like they don't want you to hear the same thing twice, or too often—he's got a new character now, almost like a new member of the band turns up, and you go, who is this crazy voice? To me, it evokes *The Phantom of the Opera*. It sounds like this grotesque romantic creature offering his love [*laughs*]. So, they set this scene with this extraordinary theatrical beast that you haven't heard before, and then it's all outro [*laughs*]—intro, scene-setting, outro, gone! [*laughs*] It offers so much, and then just as you sit down and think this is gonna be epic, it's over.

POPOFF: Is there something quintessentially British about what they do here, and just the whole package that is Queen?

SHULMAN: When they first formed is when my first band morphed into Gentle Giant. We were all experimenting in different styles of music, and a lot of bands were influenced by the R&B and soul from the USA, which the USA never even understood. But not Queen, really. And you hear the results in something like "In the Lap of the Gods." Queen took in the idea of English orchestration in their vocals and what at the root is classical, or certainly some part of it.

Led Zeppelin and Deep Purple, they were very much influenced by American blues. They stole some of the licks. Queen used them, but didn't steal them, and utilized a lot of English churchy-sounding vocals and qualities. They were quite English in that respect. But everyone was morphing into different things at that time. They weren't tagged into the progressive world, they weren't tagged into the hard rock or metal or pop world. They had everything. They could go anywhere and say anything to any audience.

POPOFF: And what about "Dear Friends?" Deep track, that one.

MYERS: Yes, I mean, there's so much energy and sonic information thrown in your face with "Stone Cold Crazy," and with such speed, you then go immediately to a blackout, like solo spotlight on a piano and the simplest production you could imagine, with this totally relaxed pace. It's almost a lullaby coming at you with, with gorgeous sort of church choir harmonies coming halfway through.

Sequentially, it's perfectly chosen. Each song throws the other one into relief. Now, that can make for an uncomfortable experience. It can make for a poorly judged album if you keep switching style so much. It takes real artistry to put those styles in. Nothing outstays its welcome. Each change is welcome, including complete palate-cleansers like these. Such artistry. A lot of bands try it and it doesn't work and you just end up with a disjointed album. What you've got here, I think, is a perfect piece of theatrical rock. On top of that, you can feel the boiling energy of a band with something to prove.

POPOFF: And back in reality, in the shops, Queen had to make it work.

WRIGHT: Definitely. If they had followed the debut and *II*, and done Queen *III*, we probably wouldn't be talking about Queen. They needed to hone in, and I wonder what Roy Thomas Baker's role was. Producers have to let the artist be the artist, but I've interviewed a lot of producers, and at some point, they were there to make sure the band made money. If Queen had put out another album that wasn't commercially successful, they probably were in danger of sliding irreparably backward.

SHULMAN: When we were recording next door to them, you could tell the guys were very, very bright; they weren't a bunch of bozos. They knew where they were going and were completely original. I don't think there's any other band like Queen. They had this credible front man, a great sidekick in Brian, the great rhythm section. And they always played music that was contemporary to the times. I guess David Bowie comes close but not really. When I reflect, you

OPPOSITE: Freddie and Brian onstage in 1975. "Brighton Rock" was a massive showcase for Brian's amazing guitar work and introduced his multilayered harmonies that would become a feature of the live shows.

could tell they were never going to be small. They were never going to be a club band. They were always going to be huge.

POPOFF: Patrick, can you explain the place of this record in the Queen canon?

MYERS: I'd say that *Sheer Heart Attack* marks an advance in terms of songwriting and editing. I did a radio course once, and writing a radio drama is the worst thing on earth because you're dealing with just voices to make this drama. And the guy running the course said, "Beware the 'Aw, shit' moment" [*laughs*], where listener goes, "Oh, sod it" and turns the dial and you've lost them. And I think Queen knew, "Right, okay, we're inventive, we can twist and turn on a sixpence"—literally, in Brian's case—"but we don't want to lose our audience. We've got this great big treasure trove of ideas we can throw at songs, but let's get the structure so tight and so catchy and use all the best bits."

But it's not like they suddenly threw everything out the window and made a commercial album. They distilled the extraordinary qualities they had into something more commercially presentable, which is totally different from upending what you're doing and delivering a commercial album.

And that's the artistry of *Sheer Heart Attack*. Anyone can turn around and go, "I'm gonna do lots of uptempo four-on-the-floor numbers and we're gonna get three fucking hits out of this." Record companies are begging bands to do that constantly. So, they opened with a Victorian pocket melodrama that goes into a huge guitar solo and *still* made one of their most commercial albums. That's real artistry.

And yet as I say, they had something to prove. Even if it bombed, Queen were going to make damn sure that people would look at that album and go, "Why did they not become the biggest band on the planet?"

RELEASED NOVEMBER 21, 1975

SIDE 1

1. **Death on Two Legs**
(DEDICATED TO . . .) 3:43
(MERCURY)

2. **Lazing on a Sunday
Afternoon** 1:08
(MERCURY)

3. **I'm in Love with My Car** 3:05
(TAYLOR)

4. **You're My Best Friend** 2:50
(DEACON)

5. **'39** 3:25
(MAY)

6. **Sweet Lady** 4:01
(MAY)

7. **Seaside Rendezvous** 2:13
(MERCURY)

SIDE 2

1. **The Prophet's Song** 8:17
(MAY)

2. **Love of My Life** 3:38
(MERCURY)

3. **Good Company** 3:26
(MAY)

4. **Bohemian Rhapsody** 5:55
(MERCURY)

5. **God Save the Queen** 1:11
(TRAD. ARR. MAY)

PERSONNEL:

FREDDIE MERCURY – *vocals,
vocal orchestration;*
BRIAN MAY – *guitars, vocals, toy koto, harp,
genuine Aloha ukelele;*
JOHN DEACON – *bass, double bass,
electric piano;*
ROGER TAYLOR – *drums, percussion, vocals,
vocal orchestration*
RECORDED AT SARM, *London;
Roundhouse Studios, London;* TRIDENT
STUDIOS, *London;* OLYMPIC STUDIOS,
London; SCORPIO STUDIOS, *London;*
LANSDOWNE STUDIOS, *London;
and* ROCKFIELD STUDIOS, *Rockfield,
Monmouthshire, Wales
Produced by* ROY THOMAS BAKER
and QUEEN

OPPOSITE: Their own genre. Live at Nihon
Budokan, Tokyo, March 22, 1976.

4 A NIGHT AT THE OPERA

WITH CHRIS CAFFERY, DAVE ELLEFSON, ROGER MANNING JR., AND SIR PAUL MCCARTNEY

33C 062-97176   SLEM-649

*Queen
A Night At The Opera*

ESTEREO   EMI

Queen became part of the pop music fabric with *Sheer Heart Attack* and "Killer Queen," but little did their fanbase know they were totally broke and about to have a nasty breakup with manager Norman Sheffield, the band's feelings for the man documented on this record's "Death on Two Legs (Dedicated to . . .)."

A Night at the Opera was do-or-die for Queen, and lore has it that it was the most expensive record made up to that time. The band's faith in what they were doing was warranted. Not particularly a different band than the one that patched together *Sheer Heart Attack*, Queen found a way to make every sound sculpture on the new album a polished diamond. Proggy "Death on Two Legs" and "The Prophet's Song" are aggressive and angular hard rockers despite the art, the latter featuring a symphony of acapella vocals. The band regarded "The Prophet's Song" so highly that it was suggested as lead single over "Bohemian Rhapsody."

Yugoslavian and Belgian pressings of "You're My Best Friend," John's first hit with the band.

"You're My Best Friend" is John Deacon's first hit for the band, distinguished by its pervasive Wurlitzer electric piano that Freddie called horrible. "Love of My Life," written for Freddie's girlfriend, Mary Austin, is practically full-blown classical. The song later took on a life of its own when the *Live Killers* version released in 1979 became a massive hit in South America. "Sweet Lady" and "I'm in Love with My Car" are earthy rockers, while "'39" is an amusing yet yearning sci-fi folk song sung by Brian.

Perhaps most odd are three compositions in the '20s and '30s spirit of "Bring Back That Leroy Brown." Do "Lazing on a Sunday Afternoon," "Seaside Rendezvous," and "Good Company" indicate a sense of humor, timelessness, or, combined with "Bohemian Rhapsody," a willful decoupling from rock (or all of the above)? All three are delightful pieces of the plush expanse of an album that should be regarded as one of the decade's top production *tours de force*.

"Bohemian Rhapsody" serves as the album's microcosm, a demonstration platter of all that Queen could do, and a frequent candidate—alongside "Stairway to Heaven"—when rock historians and fans ponder the idea of "the greatest song of all time." Queen had already brought a few dozen groundbreaking creative moments to rock, but here the listener's sensory circuits and logic are flooded with propositions, one briskly arriving upon the last. While "novelty hit" is usually a disparaging term suggesting gimmickry, "Bohemian Rhapsody" was novel in the highest sense of the term and could not be denied hit-single status. Common sense might have dictated that it was too dizzyingly disorienting to be a hit (and at six minutes, too long), but with this one track, Queen dragged the masses along to the museum and educated them.

"Bohemian Rhapsody" would be the band's first UK No. 1 single, propelling the album to the same spot in four nonconsecutive weeks. *A Night at the Opera* peaked at No. 4 in the US and was the band's first platinum record there. As Brian suggests, Queen might have been sunk had the record not caught the imagination of record buyers. Instead, the band was heralded as rock royalty. And why not? Who would be so self-assured as to not choose to end the album with "Bohemian Rhapsody," let alone follow it with their own ostentatious version of "God Save the Queen"?

POPOFF: So *A Night at the Opera*—what are the main adjustments after *Sheer Heart Attack*?

CAFFERY: Well, *A Night at the Opera*, is like going from *Paranoid* to *Sabotage*. These guys were, like, "We're going to mess the world up now and really hit our stride and show our personalities." And that is straight out of the gate: "Death on Two Legs," just the way that is written and the confidence in the structure of the song and the background vocals and the daring-ness in the music. You could feel the talent. It's like, "We're gonna make a record and we're going to do it better than anybody else can, and on top of that, it's gonna sound like us."

MANNING JR.: As a group, they finally arrived at what they'd been striving for with the other three records. And I think the songwriting is just stronger. I imagine they were all shooting for the same thing out of the gate at the beginning but weren't necessarily the writers they would become. They weren't necessarily visionaries as far as, " What's our vision, what do we want to say to the world?" And what tools do we need to say it? What's gonna be the vehicle for that? And I think that all comes together on *A Night at the Opera*.

Israeli sleeve of *A Night at the Opera*, 1975. As a group, Queen arrived at what they'd been striving toward with the first three records—a multilayered, signature sound, and an oeuvre to build upon.

It's that beautiful marriage of, we're going to risk it all, we're really pushing the envelope. Because at that point, you can't care anymore what the public thinks. But as far as the record companies were concerned, it was, "These guys need to have a hit or I don't know how much longer we can support them."

"Killer Queen" did just fine in England, but *Sheer Heart Attack* did not, and it certainly wasn't a big record in the States. No one knew who they were. That didn't happen until *A Night at the Opera*, and it was all because of "Bohemian Rhapsody."

ELLEFSON: My introduction to Queen, Christmas '76 or '77. My brother and I were each given a cassette. He got Heart, *Dreamboat Annie*, and I got *A Night at the Opera*. I put the cassette on, which was cutting-edge technology at the time—we had a player in our Wurlitzer organ [*laughs*]. So, I put it in, very different from Kiss and other music that I had, American FM rock, Bachman-Turner Overdrive.

What first happened was, I didn't know if this was a real band or some sort of rock opera. Because I had, also on cassette, *Jesus Christ Superstar*, which had Ian Gillan as the lead vocalist on it [*laughs*]. So, I'm listening to Queen and trying to draw comparisons. Who are they? What is this? And part of it I loved was [that] there was some hard rock there, with "Death on Two Legs," *wham*, out of the gate, but there was all this symphonic guitar work, and then I see in the credits, "No synthesizers"! So, it's funny—they made that very clear. But, yeah, as a kid, it was very hard to get my head around that album.

POPOFF: It's widely known that Freddie wrote "Death on Two Legs" about Norman Sheffield.

CAFFERY: That was inspired by the fact that they were burned by somebody and they wanted not only to be who they were, but to shove it down that guy's throat. I understand there was a settlement that happened between them and management because he considered the song to be slander. Personally, I never would've paid that out, but I think they got to the point where

they got so big off that record that it didn't matter. I don't think they thought "Bohemian Rhapsody" would do what it did. But I think they just wanted to get the guy out of their lives and they had the money to do it. Here it is, go away.

ELLEFSON: I wanted the whole record to be "Death on Two Legs." They come out as a straight-ahead four-piece rock band, great vocal, cool guitar tones, cool arrangement. The whole thing's like this riff. Whereas a lot of the other ones had these jazz or swing band arrangements. As a kid, that represented everything hard rock and metal was against: jazz, swing, blues. I would learn to appreciate those styles as a bass player, but at the time, it was all about the heavy tracks.

MANNING JR.: My favorite song on the record. That not only sets the tone for the whole album, but it's just badass, definitive '70s hard rock with attitude, but with such unique character and personality. *A Night at the Opera* is synonymous with "Bohemian Rhapsody," but "Death on Two Legs," that's the first track, that's your introduction. If you didn't know "Bohemian Rhapsody," that song sets the tone for the whole record. It's got these sinister, take-no-prisoners, heavy, memorable riffs that are almost as heavy as Black Sabbath but more intellectual and skilled in architecture. The melody shapes are very weird and angular, and that's why they're so intriguing.

And then you've got these great recording techniques. The music was theatrical in that every five seconds something is happening. There's ear candy all over the place. And that's completely intentional. My friend once asked, "Hey, did you ever notice how many backward cymbals there are in 'Death on Two Legs?'" It's like, they're all over the place. Well, that has an effect on the listener; you're always being ushered into a new section. They're constantly trying to hold your attention.

And like "Bohemian Rhapsody," you almost don't know whether you like it or not. It's almost like after you've heard it ten times, then you go, "Well, I kind of like this song" or "It's not my favorite; do I really like it?" But the point was that they got you to listen. And in the days before video, and before computers and all the stuff that is vying for our attention now, you had to sit down with the record. Or your friend said, "Hey, check out this song" and you had to go into his room, put the needle down, and at least give it two minutes. And maybe he had a poster. But that's what Queen's music did from the onset. And that was obviously intentional, obviously a strategy, and it worked. But it wasn't just all packaging and no content. They're master songwriters who understand great, captivating hooks.

You could just listen to Queen and look at what one guy does with one sound and figured out different ways to sculpt that sound, throughout not only one song but a whole record or a whole career. It's mind-boggling, because his neighbor down the street in Yes or in Pink Floyd is doing it totally different! But it's still a guitar! Same electric guitar plugged into the same amplifier selection and creating colors with that.

And then what you are left with, okay, it's all about the creator. The way Brian May approached this, thought about it, and then teamed up with a Roy Thomas Baker. How are we going to make the guitar that everybody has already known now for the last fifteen years, since the '50s, what are we gonna do that's different? It's part of their legacy . . . like, have you heard Brian May's guitar?

POPOFF: So, Sir Paul, what was your introduction to Queen?

McCARTNEY: To tell you the truth, I wasn't that familiar, because I was so involved in forming Wings and working on the band. We were in our very sort of early days, and the truth is I hadn't really noticed much of Queen at that point. I was just too busy to look elsewhere. But on one of my visits up to Liverpool to see my family, there was a young boy who was the son of my cousin and he was a mad, rabid Queen fan. And he was a bass player, so as bass players, as musicians, we'd just chat and have a great relationship. And he said, "Have you heard Queen?" And I said, "Well, don't really know so much about them." "Oh well, they're my favorite group." And I saw them through his eyes and it was just amazing. So, it was through Andy Harris, who is my little second cousin. And he was so keen on the band and I liked him so much, I thought, you know, there must be something here. So, I started listening to them and then became a fan myself—through Andy.

But, yeah, great music is basically what it's all to do with. Freddie was a great singer and songwriter and they were all great players and they made very good records. So, their music, first of all, and then their showmanship second. But in the writing and the playing, that's where it all lives or dies, and that's what they were so good at.

POPOFF: Chris, how about a few words on Brian May? As a guitarist yourself, I understand you use both metal and plastic picks. And, of course, both Savatage and Trans-Siberian Orchestra have often been compared to Queen.

CAFFERY: Joel, in TSO, uses metal picks sometimes. In my in-ear monitors on stage, I'm in one ear and Joel is in the other, and I can tell when he's using the metal pick. There's such a difference in tone, in the way that the notes hit you. Because it's—to quote Anvil—metal on metal. And Brian using his sixpence as a pick on "Death on Two Legs," when he's stabbing the guitar notes, you can tell something is picking those strings that's giving it a different sound.

Brian made his own sound. He even made his own guitar to make that sound. You can buy one of these new digital effects boxes and it says Brian May this or Eddie Van Halen that. But it takes Brian May to make Brian May. And what was amazing is that he made that one particular sound work in every Queen song. All of these songs had different colors and flavors, but he made that one sound work in everything.

His guitar solos are very isolated in the songs. It's funny that Queen has these impossible-to-re-create vocals, but also incredibly achievable production in the guitar, bass, and drums. They never really layered tons of guitar tracks. There were harmonies and stuff, the guitar solos. But they never really layered rhythms behind it when he went to do that solo; you would sit there and go, oh my God, this is so bare live. As well, he did something with the tone; there's a push in this one register of the midrange. And that guitar he was playing, it has a hollower kind of body and that gave him a specific sound.

ELLEFSON: I love how Brian played and I thought his tone was very weird. I subscribed to *Guitar Player* magazine. It was like the only guitar magazine in America, pretty much, when I was a teenager, and I would read how he used this coin instead of a pick, and he had his handmade guitar through a Vox amp. I mean, he was so British and so different. He looked British, he sounded British. Everything about him was so not a Les Paul into a Marshall. He was so not the status quo.

And that's what was cool about Queen in general—nothing was status quo. John Deacon played a Fender Precision bass through these acoustic amps, which had that very bassy sound. John Paul Jones did the same thing. And I liked that the drummer sang. Each was unique. They were almost like art students who got together and created a rock 'n' roll band.

You know, Brian, he's got such a calmness and a warmth about how he plays and about who he is. As I later got to know him in my professional career, he truly is that guy [*laughs*]. And that's the thing about all the guys in Queen: their personalities really seem to come out in their performances.

POPOFF: Sticking with the heavy ones for the moment, what are your thoughts on "Sweet Lady"?

MANNING JR.: "Sweet Lady," good Lord, that's like progressive hard rock without it sounding like Rush. It's heavy, very intricate. "Sweet Lady" is just such an amazing hard rock song. It's musicianly, but you still want to bang your head. Again, it's got that Sabbath heaviness, but it's on Queen's terms. Very inspirational. When I first tried to write songs on guitar—because as a keyboard player it's very hard to get that heaviness I wanted—I was hoping to get even remotely close to the neighborhood of the riffs on *Night at the Opera*, to convey that level of attitude. And that amazing arranging ability.

ELLEFSON: "Sweet Lady" could've been on a Styx record. Hard rocker, ripping guitar tones, and just so cool.

CAFFERY: "Sweet Lady" has one of my favorite Brian May solos ever. If you look at the Queen catalog, there's not a lot of songs where he really opens up like that and has that amount of time to do it. Plus, his tone—it reminds me sometimes of early Uli Jon Roth. Uli was using something that Jimi Hendrix had, which sounded like a mute inside a trumpet. And I could hear those similarities between Uli Jon Roth and Brian May. Not that those two even really knew who each other was at the time. But they both sometimes had this dry sound that comes from Hendrix.

And I love the time change. That's something that most other bands wouldn't even try to do. I know in prog rock it's normal, but just a regular rock band is not going to flip the time around. I understand that was very difficult for Roger to record on drums.

POPOFF: What do you make of there being no less than three of these vaudevillian-type numbers on the record?

MANNING JR.: I applaud it, and at the same time if I have too much of it, I have to turn it off. It kind of bums me out after a while because it's so, so playful and silly. That music is from a different era with a different social consciousness both in England and America. That

vaudevillian time has a great romance to it. It's why Freddie liked it; it resonated with him. It was part of his personality, so he was looking for a way to incorporate it in this rock setting. For me, it can be overkill. It's obviously part of that album's sound, but to me it came off as silly, even though they're masterfully executed.

ELLEFSON: I remember hearing "Lazing on a Sunday Afternoon" and my reaction being what the hell is this? Very bizarre. Again, I'm like, who are these guys? What kind of an album is this? I was used to hearing *Destroyer* with "Detroit Rock City," where it's almost like a concert. But, hey, they called it the Roaring '20s, and musically, Queen took you back to that era. I remember thinking this is like my grandparents' music or something. So, to be honest, I skipped over those—and with a cassette, it was hard [*laughs*]! Those songs kept me from becoming a really dyed-in-the-wool Queen fan as a kid because it was just too diverse.

CAFFERY: "Lazing on a Sunday Afternoon" is just fun. It's got that "Hello My Baby" vibe. It's impossible to listen to that without smiling. The vocals gave it a distinct personality, where he's sort of saying, "Don't take me too seriously."

POPOFF: Where does this vaudeville tradition come from with Queen, with British musicians?

McCARTNEY: Our parents, basically. Our parents' generation. It was there when we were kids, when we were in short trousers growing up. It was all around. It was on the radio, mainly. Through the BBC, you were exposed to a lot of music. And there were quite a few request programs where you'd hear quite a variety of music. I mean, you'd go to a local park and there might be a brass band playing. Your parents would have stories of the music hall. My dad used to work in a music hall. He was operating the spotlight, which was called the limelight because they actually burned lime to make the strong glow, which you focused down into a beam. So, he was exposed to all of that and we knew all these tunes and could play them on the piano. And that also meant that all my aunties and uncles were exposed to this music and knew it all. They knew it by heart. So, not only on the radio, but we were also hearing it live, you know, from our families. There was just a lot of that around.

Canadian pressing of "You're My Best Friend" b/w "'39."

POPOFF: These songs pack in a lot of production.

MANNING JR.: Yes, well, *A Night at the Opera* was recorded through a Trident A-Range console, but there's no nuance to it. They were just pinging the meters, frying the input as hard as they could without getting a crazy, unpleasant distortion. There's natural distortion, but what happens is, just like when you hit tape too hard, you get a natural compression.

Not that other people weren't doing that, but again, everything with Queen is in-your-face and overt. And that comes as much from the sonics as it does from the songwriting and the performances. And a lot of the Queen sound was pushing the gear of the day to its maximum and not necessarily being obsessed with a clean signal. They didn't mind it being a little rough around the edges. Some people call that "putting fur on it." There's also a tendency to lean on the room mics for both the drum set and for the guitar amps.

POPOFF: What about the others of this set?

CAFFERY: "Seaside Rendezvous" is one of my favorite songs on the record. That's another one where you can't listen to it and not smile. And the human orchestra in the middle of it is the craziest thing ever [*laughs*]. I want to steal that one day.

But those songs, I wonder where that influence came from. What were they listening to? Who was a fan of what? Because you need to have a lot of influence for something like that, whether it was who taught you how to play piano or growing up with a lot of ragtime as a kid. It couldn't have been a slight influence, because it's really hard to pull it off with such skill and conviction. To do it at that level and to have it that believable—the knowledge of that music has to be more than slight.

And then the third one, "Good Company," I thought was very George Harrison–like. From what I understand, that's one of the only songs that Queen had done that Freddie didn't have anything to do with.

POPOFF: John has a bit of a hit on her with "You're My Best Friend."

MANNING JR.: Our silent friend on bass. It's so wonderfully bubble-gum pop. And yet it still sounds super-confident when Queen does it. Beautiful song, simple, straightforward sentiment, like all his songwriting. It gives Queen a great opportunity to not only do their incredible guitar arranging, but also the harmonies. It's almost like they finish the record and

Queen was just one British band that helped carry the nation's vaudeville and music hall traditions into the rock era. Freddie's increasing confidence in his towering voice and showmanship made him the perfect ringleader for this band— and movement—to rally around. Masonic Temple, Detroit, February 1976.

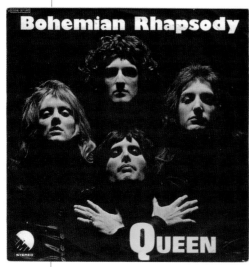

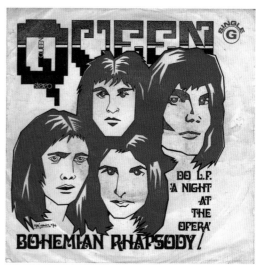

The international success of "Bohemian Rhapsody" opened the gates for Queen to do anything they pleased. **CLOCKWISE FROM TOP LEFT:** Belgium, Japan, France, UK, Germany, Denmark, Portugal, and Italy.

they're like, "It would be really, really great if we had a song like this." And then he shows up with it. Perfect. It helps balance the album.

ELLEFSON: Cool song, obviously, with a complex bass line. John wrote it about his wife, Veronica. Looking back on it, here's a guy, very understated, writes a song about his wife and it turns out that it's one of the biggest Queen singles ever. And then after the group disbands after Freddie's death, he doesn't come back with Roger and Brian in the new Queen and it's probably because he's at home with his best friend, his wife [*laughs*]. So, in a way, that song sums up who John Deacon is.

CAFFERY: I love that song. It's one of the songs where you say, "I can name that tune in one note." You don't even need to go past the first note. Years later, it's one of the most recognizable Queen songs. Very friendly too.

But another one that I really like on there is "Love of My Life." That's one of those that every Queen fan knows word for word, note for note, and will sing it. That comes over PAs and bars and people just sing every word. I know even when they played it live sometimes, they didn't even sing—the audience did it.

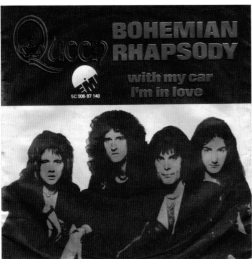

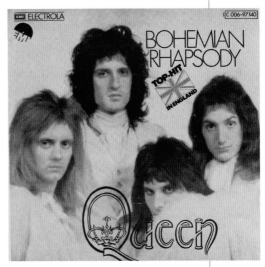

McCARTNEY: With John, I think, often bass players that are in bands like that tend to try to keep out of the way a bit. And in my view, John did that very well. It's sometimes quite a skill to be reasonably minimal. I think, for instance, of Adam Clayton in U2—again, he keeps out of the way. Not like me. I tend to be sort of more melodic. Still, Queen, I think they're all excellent players and you can't deny that when you hear the music. They make a hell of a noise.

POPOFF: We should talk about Roger's song "I'm in Love with My Car," which is perhaps the most straightforward thing on the album.

MANNING JR.: A welcome addition. A handful of groups contributed to what became an absolute movement and scene in England at the time, whether that's Mott the Hoople, Bowie, Slade, or David Essex. And Roger is very tied into that. He tried to keep Queen competitive and relevant in that scene, but not in a pretentious way. Not trying to be something they're not. Yeah, he's the racer boy. With all of Queen's frilly clothing and flirting with their feminine androgynous side, Roger's got the Teddy Boy thing and the Suzi Quatro leather thing front and center. I love Roger's contributions to all the records.

ELLEFSON: Amazing song. I love the bigness of it all and I love Roger Taylor's voice. As much as I love Freddie's voice, Roger's had an edge. Plus, he looked like Rod Stewart and was the cool rock star of the band.

CAFFERY: This is one of those where Freddie didn't write it and he had very little invested in it. Unlike "The Prophet's Song," where even though he didn't write it, you could tell he loved the song so he worked very hard on it. It's like he just walked away from this and let them do it on their own. Production-wise, I don't think it rises to the level of everything else. As far as the sound, it's left pretty raw. And it wound up being the B-side of "Bohemian Rhapsody." I would love to have written the song that was the B-side to "Bohemian Rhapsody."

POPOFF: Who can forget "Bohemian Rhapsody"? What did you think upon hearing it for the very first time?

MANNING JR.: It was, "What the hell is this? I don't even know if I like it or not, but it's got my attention." It's weird and the vocals are so unmistakably different. I've heard harmonies before, but it doesn't sound like the Beach Boys. And just when you think it's a bunch of guys doing weird theater, they kick into all this heavy rock. So epic. I still marvel, not that people liked it, but that that it was such a universal hit. That "Bohemian Rhapsody" was an international hit and so globally accepted and had such a large audience blows my mind. That just opened the gates for Queen to do anything they wanted. It was absolutely a game-changer for them.

Album closer "God Save the Queen" was perhaps a cheeky self-reference, but it also marked the band as quintessentially British.

ELLEFSON: Same reaction: "What is this?!" But it was so hooky that it caught you. Because the thing is, usually track one or track two are the biggest singles on a record. Here, the second-to-last song is "Bohemian Rhapsody"—if you were turned off by the record early on, you wouldn't have even discovered it. So, first time, just because I let the cassette play, I discovered it and it was like, oh, check this out.

McCARTNEY: The writing of the whole piece is phenomenal, and then the execution of the harmonies, the lead singing and the playing, is classic. It's an all-time classic track. Freddie as a singer is a given; he was an excellent singer as well as songwriter. He had a great voice and was a great theatrical presence. I don't think anyone could deny that. They were a great band.

CAFFERY: That song is so good, I don't think it should be that surprising it was so huge. You know, luckily, prog rock had some stuff that was making it to radio, and people's ears were opening up to longer songs; it wasn't about the three-minute hit anymore.

It's got that really raucous guitar, the *Wayne's World* guitar part—you're always going to think of that movie when you hear it [*laughs*]. It was the perfect song of its kind. And the lyrics are one of rock's great well-kept mysteries. No question, Freddie escaped into that song and was trying to do something very special.

POPOFF: At the close of the album, we get a rendition of "God Save the Queen." This marks the band as quintessentially British. Are there other markers to that effect?

McCARTNEY: Well, I mean, they are all British, except Freddie. And Freddie was educated in Britain. So, they all have a Britishness due to their upbringing, even Freddie. And they have a British sensibility in the music because they grew up during the time of the '60s explosion and were heavily influenced by '60s music, including the Beatles. Plus, I think their songs are not only good music and catchy, but there's a nice tongue-in-cheek quality. In other words, I think they're rather witty songs. Which appealed to me. Funny, I only met Freddie once, when we were recording in the same studio in Barnes in London, Olympic Studios. I was doing some recording there with Wings and he was in a next-door studio. We met and he was very charming, really terrific. I remember chatting about the bits of music we were making. A little smaller than I'd expected. I didn't know he was not a tall guy. Because it wasn't obvious from pictures. You know, he obviously wasn't tall, but his persona was tall.

POPOFF: To explore this a little further, is there also a Britishness simply to the fact that Queen were recording, at various times and in various territories, for the venerable EMI, Capitol, and later Parlophone.

Promo poster for *A Night at the Opera* tour, 1976.

McCARTNEY: Sure. Growing up in England, record labels were very important, and very sort of atmospheric. You know, you could just look at a record and just enjoy looking at the label—you kind of fell in love with the artifact. Something like a Parlophone record was a beautiful thing. When we had an option to be signed to an EMI label, they mentioned a couple of labels that we could possibly be signed to. When we heard that there was a possibility of Parlophone, we jumped at that because it was just one of those iconic names that we were sort of in love with.

And I suspect a lot of people do that. I could only guess, but maybe the Stones went to Atlantic for largely that kind of reason. This glamorous label with Ahmet Ertegun and things like that came first. But just the idea of being part of the EMI family in the beginning was some kind of honor. There's a lot of tradition there. And for us, it was . . . it still is. I'm actually back on Capitol, through the machinations of the business world. And I'm kind of proud of it. Because I remember sitting with, in that case, this purple label with the Capitol building on it, or the sleeve it came in, and staring at it for hours like it was a piece of art. You just had to look at it and your imagination went wild. So, yeah, I think there is something to do with that iconic rock 'n' roll tradition that the Beatles and I think Queen would probably admit to.

POPOFF: Cool. To sum up, does this record help us at all to define what genre Queen fits? Are they a prog band, a hard rock band, a glam band?

ELLEFSON: I think Queen is their own genre. Because of their age, they were certainly coming out of the glam thing. But then they would go on and do *The Works* and *A Kind of Magic*. Really, they're like U2. They really planted their flag, defied all commercial pressures, and yet thrived and invented their own genre. I guess they're genre-proof, which is pretty incredible. And they became—and still are—royalty in the UK. In a way that we in America can't even comprehend. They are the royal family of rock. They became everything that their name said they were [*laughs*]. And that's a pretty cool thing, too, to be so bold as to call yourself Queen and then to grow into that. They became one of Britain's most aristocratic and iconic bands, really, only second to the Beatles.

Queen may have become part of the pop music fabric after "Killer Queen," but little did their fans know, they were totally broke.

RELEASED DECEMBER 10, 1976

5 A DAY AT THE RACES

WITH HANSI KÜRSCH, NINA NOIR, AND DARIUS RUCKER

SIDE 1

1. **Tie Your Mother Down** 4:47
   (MAY)

2. **You Take My Breath Away** 5:09
   (MERCURY)

3. **Long Away** 3:34
   (MAY)

4. **The Millionaire Waltz** 4:55
   (MERCURY)

5. **You and I** 3:27
   (DEACON)

SIDE 2

1. **Somebody to Love** 4:56
   (MERCURY)

2. **White Man** 4:59
   (MAY)

3. **Good Old-Fashioned Lover Boy** 2:55
   (MERCURY)

4. **Drowse** 3:43
   (TAYLOR)

5. **Teo Torriatte (Let Us Cling Together)** 5:54
   (MAY)

PERSONNEL:

FREDDIE MERCURY – *vocals, piano;*
BRIAN MAY – *guitars, vocals, guitar orchestration, slide, harmonium piano, plastic piano;*
JOHN DEACON – *bass, acoustic guitar;*
ROGER TAYLOR – *drums, percussion, vocals, electric rhythm*

GUEST PERSONNEL:

MIKE STONE – *vocals*
Recorded at SARM *East Studios, Whitechapel, London;* WESSEX SOUND STUDIOS, *London; and* THE MANOR, *Shipton-on-Cherwell, Oxford*
Produced by QUEEN

OPPOSITE: Timeout from rehearsals at Earls Court, 1977. To show their vision was theirs alone, Queen self-produced the follow-up to their incrementally successful *A Night at the Opera*.

Proving that their vision had been theirs alone all along, Queen self-produced the follow-up to *A Night at the Opera*. Roy Thomas Baker was gone. His longtime engineer, Mike Stone, was kept on, admired for his deft stacking of vocal harmonies (and their sympathetic placement in the mix), which run riot all over *A Day at the Races*. Stone sadly succumbed to the demon drink in 2002, when he was barely fifty years old and having just been tapped to remaster the Queen catalog for reissue.

A bull-headed producer might have pushed Queen to make greater leaps forward. *A Day at the Races* was not that, but rather a record that matched up almost song for song with the architectural underpinnings of its predecessor. The irony of that is that the record *A Day at the Races* somewhat mirrors (visually as well, with the white-to-black cover arts) had represented such a disorienting chimera of styles. In 1977 (following the album's release mid-December 1976), fans and critics alike noticed this, satisfied in having Queen

pegged for the first time, after having been confounded by "Bohemian Rhapsody." And despite the quilt-work of styles all over *A Day at the Races*, the band took care to create more discernibly shaped and rounded songs. Deemphasized was the prog of "Bohemian Rhapsody," "Death on Two Legs," and "The Prophet's Song." Instead, Queen's ultimate expressions of songcraft on this album were displayed in the spare ballads and in "Tie Your Mother Down," which could have boogie-woogied without glaring distinction on *Fool for the City* or even *Love Gun*.

The record's only other heavy song, "White Man," verges on metallic, with Brian aptly pounding home his tale of indigenous protest with Geronimo riffs found in Sabbath before and Soundgarden after. "White Man" is also an example of how Mercury could inject aggression into a hard rock vocal through sheer power and projection rather than screams and growls.

In fact, it's at the vocal end of things that *A Day at the Races* excels. "You Take My Breath Away" is entirely the creation of Freddie and Mike Stone, an example of how far Queen could take inspired chorals. Producer and band utilize reverse recording and the song washes carefully into the record's next track, "You and I." "Teo Torriatte (Let Us Cling Together)" is the band's tribute to Japanese fans, and like "Las Palabras de Amor" from *Hot Space* even includes non-English lyrics in the chorus. Also of interest, the song ends with the same harmonium passage that opens the album, an idea May assessed as "a never-ending staircase."

"Somebody to Love" combines both dynamics, with Queen creating what is perhaps the most emotionally torrid of their smash hits upon a frame not much less traditional than that supporting "Teo Torriatte," then loading it up like a Mardi Gras float. Vaulted gospel vocals are what this one's all about, but Roger Taylor also shines, as he does on much of Queen's balladry, with his simple yet exacting percussion.

In the harsh light of punk, *A Day at the Races* and the band making it were no longer the talk of the town. Sure, Queen was big, but they were also establishment. "Somebody to Love" and "Tie Your Mother Down" were just two more Queen hits, nothing shocking like "Killer Queen" or "Bohemian Rhapsody." Also, since about 1975, there had been a shift away from the UK in terms of hard rock, with 1977 being big years for the likes of Kiss, Aerosmith, Ted Nugent, Blue Öyster Cult, Heart, and UK transplants Foghat. Into this landscape, Queen, one of the world's most relentlessly surprising and individualistic bands, delivered something familiar. Nonetheless, *A Day at the Races* blasted to No. 1 on the UK charts, hitting No. 5 in the United States and finding the top spot in Japan, the only territory in which "Teo Torriatte" was issued as a single. Canada bought the record in platinum quantities as did the US. Perhaps more importantly, "Tie Your Mother Down" and "Somebody to Love" would only grow in status over time.

POPOFF: What are the main adjustments from *A Day at the Races* to *A Night at the Opera*? It's difficult not to look at them as a tidy pair, is it not?

KÜRSCH: Yes, I tend to look at them as twins. They have so much in common in terms of the structure and even song-to-song comparisons. But I would say *A Day at the Races* is the more mature album, and to a certain

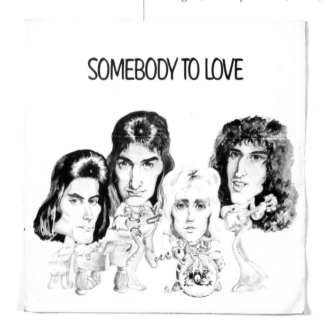

"Somebody to Love" b/w "White Man," UK, 1976. "Somebody to Love" would grow in status over time, arguably becoming the most beloved Queen anthem of all time—not the most famed, but the most cherished.

SOMEBODY TO LOVE

extent, it defines the end of an era. Compared though, maybe influenced by the artwork, I see *A Day at the Races* as darker but also just better, more ambitious, no filler, the superior album.

RUCKER: It might have been a little ill-received compared to *A Night at the Opera*. I'm sure it was for some people. But, you know, when you come up with an album with that many good songs, I'm in. Being a radio kid like I was, it was more about the singles than the whole album. Because back then, it was hard for me to afford albums [*laughs*]. But for me, when a Queen record came out and you heard it on the radio, you always wanted to run out and get that 45. Those are moments I'll always remember. Like when "Bohemian Rhapsody" came out, all I wanted to do was know that song. You'd get the 45 and take your time and you'd go back and forth. Over and over, I listened to that and that's how I got into Queen.

POPOFF: The album opens with a bang, "Tie Your Mother Down" being quite rock 'n' rollsy for the band, even containing a slide solo and a boogie woogie chorus.

RUCKER: Great song, and different for them, a shuffle. I mean, another example of Queen delivering something you don't expect, but once you listen to it, why didn't you expect it? [*laughs*]

Great live song too. You watch Freddie perform that; Freddie was so confident on the stage. You watch the old tapes of those concerts, and Freddie's so amazingly confident in what he's doing onstage. And it never seemed like it was choreographed. It was Freddie being Freddie.

KÜRSCH: Again, with the matchups, it's in the tradition of "Death on Two Legs," but it's more to the point, more aggressive. The performance is enormous and it's a different type of hard

Queen at the Tokyo Prince Hotel's garden, April 20, 1975. As with its predecessor, *A Day at the Races* opened with a cracker of a song, namely "Tie Your Mother Down."

rock from the band. There's an anger in the vocals, which I've never heard in any other Queen performances before. And the fact that Brian May wrote it in 1968 makes it even more spectacular and respectable. And that slide solo . . . Brian's solos have influenced so many lead guitarists. I remember having a session with Kai Hansen from Gamma Ray in the late '80s or early '90s, and he was referring to that solo over and over again, which gives you an idea of how influential it is.

NOIR: I agree that the two records complement each other, with the artwork and both titles taken from the Marx Brothers films, and even being somewhat in the spirit of those movies, given that they were from the mid-'30s and Queen revisits the music from that era on both albums. And, yes, they start with "Tie Your Mother Down," which is really a heavy blues-rock song. Our tribute band, Killer Queens, sometimes opens our shows with that song and we've learned that we can't play it next to "Crazy Little Thing Called Love" because they're too similar.

Copping a couple of album titles from Marx Brothers films was fitting, given that both films were from the 1930s, a period Queen revisited musically on both albums.

They've got the same kind of swing feel and similar chording. The slide solo gives it an almost country feel, especially nowadays when we consider country as more rock—"Tie Your Mother Down" would almost fit modern country.

POPOFF: Hansi, your band, Blind Guardian, called your seventh album *A Night at the Opera*. What inspired you guys to do that?

KÜRSCH: That was because (a) we were Queen fans and (b) we liked the humor, and we knew that the Queen guys had a sense of humor as well. And many people were considering us the Queen of heavy metal, put it that way. Plus, it was a super-ambitious album with so many multiple vocal layers that we thought, well, it would be a nice treat to call it *A Night at the Opera*. People were really insulting us and were really, really angry. They thought we were being arrogant and too ambitious.

But it was never our goal to say we are the new Queen or we are on the same level as Queen. It was a joke and a tribute and a bit of fun. And we also felt that the title really fit the music because we had some orchestral elements on there and, as I said, multilayered vocals as well. So, "Opera" was our reference to the music itself. But like I say, when we were accused of stealing the title, I knew that it was stolen from the Marx Brothers, so I didn't really see the big offense, put it that way.

POPOFF: "Tie Your Mother Down" was played widely on the radio, but "Somebody to Love" was a much bigger hit. Why do you think that song has endured and grown in stature over the years?

Though Freddie's falsetto became a hallmark of Queen recordings, in concert he would take the lower notes and leave the highs to Roger. The Playhouse, Edinburgh, Scotland, September 1976.

"Good Old-Fashioned Lover Boy" and "Death on Two Legs (Dedicated To. . .)" b/w "Tenement Funster" and "White Queen (As It Began)," U.K., 1977. "Good Old-Fashioned Lover Boy" delivers grandeur rarely heard from other rock composers, evoking Oscar Wilde, burlesque, and even Weimar Germany.

KÜRSCH: One thing about Queen is their ability to incorporate so many surprising things in one song, and things that appear easy but are quite complicated. The two main aspects of this song, though, are the huge choirs and the 6/8 approach. Not unheard of for Queen, but most bands ignore 3/4 or 6/8 beats. Queen do it so spectacularly that people do not even recognize that it's not particularly rock 'n' roll [*laughs*].

RUCKER: "Somebody to Love" is my favorite Queen song ever. Freddie's vocal . . . oh, man, I think about it now and I'm getting chills. When he gets to "Can anybody find me somebody to love," when he hits that high note and then the bridge, "Everyday I try and I try and I try/But everybody wants to put me down," it's so groovy and unlike anything else they were doing. His vocals are genius and have that opera feel with the backgrounds.

"Somebody to Love" is definitely a ballad, but the production and the way they play it, it's like a heavy metal song. But Freddie's vocals take it to a whole new level, a place where as a singer you just go wow, goddammit, he delivered like hell. His range . . . he had this incredible falsetto that was so strong, it's not even like singing a falsetto; it's like he's singing in full voice up there, and then he can come down and go "Crazy Little Thing Called Love" and sound amazing. And then the backing vocals on "Somebody to Love" are genius. Brian and Roger could both be dedicated lead singers.

NOIR: Every time we perform that song the audience loses its mind. It's got a gospel, preaching feel to it, which you don't really hear in a lot of their music. Being that it's coming out after four albums, you'd maybe have expected to hear something similar before. It's a showcase for Freddie as well. I'm a voice teacher as well as a professional singer, and I study Freddie's voice a lot, as you can imagine, and I find him fascinating because he does things that are technically incorrect. Like he brings his chest voice up way too high, almost to the point where he's screaming, but it creates this really intense tone that I think the audience has fallen in love with it. He's not really singing as correctly as he probably should, but that creates a raw emotion that everybody just goes crazy for.

It's interesting to sing Queen, because I have to do so many different styles. Freddie's got a four-octave range and he uses most of that across the catalog.

POPOFF: Hansi, how about you, also from the standpoint as a singer?

KÜRSCH: For me, the most significant thing about Freddie is that he has a three-and-a-half-, four-octave range, and he could sing songs in any part of his range and they would sound like Freddie. His ability and easy adaptation to switch from chest to falsetto without losing the intensity and the dynamic is outstanding.

As well, he keeps songs in a certain range where he shines through best, usually around two octaves. And for a lead vocalist, that's quite a lot. It's an honest, very clean voice. He barely has any roughness, even when he does the heavy stuff, which is also very unique, considering also that he kept it up for almost twenty years.

But what shines through most, like with Peter Gabriel of Genesis, for example, is the character, the personality, which is very warm. You feel very comfortable and close to it. The way they produced, especially the first albums, it's like he's in your room. He's not hidden at any point. He's the front man and the shining star. Obviously, Brian and Roger have great talent, but it's Freddie who shines through.

POPOFF: And Freddie uses his falsetto a lot too.

NOIR: Especially during recording. But if you watch live performances, he doesn't do that live. He chooses lower notes and Roger Taylor comes in and sings the high notes. Freddie will do some of them, but he won't do it in his head voice, he'll do it more as a belt. And I think that's mostly because when you're in a rock setting, you have a really loud band behind you, and if you use your head voice, it disappears. But in recording, he uses it and he sounds beautiful. He should've used it more live, but I think at that time, they didn't have the techniques for live sound to balance his voice so you could hear the head voice. Now you can do that.

POPOFF: And again there are links here to music of the '20s and '30s.

NOIR: We started doing "Good Old-Fashioned Lover Boy" because it's one of my favorites and it's so campy. It's actually very typical Queen, but not necessarily the sound that they are famous for. But it's a style you hear routinely on the '70s albums, with almost a musical theater style of singing.

The song on here that I wish I could perform is "The Millionaire Waltz." Amazing. I love where it goes. It starts off with lots of fast piano and then it takes you on this long journey,

BELOW: Brøndbyhallen, Copenhagen, Denmark, May 12, 1977.

OVERLEAF: Queen had a knack for incorporating many surprises in a single song—chords, trills, and frills that appeared easy but were musically quite complicated.

and by the end of it, you feel like you've listened to four songs. Queen fans often compare it to "Bohemian Rhapsody," which is high praise. It's very difficult to do that one live. There are a lot of Queen songs that Queen wouldn't even do live.

RUCKER: Most people, I guess they'd hear it as '20s music or vaudevillian, but to us it was Queen and you didn't even think about it. Shuffle, rockabilly, funk, synth-pop, whatever—when they did it, that was just Queen making great songs.

KÜRSCH: "Good Old-Fashioned Lover Boy" and "Millionaire's Waltz" deliver humor and grandeur that you rarely hear from other rock composers, although it reminds me of the creativity of the Beatles. They evoke Oscar Wilde, burlesque themes, even the Weimar Republic. Here in Germany, we had our first democracy between the Great War and World War II, and this period has been called the Republic of Weimar. Berlin in the '30s was influenced by Paris fashion and New York and there was established a colorful art and music scene with a shady reputation. And so that cabaret feel is in some of these Queen songs. Freddie even crosses into a slightly German approach at times, with his pronunciation and delivery of some of the words.

As a listener, you sense that Queen takes it very seriously and that they are careful in their adaptations of these things from the past. Sonically, there's somehow this dusty patina that fits the scene. And with Freddie's ability as an entertainer, he shines through.

POPOFF: But as we know, as with Pink Floyd and even Kiss, there are other good singers in this band. What do you make of Roger's lone song on here, "Drowse"?

KÜRSCH: Both Roger Taylor and Brian May are perfectly fine lead singers—they could've done it themselves. Roger has a fabulous voice. He's so high-pitched when he does the choir stuff, beyond imagination; there's no other vocalist I know that can go as high as Roger Taylor. Just like "I'm in Love with My Car," oddly, "Drowse" has a very strong 6/8 pattern, but there's so much more going on. It's almost like listening to a different vocalist than "I'm in Love with My Car." Here it's more of his softer voice.

ROW (1) SEAT

A 25

FLOOR

Retain Stub — Good Only
No Exchange — No Refund

TUE.
8:00 P.M.

FEB. 1
1977

Davis Printing Limited

"QUEEN"

PRICE-7.00+RST .70-$7.70

ADMIT ONE. Entrance by Main
Door or by Church Street Door.

Maple Leaf Gardens
LIMITED
CONDITION OF SALE

Upon refunding the purchase
price the management may
remove fr⌐ the premises

NOIR: "Drowse" reminds me of the psychedelic side of the Beatles. The 6/8 signature gives it a swing feel. It's so spacey, you almost don't realize it's Roger Taylor when you first hear it. You're like, wait, what band is this now? [*laughs*]. I really think Roger was the most underrated rock singer of his time. He's put out albums that haven't really been embraced. And, man, every time he writes a song for Queen, it contributes another dimension to the album. On *II*, his song "The Loser in the End" is almost Zeppelin-like.

He's got a really awesome high vocal, but he's got lots of vocal fry, a technique used to create that edgy rocker sound, where the voice sort of rasps out. You don't want to put a lot of pressure on your voice to make it do that, so what we do is back off the vocal chords to the point where they're barely touching and it gives you that raspy, growling sound without doing a lot of damage.

POPOFF: One that rarely gets talked about is "White Man," which, really, is one of the band's heaviest songs, almost Black Sabbath in nature.

KÜRSCH: Sure, and as I said before, there's that tendency to match up songs to *A Night at the Opera*, and here one can think of "Sweet Lady" or "The Prophet's Song," but *A Day at the Races* always wins the matchups for me and "White Man," in comparison, is the better song. Its dark approach captured me from the very first moment. I like the reprise, the false ending. It's a perfect heavy rock song, although if I had to pick a favorite on the album, it's "Teo Torriatte."

With "Bohemian Rhapsody" concluding *A Night at the Opera*, I couldn't imagine how these guys could come up with something as big or as impressive to close *A Day at the Races*, but I really think they accomplished that with "Teo Torriatte." It's both harmonic and moody and even though it has nothing in common with "Bohemian Rhapsody," apart from its quality, it's on the same level for me. It has such great piano parts and a very nice singalong choir. I would kill to have written a song like that; it's in my top five Queen songs ever.

NOIR: I love "Teo Torriatte." When I first heard this album, I was so confused when they started singing in Japanese. This is the song that makes them so wildly popular in Japan. I've heard from people who go over to Japan that they have lots of Queen tribute nights over there with multiple Freddie Mercuries coming on stage in all the different Freddie Mercury fashions. "Teo Torriatte" is just an uplifting ballad that brings everyone together.

POPOFF: As you say, that's the closer of the album, but the closer of side one of the original vinyl was John Deacon's only song on here, "You and I," a jaunty number. He's somewhat of a stealth pop craftsman, isn't he?

KÜRSCH: Yes, I'd agree with that. I'm a big John Deacon fan. I like the way the album is dominated by the piano, and that's a characteristic of "You and I" as well. It connects with "You're My Best Friend," I suppose. But I like the acoustic performance, the easy accessibility and simplicity of the song. It's a welcome organic part of such a bombastic album.

POPOFF: Nina, as a vocalist and vocal coach, what are your thoughts on "You Take My Breath Away," which is possibly even more elaborate of voice than "Somebody to Love"?

NOIR: That's the song I would consider most Queen-like on the album. Very intense vocal, unique. As soon as you hear it, it's like, only Queen could do this. It's so layered that you're drawn in immediately.

RUCKER: Queen's one of those bands you want to listen to with the headphones on. Because there are so many little quirks, little vocal or guitar things they do, a little hook here or there you might miss, and that makes for entertainment. That makes you love them even more when you sit and listen. That's one of the things I love about them. You listen to a song like "Take My Breath Away" or "Bohemian Rhapsody," you think you're hearing everything, but you're not until you put on headphones and you really listen and realize, "Wow, I've never heard that before." That's what Queen did, and I'm sure they did it on purpose.

POPOFF: We haven't talked about Brian May much in the context of this album. He wrote "Long Away"—spirited, buoyant, a bit folk, maybe somewhat Celtic—and "Teo Torriatte," but also the two most guitar-centric songs: "Tie Your Mother Down" and "White Man."

KÜRSCH: It's no secret that Blind Guardian is a Queen-inspired band, but even if you are inspired by Queen, you cannot cover what they have done throughout their career, musically, because they have such an enormous range. But Brian May is really the biggest personal interest, especially in our field of heavy metal. He has influenced many, many heavy metal guitarists. Nowadays, guitarists have so many conveniences because of the pickups we have, for example. But, you know, he designed his stuff, guitars and pickups, with the help of his father, although when it comes to pickups, he had microphonic issues with what they did and moved over to Burns Tri-Sonics. Still, so much of who Brian is comes from this homemade quality to his thinking.

From a performance standpoint, he is the founder and inventor of that multiple-harmony lead style that is an obviously big influence on Blind Guardian. I haven't met Brian in person, and I don't know how much of it is acting, but he seems to be a very nice fellow as well as very intelligent. You can hear that in his playing. He has his own sound, his own style, and over time, he improved it and perfected it. So, as the master of multitracked guitars, of layered solos, but also through his innovative work with effects, he's got to be considered one of the most outstanding guitarists of the '70s.

POPOFF: And surely he was a big part of producing *A Day at the Races*, officially the band's first self-produced album. Did Queen succeed at producing the record themselves?

KÜRSCH: Absolutely. From my point of view as a musician, I think it's the best-sounding of the old Queen albums. I like what Roy Thomas Baker did, but everything about *A Day at the Races*, from the point of view of a musician, is very professionally arranged and produced, and everything sounds serious and expensive. It's up to the highest technical standards, but it's restrained enough so that you can discern and hear every individual instrument. I think it sounds perfect—it's flawless.

POPOFF: But it's interesting. As much as a heavy metal guy as you are, your love of Queen doesn't end with a traditional album like this.

KÜRSCH: No. I mean, exactly like you, and being the same age as you, I didn't like *The Game* so much when it came out. And when I started my career as a musician, Queen was not on my radar for the first year because I was only listening to heavy metal. But just like with *Jazz* or *A Day at the Races*, which I loved instantly, the older I got, I'd say by the end of the '80s, the band and I rediscovered Queen again.

I began to appreciate and start liking even the '80s stuff, which I had my issues with when the albums were released. But listening back now, you just say, well, stroke of genius [*laughs*]. There's nothing wrong with those albums; it was just a different mindset. But at the time, as a kid of the '70s, I grew into punk and heavy metal, and maybe I had to grow a little bit to understand what Queen was all about. And when my own career moved forward, I began to realize a band needs artistic freedom. This is maybe the point when I started appreciating the later albums more and more.

POPOFF: Cool. And Nina, any closing thoughts? Your relationship to the Queen catalog has got to be a strange one. I'm thinking that *A Day at the Races* is one of the few Queen albums left that you can go to when you're sick and tired of all the records that overshadow it, the big hit albums full of songs we are constantly bombarded with on the radio.

NOIR: Yes, it definitely has that vibe to it. That's probably one reason we listen to it a lot on the road. You're right—we get tired of Queen because we perform Queen all the time, so listening to albums that have a lot of the hit songs is kind of hard. Another album that we listen to a lot is *News of the World*, which has the same kind of "deep cut" thing.

But no, as a band, we definitely consider *A Day at the Races* to be at the top of the list; it's a favorite for all of us, which is probably why we have chosen so many songs off the album to play live. But, yeah, no question, when we're going on long road trips and we want to listen to Queen, this is the record we'll throw on.

POPOFF: Darius, any final thoughts on this record?

RUCKER: *A Night at the Opera* and *A Day at the Races*, when I was a kid, myself and my buddies, those were the records that formed our love for Queen. Those, and before that, probably "Killer Queen," made Queen what they were and let the world know who they were. "Somebody to Love" and "Tie Your Mother Down" were anthems that had you singing along, but also had you listening to and reading the words.

But I think also about those songs and how they blossomed live. Queen left us great music, but they also left this great stage show. Any time you see Freddie on stage, you just remember how great a live band they were. Their legacy will be delivering albums like *A Day at the Races*, but it will also be the fact that they brought it live.

Brian designed much of his gear—including his guitar and its first pickups—with his father. He later switched to the Burns Trisonic pickups seen here after experiencing microphonic issues with their predecessors.

NEXT: Backstage
somewhere in the American
Midwest during the North
American leg of the *A Day
at the Races* tour,
January 1977.

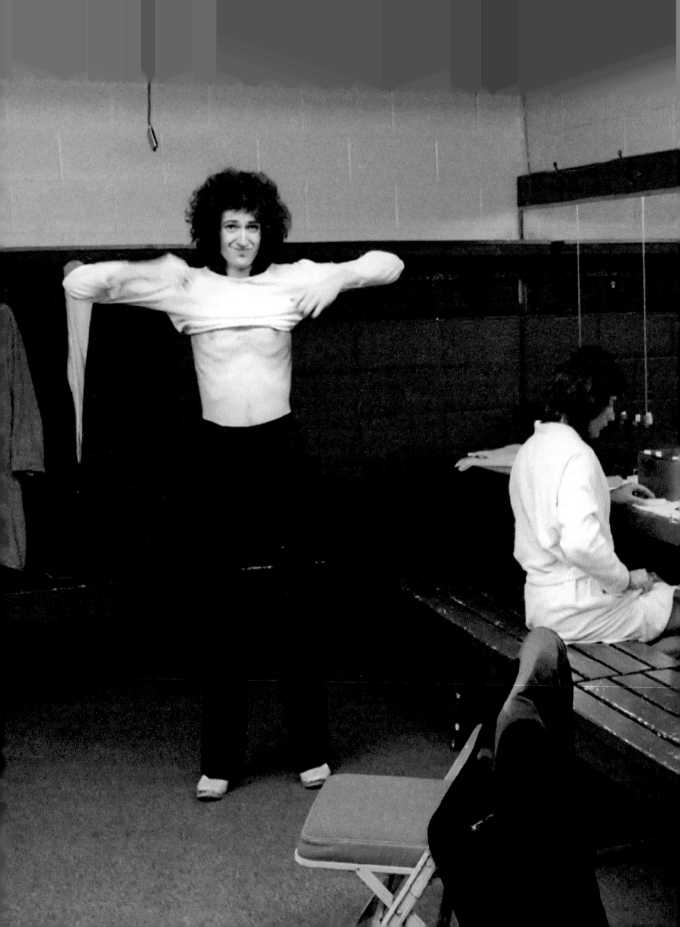

RELEASED OCTOBER 28, 1977

6 NEWS OF THE WORLD

WITH DAVID ELLEFSON, ROGER MANNING JR., SIR PAUL MCCARTNEY, AND JEB WRIGHT

SIDE 1

1. **We Will Rock You** 2:01
   (MAY)

2. **We Are the Champions** 3:00
   (MERCURY)

3. **Sheer Heart Attack** 3:24
   (TAYLOR)

4. **All Dead, All Dead** 3:10
   (MAY)

5. **Spread Your Wings** 4:36
   (DEACON)

6. **Fight from the Inside** 3:02
   (TAYLOR)

SIDE 2

1. **Get Down, Make Love** 3:51
   (MERCURY)

2. **Sleeping on the Sidewalk** 3:05
   (MAY)

3. **Who Needs You** 3:07
   (DEACON)

4. **It's Late** 6:26
   (MAY)

5. **My Melancholy Blues** 3:33
   (MERCURY)

PERSONNEL:

FREDDIE MERCURY – *vocals, piano, cowbell;*
BRIAN MAY – *guitar, vocals, maracas;*
JOHN DEACON – *bass, acoustic guitar,*
backing vocals;
ROGER TAYLOR – *drums, vocals,*
bass guitars, guitars
Recorded at SARM WEST, *Notting Hill,*
London, and WESSEX SOUND STUDIOS,
London
Produced by QUEEN;
assisted by MIKE STONE

OPPOSITE: Freddie performs on the
News of the World tour in Detroit, Michigan,
November 18, 1977

News of the World is a record whose narrative is completely overwhelmed by its two smash singles. Yet appropriately, "We Will Rock You" and "We Are the Champions" are two very different songs, their contrast demonstrating the range we've come to expect from Queen.

However, they are linked in one other respect—and linked with the rest of *News of the World* as well—in that both belie a certain simplicity. *A Day at the Races* was viewed, generally, as ponderous and finicky, and the band endeavored this time out to make more of a rock 'n' roll record. It doesn't escape attention that recording right next door to Queen at Wessex were the notorious Sex Pistols, crafting their own great record for 1977, *Never Mind the Bollocks, Here's the Sex Pistols*. Punk was in play, more so in the UK than in America, and a war of words was being waged between the new guard and the old, of which Queen . . . well, they step right in it, don't they?

Set against every previous Queen album (except, arguably, the debut . . . and even set against *Jazz*), *News of the World* is an inspiring garage

rave-up, tough on the guitars, bass, and drums, especially the ferocious "Sheer Heart Attack," the feisty "Fight from the Inside," the unheralded blues of "Sleeping on the Sidewalk," and the Zeppelin-esque "It's Late," a soaring, powerful anthem featuring cathedral-vaulted vocal harmonies and pretty much the album's only nod to labored production.

"Spread Your Wings" is just as languid and grand, although closer to the celebrated power ballad space Queen commanded so well, as demonstrated in world-beating fashion on this record with "We Are the Champions" (written, according to Freddie, two years previous!). Further feeding the premise that this is more of a rock 'n' roll record are "My Melancholy Blues," the jamming basement electrics of "Get Down, Make Love," and the quiet arrangements of "Who Needs You" and "All Dead, All Dead."

Another distinguishing feature of the album is that Roger Taylor and John Deacon each write two tracks. As usual, pinning the enigmatic Mr. Deacon to any one style proves futile. "Who Needs You" is practically Hawaiian folk, while "Spread Your Wings" sounds like classic Freddie. Roger, on the other hand, remaining on pattern, turns in the record's two hardest rockers, playing almost all instruments on both tracks and singing with his usual tough sneer. "Fight from the Inside" is a song of uncommonly forceful rhythm for Queen and an omen of things to come.

At the business end, "We Are the Champions," which hit No. 2 in the United Kingdom and No. 5 in the United States, propelled *News of the World* to quadruple platinum in America, triple platinum in Canada, and platinum across much of Europe. "Spread Your Wings" was issued as a single in the UK, rising to No. 34, while "It's Late" was offered in the US, Canada, Japan, and New Zealand, barely troubling the charts—surprising given how passionately the band performs the track. Set against the likes of the album's ridiculously digestible dual smash anthems, "It's Late" sounds like "Bohemian Rhapsody," except it's nothing more than joyous power trio rock forged in spirit of Led Zeppelin or the Who. As this writer's favorite Queen song, it's a travesty to me why it wasn't a bigger commercial smash.

All told, Queen found themselves emerging from 1977 victorious, both commercially and critically. What's more, *News of the World* wasn't a band resting on its laurels, nor was it a band retreating into the studio to sculpt expensive prog for a select elite to enjoy. Queen absolutely shocked the world with the metronomic simplicity of "We Will Rock You," and those brave enough to explore the rest of the record were beneficiaries of that song's promise. Although not always soaked in guitars, *News of the World* managed to sound like the jam of a crack band dishing out their business with an urgency that would make any punk band proud.

POPOFF: Roger, growing up in Northern California, what was your take on what *News of the World* did for Queen's career, at least in America?

MANNING JR.: I remember being a kid and we all knew Queen through "Bohemian Rhapsody"; that was the most internationally popular song, although there were several albums and they were established already.

A Day at the Races didn't make any noise, really, completely overlooked even though it's a great follow-up. And then you get to *News of the World*, which I felt I was part of and a voice of—"We Will Rock You," "We Are the Champions," they just slammed that whole record as a listening experience. It just solidifies that, okay, Queen is officially now one of the major forces in the rock pantheon, one of the top five or certainly ten biggest, most influential bands that had everyone's attention in '77, '78. And it's because of *News of the World*, at least in America. That

"We Will Rock You" b/w "We Are the Champions," Canadian pressing— a one-two punch of the biggest songs ever piped into in sports arenas.

OPPOSITE: Deacon and Taylor tinker with a Polaroid camera backstage. Deacon scored two writing credits on *News of the World*: the story song "Spread Your Wings" and the Spanish-tinged "Who Needs You."

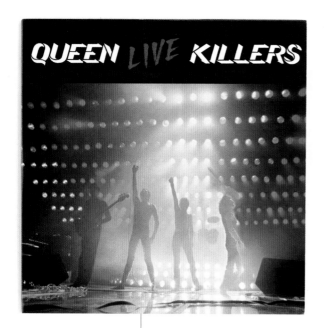

The fully fleshed-out, fast rock 'n' roll version of "We Will Rock You" would see official release on 1979's *Live Killers*.

record just solidified everything. And then people, were like, oh, what are they gonna do next?

POPOFF: Why were "We Will Rock You" and "We Are the Champions" so dominant?

ELLEFSON: Right away out of the gate, it's the production. Once Brian May comes in, you're struck by this peculiar tone that's not a Les Paul through a Marshall. It's not a standard-issue hard rocker tone—it's totally him. And then you realize, that's all it is, drums, guitar, and vocals—that's it. And Freddie's just killin' it on the vocal. Before there was metal, you were going, "This is metal," you know?

And suddenly there's that hard stop and they transition into "We Are the Champions." So, first this weird transition and then another song with a long, involved intro. The song builds to this huge crescendo in the chorus and we've got a one-two punch of the biggest songs ever used in sports events. Everybody in hard rock and heavy metal is trying to write one of these, but Queen has the clear winners. There is nothing more instantly recognizable as the drumbeat in "We Will Rock You." As they say, if you can make your tune known within one measure, that's a hit. And there it is: three or two or even just one beat and you know it's Queen and it's "We Will Rock You."

WRIGHT: First off, I think it was marketed well. Maybe I'm being naïve, but the track listing, if you put those in different places, it doesn't work. If you put those on a single and it's not side A and side B, it doesn't work. If you don't have FM radio stations following them back-to-back, it doesn't work—I don't like hearing just one of them. Even on the live album, where you just hear the fast version of "We Will Rock You" but it's followed by "Let Me Entertain You," I don't like that.

As for the lyrics, even though "We Will Rock You" is more about machismo and not a particularly deep lyric, is this not perfect for the year? In '77, rockers, we all had mullets, only you didn't call them mullets—it was just long hair. That was our attitude, man. And in post-Vietnam, there's nothing to protest. There's just beer, arenas full of rock, looking for girls, and, man, "We Will Rock You" is a song full of testosterone.

And then Freddie sneaks in with this anthem championing the downtrodden, which I think he's also representing the struggles of being a gay man in a society that doesn't like gay men. But his lyrics are ambiguous enough, any of us relate to it. I think human beings always tend to feel like the underdog. If you're halfway human, you feel like you're always fighting for something. And I think if you take that first song of rock 'n' roll guitar and powerful drums—they aren't even drums; that's more powerful than drums could be—and that level of testosterone, and follow it up with something that has to do with the underdog becoming the champion, how could it not be a hit? And then of course there's sports [*laughs*]—the stomp, stomp, clap is still done today. There are kids doing that at games who probably don't even know it's a Queen song.

MANNING JR.: Certainly "We are the Champions" has that lyric that made it very easy for sports organizations to adopt it. But "We Will Rock You" worked famously, as well, because it was such a chant, a march, and so easy to assimilate, and it makes so much sense. It was a fully fleshed-out rock 'n' roll song, and the tempo was double time, but you hear the half-time pulse for the final album version. The original was twice as fast, which we get on *Live Killers*.

That song represents such an epic moment in rock history, because you're not given the chords. As a listener, your ear has to fill in the chords because that's the only way melody can function: it has to be set against a chord progression. So as a listener, your brain fills it out for you. And it's not a particularly involved chord progression, which helps. But your brain still does that. As a listener, it's very seductive. You immediately pay attention, the starkness pulls you in, just like in a lot of hip-hop, and you have to fill in the blanks. That in and of itself is so gargantuan, it's brilliant. Super-trained, schooled music people would've never come up with that. It takes conceptual artists to come up with that.

And as the legend goes, they were suspect of the almost generic obviousness of the original version. They're like, this is just a fast rock 'n' roll, blues number and we're better than that. We're more special than that. How can we make this song more special? Whether it was an accident or not, somebody had the idea, hey, let's just strip it away. Those big chants and that choir is so bonehead Ramones, Dada, simplistic. I didn't go to art school, but it's almost abstract. It's simplistic to the point of infantile.

But that is rock in all its glory. They're showing the world, "We know how to do this better than anybody. We're helping continue to write the rock 'n' roll history book that started in the 1950s with Jerry Lee Lewis and Elvis and Little Richard. This is nothing but a continuation of that."

News of the World was recorded amid a war between the old guard and the new punks, and was perhaps one reason behind Queen's decision to make a less finicky, more straightforward record.

The Roger-penned "Sheer Heart Attack" was half-written earlier during sessions for the album of the same name. Roger played guitar, bass, and drums, and provided some of the vocals on the album cut.

POPOFF: Just to clarify, when you were talking about filling in the chords, do you mean the verse or the chorus?

MANNING JR.: All of the above. And what's great about that is any listener, whether they've gone to music school or not, can do that. So, it's a very communal song. Chanting, pounding your fist, stomping your feet—that's tribal. Add the fact that you can adopt that to sports events, and you basically can't write a bigger international hit.

Follow that up with "We Are the Champions," one of my favorite Queen songs of all time, simply because I love the melody and the chords. It's executed—just like all Queen songs—with the idea of keeping the arrangement stark but loading up the background harmonies. And then when they come in, or when the guitar solo comes in, it sounds much larger than life. Queen is about being so overt to the point of reaching through the speakers, grabbing the you by the throat, slapping you in the face a few times, and saying, "Pay attention."

McCARTNEY: "We Are the Champions" is another great Queen anthem. I must say, I admire a song that can be so readily played at a sports event, and that song has gotten the hell played out of it and it works every single time. It's a rousing anthem. Funny story, we were in Japan a few years ago, and it was my wife, Nancy's, birthday, so we were throwing her a surprise party. And we got two tribute bands to liven up the evening. One was a Beatles tribute band that I ended up going and singing with, making their day [*laughs*], and the other was a Queen tribute band.

And they were great. All they did was they substituted a G for the Q, so they were "Gueen." And they really had it down. There was moment during the party when they were playing and I was just sitting there—here's the party, something to eat, something to drink—and I was in a very mellow mood. And I got really quite emotional because I listened to these Japanese guys singing this Queen music. And I was thinking, oh my God, the power of music. And in this case, the power of English music that these people on the other side of the world had been so impressed that they learned to play it, to sing it, they'd learned Freddie's show, his actions, and I just got very sort of emotional, thinking of how powerful, this little island of England sending out these messages to the world. So, yeah, I fully appreciate the reach of the music—it's fantastic.

POPOFF: Next up is possibly the most heavy-metal song of the entire Queen canon. What is the significance of "Sheer Heart Attack"?

ELLEFSON: You get through these two opening tracks and they're just blistering, each in its own right, and then suddenly "Sheer Heart Attack" comes in and it's just this benchmark for everything that you could do as a metal band. It's right there in that one song. That whole down-picking thing became not only the basis of punk rock, which was certainly alive and well by that time, or was becoming alive and well in 1977, but what we would later do in thrash metal. Thrash is just tons of down-picking.

Deacon on the *News of the World* tour, 1978.

"It's Late" finds Queen embracing their classic rock and even blues rock roots, however slight the latter may be.

So that song is basically delivering the template of how to play what would become thrash metal—and it's coming from Roger Taylor, who not only wrote it but plays all the guitar, bass, and drums, but also provides some of the vocals. In fact, me and Anthrax drummer Charlie Benante were discussing this because Charlie knows all these Queen tunes and is a great guitar player. I drew the comparison between Roger Taylor playing "Sheer Heart Attack" and Charlie Benante writing Anthrax songs on guitar. He's kind of the modern-day version of that. Even in Megadeth, when Nick Menza would write songs on guitar, he would have this kind of not highly skilled way of playing that would remind me of "Sheer Heart Attack." It's a drummer trying to play an instrument that he's not really great at, but that's what makes it so friggin' cool and so raw.

Also in the middle of that song there's that Rototom drum fill that they put the flanger on that was just friggin' iconic! I love that the whole song was Roger.

POPOFF: Another interesting thing is that song was half-written during the *Sheer Heart Attack* sessions, and that's why it's called that.

WRIGHT: Zeppelin did it with "Houses of the Holy," put that song on *Physical Graffiti*, the album after *Houses of the Holy*. AC/DC I know did it with "If You Want Blood." The thing people overlook in "Sheer Heart Attack" is that this is where Taylor really shines vocally. As he did on "Bohemian Rhapsody," he does his high notes. His guitars scream and so does he. It makes you think maybe Roger wanted to be in a heavy metal band. I don't know if Queen ever had a heavier song.

MANNING JR.: It's true, the song is so metal, but I think it was Roger Taylor's attempt at being as in-your-face, fast, and punk as he could be at that time. But you can't get away from those awesome, forward-thinking harmonies. That's a really interesting chorus hook. It's super-catchy and it sounds very much like Cheap Trick. And that's not something you can train for or practice. You can't practice having all the harmonics add up as sweetly as they do for Crosby, Stills & Nash or the Byrds or Queen or the Carpenters or Fleetwood Mac. It either sounds good out of the gate or it doesn't. And so much of Queen's trademark is their unique sound when they sing together.

POPOFF: Paul, really, what Queen is doing with "Sheer Heart Attack" is what you did with "Helter Skelter." Would you agree there are parallels there?

McCARTNEY: Sure, yeah, I think that what heavy metal came out of was a desire to rock. And to rock big and dirty and loud. And for that you don't need rules. You talk about what made us do "Helter Skelter," it was just a desire to rock dirty and rock loud. And when I listen to it now, I think, oh gosh, I thought it was louder and dirtier than that. Because times have changed, you know. But I think it's just that, if you're in a rock 'n' roll band, your soul is anchored in the sea of rock 'n' roll and so you want to do it. You want to participate to your fullest. And sometimes that means being dirty, being loud.

You know, guitarists are famous for turning up to 11. And that's a very understandable desire. Still, now, when I get with my band and we're at a soundcheck, just strapping on my electric guitar and kicking in a pedal, turning it up, that's the spirit that goes through rock 'n' roll—it's a thrill. Anyone who has ever owned an electric guitar and put it through an amp knows that thrill. I think that's where it all came from, the desire to just thrash it out. That's why we did "Helter Skelter." And I'm sure that's probably why the guys did "Sheer Heart Attack" and those songs, being essentially the precursors of heavy metal. And I'm sure that's why the heavy

The Frank Kelly Freas cover of *Astounding Science Fiction*, October 1953, inspired the *News of the World* album art.

metal then pretty much just did *it*, you know? I think it's just great. As Brian would probably tell you, it's an addictive feeling.

POPOFF: In Brian May's view, *News of the World* was somewhat back to the roots after two very complex records. That makes a lot of sense, particularly in "Sheer Heart Attack" and perhaps "It's Late."

MANNING JR.: Absolutely, "It's Late" is it for me. That fast section, if anybody else did that . . . it's so kind of average, post-Beatles with the guitar intervals, it's practically southern rock or something. But when you put it in the hands of Queen, it's so heavy and has such a distinct character. I enjoy that sort of double-time instrumental jam even though it's Bar Band 101.

In general, this type of execution and style of music usually bores me to tears, frankly, but Queen do it so well and so above their peers. It's really Led Zeppelin syndrome, like, "Zeppelin, oh, British blues." No, no, no. That's what their roots are, but Led Zeppelin expanded so far beyond and into so many interesting and clever areas. They took that genre as far as it possibly could go and completely redefined it.

That's what Queen does for me too. They take all the clichés and stereotypes of classic rock and redefine them. "It's Late" starts so average, but when they go to that fast part, again, it really shows that here's four guys, or three, I should say, who are really playing well together, they're very practiced, it breathes, it's organic, it has movement, it's so not by the book. It's like they're writing the book. They're showing everybody how passionate it can get, how extreme it can get, just how intense it can get.

They're taking whatever rock 'n' roll cliché and forging new paths. Rock 'n' roll had really only been around for fifteen, twenty years at that point, but they're making it their own, taking Chuck Berry and Jimi Hendrix into a whole 'nother zone, with mastery and high artistry. And that song for me really demonstrates that. There are so few rock combos that play that well together, it reaches the level of jazz trio or jazz quartet. I mean, that's what you become a jazz fan for. But when you've got a rock 'n' roll ensemble that demonstrates that, to that degree, it's just so exciting. It was exciting for me as a kid and it's exciting for me now.

POPOFF: And how would you assess Brian's role as a guitarist on this record?

WRIGHT: As cool as "We Will Rock You" is, I don't know if it's as cool without him bringing in that riff. If you go to other songs like "Now I'm Here," any of them with the little guitar call-and-response stuff he does, or the repeats, where he's using the harmonizer or whatever, that's brilliant, too, but this is more straight from his fingers into your gut.

In general, he's understated. He doesn't show off enough for me personally, but he can hit you with notes that are amazing. I would guess that Brian May spends hours twiddling his knobs to get his tones. Nobody sounds like Brian May. He sticks mostly to the pentatonic scales, but he does it in ways that I would never think of doing. There's some classical, some Spanish; he's obviously well-versed, but when he's just being raw, like in "We Will Rock You," I don't think he's ever better. Different album, but the solo in "Dragon Attack," where's he's basically saying "I can rock as hard as anybody else," he does it with one note in that solo. When you could cut glass with a guitar note, to me, you're pretty damn good.

McCARTNEY: I remember meeting Brian May at the Queen's Jubilee concert. I'm sitting with Eric Clapton and he came over and shook our hands. "Eric, oh my God, gotta thank you, I've gotta thank you. Because without you, I wouldn't be playing guitar." You know? And then he turns to me and says, "And Paul, I've got to thank you, because without you, there wouldn't be a group, Queen." I was very honored by that. And he was so nice and genuine, that when he left, one of the people we were with said, "Oh my gosh, he's so humble, isn't he?" And Eric turned to that person and said, "The great ones usually are." And that stuck with me, that phrase: "The great ones usually are." It's a very telling phrase. So, Brian, all of them, they were just great guys, great music.

I also like Brian because we are fellow animal activists. When cruel campaigns come about, we are there opposing them. So, I like his sensitivity to the plight of animals. We have a big badger cull in the UK. They're blamed over here for a lot of things, and he and I both think that it's not as necessary as the government thinks it is. On that front, we're sort of soulmates.

But I think his guitar playing is fantastic. Queen were sort of the next generation after Clapton; it was more flash and shredding. But he's technically super-proficient and I think very tasteful. And like I say, we have a lot in common and I find him very easy to get on with.

POPOFF: As a side note, I'm interested, Paul, in what you thought of what Brian did after this era, where in the '80s, he sort of put aside the guitar and there were a lot of synthesizers and drum machines. Were you on board then, still? I mean, one could frame it as fearless artists following their muse.

McCARTNEY: Well I think it is that, but it also is moving with the times. Nobody wants to feel that their current music is antique. When there was a fashion for synthesizers or drum machines, a lot of people followed that. Because it was the sound of the times. I think in pop music, one of the things is, you want your music to exist in the now as well as in the past. I would think that's what they were doing. And I don't think there's a need to defend it. That was the sound then. Now it sounds more dated. You couldn't blame them for moving with it. Queen were always an up-to-date band.

POPOFF: Back to *News of the World* . . . As Jeb alluded to, there is quite a bit of bullish, aggressive guitar rock on this record. Even "Get Down, Make Love" becomes a wall of sound.

MANNING JR.: Yeah, but "Get Down, Make Love" was such a progressive, forward-thinking, highly conceptual artistic tune. It's a huge exercise in sound design, particularly with Brian May's guitar. It's almost creepy and sounds like science fiction. And it's highly, highly sexualized. It's kind of a tall order, but I demand that I be transported somewhere. That's a lot easier to do if you're doing instrumental music or progressive rock, for example, where you have seven, fifteen, twenty minutes to take your time and transport the listener. But if you're asked to do that in a three-and-a-half-minute pop song, that's very much a challenge.

My favorite music has always done that. It's personalized, it's all subjective, but the Beach Boys could do that, Queen could do that, Pink Floyd could do that. And "Get Down, Make Love" just puts you in some crazy '70s porn underbelly where, for a kid, whether you know what's going on or not, something otherworldly is conveyed. Some sinister "My parents told me not to open this door and walk into this room" kind of thing.

ELLEFSON: That song didn't really hit me until the *Live Killers* album. That was where that song had an impact to me, because live the arrangement was so cool. Maybe they were trying to write their "Whole Lotta Love," but what caught my attention was the bass line. That was in

the age of disco bass, so playing the octave bass line was very reminiscent of disco. You could tell John was a really educated musician and a real bass player, but on *Live Killers*, it just gets better. It was heavier and had a bigger impact.

WRIGHT: With *News of the World*, they made more of a rock album. I don't hear as much of the pomp of Freddie that we all love, but at the same time, he's got an attitude all over this. You would not hear a song like "Get Down, Make Love" on any of the previous albums. I love the way it starts and then builds. Any time Brian May is making weird sounds, it's just so damn cool. But more importantly, it's about the raw sexuality; there's no pretending what that song is about. Except when I was a kid, I didn't really realize that it was a man, maybe, he was writing about.

POPOFF: "All Dead, All Dead" is all Brian, in the writing as well as the vocal. I can almost picture him in one of his frocks, because in a way, this is back to the renaissance music of *II*.

MANNING JR.: Even to this day, lyrics are secondary for me. If the song affects me, it affects me because of the melodies, the harmonies, the groove, the musicality. I bring this up because after I heard "All Dead, All Dead," a good friend pointed out what an amazing lyric it is and how they related to it, that they had lost several close friends, either to drugs or suicide, and family members too. And I had not. I couldn't really relate, but it really affected me when I listened to the lyric more closely. I always thought of the song as super, super sweet; it put me in this wonderful kind of melancholic and contemplative mood. But this new focus on the lyric put a whole different vibe on the song. It became even more powerful to me, which ideally, that's what a good lyric does.

POPOFF: What do you make of Brian's vocal performance on that song?

MANNING JR.: Brian, in my opinion, had the most kind of vanilla, average voice of the three, but it's very soothing. It's not particularly a lead rock 'n' roll voice with loads of presence, but it's calming and sweet and beautiful. Still, it doesn't really command attention, like Freddie's, but you have to have luck with respect to harmonizing, and Queen does. You can have a bunch of guys that sing very well and know the mechanics of harmonizing. It doesn't mean that their voices are going to blend well. But that's another gift, another bonus that Queen enjoys.

POPOFF: And how about a quick tour of a few other tracks on the record?

ELLEFSON: I really like "Fight from the Inside." I agree with Jeb that this is an album where Roger Taylor really shines. Right out of the gate, first thing you hear is his drumming and then "Sheer Heart Attack." And then suddenly "Fight from the Inside," written by Roger, sung by Roger, such a cool song. But side two wasn't so much kickass hard rock. I was glad they put that all at the back of this album and front-loaded it with the better stuff, rather than scattering it across the entire album.

WRIGHT: "Spread Your Wings," a John Deacon song, might be my favorite, speaking from the heart as a fan rather than as a rock journalist, who sort of has to acknowledge the importance of "We Will Rock You" and "We Are the Champions." I don't believe the big Mike Stone backing vocals, that super swath of vocal harmonies, are anywhere to be found on that song. But to me it's all about the story. Lyrically, it's a folk song.

"Fight from the Inside" is not one of the most popular tracks, but it's pretty interesting because it's got that cool guitar riff all the way through it. Taylor, for a drummer, always writes good guitar riffs. And he's got a cool voice, which contrasts and plays against Freddie's.

"Sleeping on the Sidewalk"—Brian May, bluesy. I'm picking on it because I don't care for his vocals, especially given the power of both Freddie and Roger. "Who Needs You," John Deacon, it's got a Spanish guitar flavor. It's okay. "Get Down, Make Love," that's get-your-rocks-off music. "Who Needs You?" That's not Queen. It doesn't have the attitude. And then "Melancholy Blues"—I'll put this way: it's a good way to end the album.

POPOFF: What does this cover art say to you?

MANNING JR.: I never really derived a particular message from it, but I loved the fantastical sci-fi aspect of it. I was a big *Mad* magazine fan as a kid, and the guy who did that illustration, Frank Kelly Freas, is a famous artist, and he did a lot of magazine art. I connected the dots and enjoyed that.

WRIGHT: First impression, to be honest, I thought it was kind of silly. I don't think it matches the music. Some albums match the music. Looking around my office, I've got all the signed shit on the walls. If I look at Scorpions *Lovedrive* or Foghat *Live*, even Kansas *Leftoverture*, those covers all enhance your appreciation of the music. *News of the World*, there's a disconnect. It's cool enough, I suppose, but it's kind of nerdy. But wasn't Queen kind of nerdy? Yeah, in a sense . . . Queen, as much as they were conquering rock stars, they're a little bit nerdy too [*laughs*].

News of the World may not have had all the Freddie pomp that fans loved, but the singer still sweat attitude and swagger all over the stage and vocals.

RELEASED NOVEMBER 10, 1978

7 JAZZ

WITH STEPHEN DALTON, HANSI KÜRSCH, AND ROGER MANNING JR.

SIDE 1

1. **Mustapha** 3:01
(MERCURY)

2. **Fat Bottomed Girls** 4:16
(MAY)

3. **Jealousy** 3:14
(MERCURY)

4. **Bicycle Race** 3:01
(MERCURY)

5. **If You Can't Beat Them** 4:15
(DEACON)

6. **Let Me Entertain You** 3:01
(MERCURY)

SIDE 2

1. **Dead on Time** 3:23
(MAY)

2. **In Only Seven Days** 2:30
(DEACON)

3. **Dreamers Ball** 3:30
(MAY)

4. **Fun It** 3:29
(TAYLOR)

5. **Leaving Home Ain't Easy** 3:15
(MAY)

6. **Don't Stop Me Now** 3:29
(MERCURY)

7. **More of That Jazz** 4:16
(TAYLOR)

PERSONNEL:

FREDDIE MERCURY – *vocals, piano;*
BRIAN MAY – *guitar, vocals;*
JOHN DEACON – *bass guitar;*
ROGER TAYLOR – *percussion, vocals*
Recorded at MOUNTAIN STUDIOS,
Montreux, Switzerland, and SUPER
BEAR STUDIOS, *Berre-les-Alpes, France*
Produced by QUEEN *and*
ROY THOMAS BAKER

OPPOSITE: Paris, June 1979. When ardent fans consider *Jazz,* talk inevitably revolves around its whirlwind energy.

It's always a hot debate: which Queen album most represents a shift and the last of a run of records marked by a certain sound.

Jazz jumps into that fray jumps like a soused bar patron with his pants on fire. For many, there was always something about *A Day at the Races* that marks it as the last of the gilded age. But then I've always seen *The Game* as the last (admittedly taking the easy route, given the starkness of *Hot Space*). But then again, considering *The Game*'s two runaway hits suggests another way to view *Jazz*: this is the first Queen record since *Sheer Heart Attack* where the discourse is not overwhelmed by talk of the hits.

And that's to its credit. When ardent Queen fans consider *Jazz*, talk and laughter revolve around its energy. *Jazz* is a whirlwind marked by happy exhaustion and more humor, both lyrical and sonic, than are found on the previous albums. "More of That Jazz," the album's final track, is therefore the distillation of *Jazz*: not only does Roger *not* want the party to end, as evident in the song's title and sophisticated Escher drawing of a riff, but he's already reliving the most fab gala Queen's ever thrown by literally replaying bits of the album that has just passed by.

And *Jazz* is a record worth the instant reminiscence. Sure, there are the moderate hits—the emotionally surging "Don't Stop Me Now" and the wide load of "Fat Bottomed Girls"—but the second stringers are like a blur of guests willing to be the life of the party. "Let Me Entertain You" and "Dead on Time" are sophisticated and skittery rockers, note-dense and action-packed to the point where one is hard-pressed to remember the last time Queen were this flash with their semi-metal (arguably, the answer is "Stone Cold Crazy"). At the other end, "Jealousy," "In Only Seven Days," "Leaving Home Ain't Easy," and "Dreamer's Ball" feature arrangements and tempos in the realm of balladry, the band offering its usual treatise on the history of pop throughout the twentieth century.

Supporting the position that *Jazz* is Queen's most lighthearted album thus far, "Bicycle Race" is compact, diamond-hard prog, but still daft, while "Mustapha" entertains and provokes with exotic Middle Eastern melodies. Finally, "If You Can't Beat Them" is a semi-hard rocker of dependable original rock 'n' roll chords, written by Deacon and soloed over for two minutes by Brian, who also plays all the guitars, rare on a Deacon song. If any song foreshadows the deep cuts of *The Game*, it's this, while "Fun It" telegraphs a line to Queen's dance track future.

Also remarkable about this stack of songs is that they comprise an album of thirteen tracks, yet there are no short snappers or idea fragments, nor anything that drones on and clobbers the conversation either. Nearly everything is plated around the three-minute mark—*Jazz* is not a rich seven-course meal that takes half the night, but rather a sumptuous buffet where partygoers pile their plates with a symphony of tastes—then return to their tables for more loud chatter and salacious rumor.

Lacking the monster hits that tended to suck the oxygen from the room on past records, *Jazz* topped out at platinum in the US and the UK, missing that certification in other key territories while nonetheless nibbling its way to sales of around five million copies the world over.

Queen would spend the following year defending the ill-received but hard-hitting *Live Killers* album before putting in for a bit of a rethink and finding Reinhold Mack and Musicland in Munich. Soon they would embrace a melange of modern music that, in retrospect, would further throw *Jazz* into high relief as the last record of a golden creative era, a wily and zestful album by a four-piece rock band operating at peak performance with Freddie as the hyperactive bonus, pumping away at his piano and singing his heart out in English, Arabic, Persian, and in-between dialects still to be determined.

POPOFF: What is the personality of *Jazz* versus *News of the World*?

MANNING JR.: Well, in the writing, you can hear Roger trying to get into some of the more youth-oriented sounds of the day. It's slightly punky, it's slightly new wave. The rest of the band doesn't seem to care about that. They're going in the same direction they've been going, and they will continue to do so up until *The Game*.

Sonically as well, especially the drums; they're trying to go for some more modernized, less classic rock sounds, like somebody is listening to the other records of the day that are getting some attention. It seems that somebody in the Queen organization was paying enough attention to what was new in music recording style to have them change at least a little bit.

KÜRSCH: With "We Will Rock You" and "We Are the Champions," you had two of the greatest Queen songs ever, but it was an album that still had a strong connection to the past. And I believe *Jazz* was the beginning of the complete liberation from what Queen had done before, a more modern approach. Queen said farewell to the epic elements they had on the older albums. And I never felt that these songs needed more. There was freshness, humor. *Jazz* reflected the times. It was a bit rebellious, even with its title.

Yet Queen stayed Queen. That's the good thing about them—first album all the way to *Innuendo*, it doesn't make a difference. But I think *Jazz* overcomes *News of the World* by almost every measure, except in the stature of the hits.

DALTON: I think both those records can be seen as the end of Queen's "imperial" phase. *Jazz* got mixed reviews. Perhaps they were pushing that sort of cabaret tongue-in-cheek style a little too far for Americans. For example, the "I Want to Break Free" video from *The Works* famously was banned in the States. The fact that they were the gayest band in the world and Americans didn't spot that for another twenty years is quite telling. So, with Jazz, they possibly embraced that kind of camp tongue-in-cheek stuff too much. But it has a lot of good stuff on it, kicking off with "Mustapha," with those amped-up Arabic lyrics, which are obviously referencing Freddie's family heritage. It's a nice eclectic mix with a lot of stylistic variety but compact, given that it's thirteen short songs.

POPOFF: What do you guys make of "Mustapha"? It's perhaps not surprising that Queen would do a song like that, but it's almost a provocation to put it down as opening track.

DALTON: Sure, when it starts, you think you're listening to some sort of experimental world music statement, and then the guitars and the drums kick in and it's as heavy as anything else on the album. That's the kind of heavy rock I like—it takes you somewhere else, while still having the muscle and dynamics of heavy rock.

MANNING JR.: It's so overtly Middle Eastern and almost cinematic, but they do it with guitar, bass, drums, and vocal harmonies. I really love that; it displays their ability and range and attention to detail. "Mustapha" was interesting and flashy and got a lot

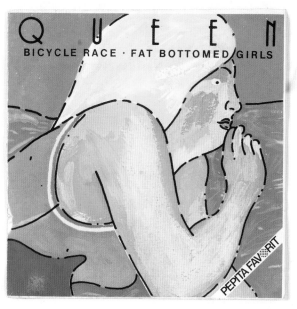

of attention; that is just so far removed from anything any artist is going for even these days or necessarily has the talent and ability and skills to do so. And yet these guys, who were considered a rock 'n' roll band, were doing that back in 1978.

KÜRSCH: "Mustapha" delivers a certain sense of humor the band always had. But for sure, it was a new sound I did not expect. I was twelve or so and a little disappointed. It was out of my capability and understanding. I liked the rocking, majestic stuff the older albums stood for, and here comes *Jazz*, opening with "Mustapha," which was not "We Are the Champions." Although I love it now.

Also, being German, this song provides so many emotional opportunities in terms of how to relate to it. Because even at the best of times, I never really knew what they were talking about. English was not even taught in school in Germany at that point. I started learning English at eleven or twelve, so I grew up not having any idea what Queen were talking about. And even more so, "Mustapha" provides a lot of space for interpretations. My mind was going crazy, thinking about this song. And then, of course, it turns out that *nobody* knows what it's about [*laughs*].

If you did a song like that today, you might be praised or you might be in deep shit. Art is not as respected as in the '70s. Those were blessed times.

DALTON: I can see why "Mustapha" might possibly have put people off at the time, particularly hardcore "disco sucks" rock snobs. And having the title "Mustapha" nowadays, certain politically extreme people might find that somewhat off-putting. But I don't think it would have in the '70s, particularly as Freddie was this kind of exotic orientalist figure on the rock landscape. I'm sure if I listened to it when I was ten or eleven, when this came out, I might've felt the same thing. Nowadays, having spent twenty-five years listening to very mediocre hard rock records, I welcome those different shades and colors and stylistic twists.

POPOFF: One of *Jazz*'s two hits is "Fat Bottomed Girls." What does this song represent, other than helping save the record from commercial disappointment?

MANNING JR.: It's such a bone-headed blues jam. It's almost a parody of a classic rock song and I think they had fun with that idea. I don't know if this is coming from Freddie leading the way or whether it's everybody, but there's so much testosterone, almost to the point of it being comical. Just this whole take-no-prisoners, in-your-face kind of thing, like Judas Priest. But Queen does it with so much more finesse and elegance and toughness. It's almost like Freddie was overcompensating for his effeminate side. It's so over-the-top, but it translates.

You've got these gigantic monster drum fills that, again, are almost comedic, the definition of '70s rock fills. The same with the background vocals. Over this simple, generic, bluesy riff. It's like, why would they bother doing something like this? Oh, because they're reminding us they do it better than anybody. It always struck me as so competitive. Not that anybody had challenged them to a duel necessarily, but they were fighting anyway. I always found that amusing.

KÜRSCH: Even that title, "Fat Bottomed Girls," they bring in more of a modern, rock 'n' roll sexuality. You're no longer thinking about the '30s and Oscar Wilde, like with *A Night at the Opera* or *A Day at the Races*.

I don't know how you can explain "Fat Bottomed Girls." It's such a funny, expressive way of just making fun of life, but somehow with the confidence and bravado in it, you come away understanding that these guys are superstars. It's a Brian May song, so the interesting opening, with that stark guitar is not surprising. He even sings it with Freddie, making this one of the heaviest songs Brian does vocals on—that's mostly him we hear on the chorus. Also, very rare for Queen, it's quite detuned, I think to drop-D.

DALTON: "Fat Bottomed Girls" got a lot of negative comments at the time, but you listen to it now, it's very tongue-in-cheek, spoofing that whole Zeppelin and Stones kind of lascivious objectification of women. It's done in such a camp, eye-winking, cabaret way that it's hard to take offense, especially when you know that Freddie was not necessarily oriented that way. I think that's quite an interesting addition to their canon. To me, Queen are a fantastic pop group who can do hard rock. They're not a fantastic hard rock band that flirt with pop. I think their conception of how pop music works is broader than the dynamics of hard rock. Brian May's guitar solos have a shiny, glamorous quality that Jimmy Page's don't, for instance. I've got a blind spot to a lot of hard rock, but to me, Brian May's like tinsel on the Christmas tree.

POPOFF: And what do you make of this album cover and, indeed, the title, *Jazz*?

MANNING JR.: Again, I see somebody in the group—or several people—going, hey, we gotta do something new. They're being influenced by new wave and punk. Pure, sweet, simple, to the point. The artwork is very pop art, not flowery, not ornamental. And maybe that translates into the songs too, being shorter and simpler of architecture.

Now that gatefold, that giant black-and-white photo of them in the Montreux studio where they recorded, that's what inspired the booklet photography for our second Jellyfish record, *Spilt Milk*. We just told all our art direction people, we want a picture that is as cool as that Queen photo. Because there was a

Roger backstage during the band's 1977 US tour. It's said that he came up with concept for the *Jazz* cover, inspired by an image he saw painted on the Berlin Wall.

OPPOSITE: "Bicycle Race" b/w "Fat Bottomed Girls," UK, 1978. "Bicycle Race" was perhaps a perfect example of the band continuing to distill a sound they were perfecting over the years—sharp, brash, and more than a little whimsical.

grandeur to it; it was monolithic, such a statement. "We may be an army of four, but we're an army, we're a force"—that's what we took away from that photo.

KÜRSCH: That cover was Roger Taylor's idea; I believe he saw a similar image painted on the Berlin Wall. New frontiers and new dimensions. Certainly not in the formal and regal tradition of what they had used on earlier albums—it's modern, clean. I can imagine how much time they must have spent on album covers. It's not like today; you have an airbrush or someone paints you a nice little picture or the record company decides. It does not have to be very expensive. But Queen, they considered the whole package, the music, the appearance of the band, the character of the band, the image of the band. The album cover had to represent visually a union of all these things, be part of one defining statement. So, I think the *Jazz* cover is spectacular and well designed for the music.

AMK BERLIN — DEUTSCHLANDHALLE
Messedamm 26   Autobus 4, 10, 65, 66, 69, 92, 94   U-Bahn Kaiserdamm   (Zubringer)

Deutschlandhalle

Freitag, 28. April 1978   **Beginn siehe Rückseite**

DM 17,—   A Night With QUEEN Concert '78

Veranstalter: Concert Büro Lippmann + Rau, Frankfurt/Main — Konzertdirektion Wolfgang Jänicke GmbH, Berlin

Kartenrücknahme ausgeschlossen   Programmänderung vorbehalten

28. 4. 1978

Vorverkauf: DM 17,—
+ Vorverkaufsgebühr   incl. Mehrwertsteuer

Buchdruckerei Bree Schöneberg   Kontrollabschnitt   28. April 1978

DALTON: The interesting thing about a lot of '70s stuff is it has dated a little less than '80s stuff. Visual grammar from different periods go out of style at different rates. And that title, *Jazz*, is quite arch and ironic. Maybe it's saying, "We can do whatever we want." And I suppose if they're not calling it *Jazz* ironically, they're perhaps referring to the album's stylistic diversity. I'm just speculating. It's a nice title. It doesn't grate, it's snappy.

POPOFF: The poster of the naked women on the bikes—what do you know about the history of that? How did that go over in the UK? It was not included in the US album.

DALTON: I know that they hired Wimbledon Greyhound Stadium and did a video with lots of naked women on bikes. At the time, I think it was probably seen as a jolly jape. But I think if they did that today, it would attract enormous derision. Different times, they say. It doesn't personally offend me, but it certainly wouldn't be what I would do if I was in the band [*laughs*]. This was when rock 'n' roll was still steeped in misogyny, even the comical, cartoonish sort of sexism that creeps into Queen at times.

POPOFF: *Jazz* generated a second hit, "Don't Stop Me Now." What is interesting about this track?

KÜRSCH: "Don't Stop Me Now" is my favorite on the album. When we did "Spread Your Wings" as a bonus track on *Somewhere Far Beyond* in 1992, this was a song we had in line for Blind Guardian. We all loved "Don't Stop Me Now," but we really did not know how to do it in our way. It's a modern Queen song, but it also has grandeur. It would be quite hard to cover for anyone. And I like the message, the intention of the song.

POPOFF: And what is Queen doing at the heavy rock end of things, aside from "Fat Bottomed Girls"?

MANNING JR.: "Dead on Time" I always remember. If you want chops and enjoy meticulous craftsmanship on one's instrument, usually you go into jazz or progressive rock—that's where you can find all the musicianship you want. And even when you hail great rock musicians like Jimmy Page, Ian Paice, or John Bonham, it's kind of understood that those guys were good, but they're not as good as jazz musicians. But Queen had chops as good as anybody at the time. They had incredible finesse. And they were all art school students; it wasn't like they went to jazz music school. But they studied and learned their craft and they get to show it off on "Dead on Time." I mean, that song, they make it sound effortless.

KÜRSCH: That song is quite technical at points. It reminds me of "Keep Yourself Alive." But "Let Me Entertain You" is probably the heaviest song. That is what Queen stands for. And they just nailed it. Great guitar riff, great chemistry as a band, and the drumming is insane.

"If You Can't Beat Them," one of two John Deacon songs on the album, is certainly one of the rocky ones—modern, great vocal harmonies, and a hook that sticks in your mind once you've heard the song. Brian's guitar solo is something that has to be mentioned because for Queen it's quite long.

MANNING JR.: Interestingly, the guy who wasn't singing ends up writing half their hits. John Deacon's just as consummate a musician as the rest of them, fantastic bass player, and clearly could write a pop song.

Elsewhere on here, "Fun It" I enjoy, because again, I can imagine Roger Taylor watching *Top of the Pops* and caring that there's a whole new younger generation—not a '60s hippie generation—that are in their teens and into bands like the Clash and Generation X and the Damned, bands that are influenced by the British glitter rock scene but are taking it to a whole new place. You see it in his writing over the next few albums, but he starts exploring that on *Jazz*. Just the title, "Fun It," is in a punk or new wave direction. That's tricky for any artist, figuring out a way to have your cake and eat it too.

DALTON: With "Fun It," you can see it pointing to their *The Game/Hot Space* period, with the disco-type stuff, but it feels like an early sketch. Having just seen Roger Taylor and Brian May singing onstage with their new lineup, with Adam Lambert, I think they are both capable adequate vocalists. I think if you're in a band with Freddie Mercury, you really have to step down and admit defeat. But it adds texture to albums, the fact that they all get solos or they all get duets with Freddie. It's not like Keith Richards who is technically a bad singer, so they let him have one track every couple of albums as a kind of indulgence. Brian and Roger are perfectly adequate singers, but once Freddie starts singing, it puts them completely in the shade. I think perhaps more importantly than their vocal skills is that it's a band of four songwriters. Each contributes entire songs, across their career, and I think that richness is a massive factor in why they are still so loved.

KÜRSCH: "More of That Jazz" is also written and sung by Roger Taylor, right? That one struck me by surprise, with all the brief samples from the songs that had just passed by—such a nice refreshment. The way Queen did it was so organic. Much simpler these days with computers, but you can tell there was thought put into it. It runs through so smoothly, within the context of the song.

POPOFF: Roger, as a studio guru yourself, how would you assess *Jazz* sonically? What does Roy Thomas Baker bring to the sound of the band?

MANNING JR.: I'd say they really honed their marriage on *A Night at the Opera*. That's when you get not only obvious arrangement changes, but the whole sonic landscape really solidifying and becoming a stamp that they carry well into *The Game*. Thing started changing with *The Game*, but clearly Geoff Workman is important too, as engineer, as he gets a big print credit in the gatefold.

You have the big, roomy tom-tom sounds. A lot of bands started doing it. The most overt things for me are the drum sound and Brian May's guitar tones. Not so much because of his ability to sculpt his Red Special with all his effects boxes, but you hear a lot of room mics on the amplifiers. Instead of using reverb effects—artificial reverb or even plates—you get simply room mics that help add to the largeness of the guitar sound.

As well, Queen arrangements are so sparse, and that allows for a level of intricacy on guitar harmonies and vocal harmonies. Most people—and my own band's been guilty of this—throw everything but the kitchen sink at it in an attempt to make it as large as possible. But the human ear can't process it and you have the reverse effect. You can get a lot more largeness, or apparent largeness, by leaving arrangements sparse and soaking the mix with a big, powerful vocal in the chorus. Or when there's a Brian May guitar solo, it's the loudest thing in the mix. There's no logic to it. It just clobbers the rest of the mix. The drums and everything else are pushed to the background and you get this gargantuan sound.

POPOFF: Hansi, any closing thoughts?

KÜRSCH: Well, what comes to mind is that these are songs you rarely see on greatest hits collections. But as I said about *A Day at the Races*, there is no filler. *Jazz* is an album you can easily listen to from beginning to end and marvel at the complexity and the speed at which the band present their ideas and then move on. The roots of Queen are there yet it's fresh and modern, so in a sense it's all about the here and now of the late '70s.

As well, across the record, there are so many sound effects, but they are so on-point that you do not recognize them immediately or are not distracted by them. You may not even recognize what they are, because they work so well in the song. On an artistic level as a musician or on the level of a listener, you will be entertained.

It's obvious Queen put a lot of thought into what they were doing. Those guys were all highly educated, great musicians and they were totally dedicated to the entire package that was Queen. They did something like eight albums in eight years. Just imagine the creativity and the artistry. And then on *Jazz*, there was not only so much that we appreciate from Queen, but these signposts to what they were going to do in the future.

MANNING JR.: I agree. As much as I like Queen's more progressive aspects, I appreciate *Jazz* because it's structured almost like a pop record. The songs are clean, honed, and direct, in these tight little bundles, and that's why I find it so effortlessly catchy. "Bicycle Race" is a perfect example of Queen distilling this sound they'd been perfecting over the years, and just cramming it into a quicker, more precise version.

The '70s was a time when the record company acted as a filtering mechanism. Once signed, it was not uncommon for record companies to give an artist at least three albums before they said, "Hey, it's not working out" or "It's kind of working out, let's keep nurturing you and hopefully by your fifth record you're gonna have a huge hit and we're all gonna make our money back."

Those days are over. But when they signed an artist or a group that had extreme talent, that was obviously a cut above the rest, they were banking on the fact that their talent is so good or they're so unique as singers, we're going to make our money back. Very often they were right and everybody got rich. Chicago, the Doobie Brothers, these bands I grew up with on AM radio when I was a kid, you had guys who came together and said, "Well, I'm pretty good and you're pretty good, but if we put our talents together, good God, we'd be unstoppable."

And Queen was the perfect example. Watch any Queen documentary and you'll quickly notice the amount of confidence that those guys had to set out to tackle and conquer the music world. If you've got that kind of artillery at your disposal, you look to your left and you're like, geez, this is one of the best guitarists ever—and he writes amazing. The guy behind me, killer drummer and he can sing way higher than the rest of us. Turn to my right, the bass player, kind of the quiet one, great writer, shredding bass player, and suddenly you see that British cockiness that we associate with so many British bands over the years was justified! It might be coming across as braggadocio, but Queen could back it up. They're not just blowing hot air.

RELEASED JUNE 30, 1980

8 THE GAME

WITH REINHOLD MACK, RICHIE UNTERBERGER, AND JEB WRIGHT

SIDE 1

1. **Play the Game** 3:28
   (MERCURY)
2. **Dragon Attack** 4:17
   (MAY)
3. **Another One Bites the Dust** 3:33
   (DEACON)
4. **Need Your Loving Tonight** 2:47
   (DEACON)
5. **Crazy Little Thing Called Love** 2:42
   (MERCURY)

SIDE 2

1. **Rock It (Prime Jive)** 4:30
   (TAYLOR)
2. **Don't Try Suicide** 3:52
   (MERCURY)
3. **Sail Away Sweet Sister** 3:30
   (MAY)
4. **Coming Soon** 2:48
   (TAYLOR)
5. **Save Me** 3:45
   (MAY)

PERSONNEL:

FREDDIE MERCURY – *vocals, keyboards, acoustic guitar;*
BRIAN MAY – *guitar, keyboards, vocals;*
JOHN DEACON – *bass, guitar, keyboards;*
ROGER TAYLOR – *drums, vocals, guitar, keyboards*

GUEST PERSONNEL:

REINHOLD MACK – *synthesizer*
Recorded at MUSICLAND STUDIOS, *Munich*
Produced by QUEEN; *co-produced by* MACK

OPPOSITE: Freddie practices "Bohemian Rhapsody" and "Crazy Little Thing Called Love" in London, a few days ahead of his October 7, 1979, performances with the Royal Ballet.

I suppose one could ponder *News of the World* and *Jazz* and find high contrasts between the two, and then similarly between those two and what preceded them. But then along comes *The Game* and one quickly has to rethink the extent of contrast in the past. Because now Queen is *really* zooming into the future, an exciting new decade, in fact, with two *au courant* tricks up their sleeves.

Three, if one counts rockabilly, which, come to think of it, is the opposite of zooming forward. But it must be discussed, of course, thanks to the egregiously incongruous lead single "Crazy Little Thing Called Love." There are also '50s rock signifiers in the elongated intro to "Rock It (Prime Jive)" and the oft-forgotten break late in "Don't Try Suicide" (*and* on the album cover, of course). But that's stretching things, really. History will remember the "rockabilly portion" of the album as being all about the smash single.

So, what is exciting and new and fresh here? Quite a bit, actually. Despite a couple of flirtations with funk on the last two records, *The Game* is essentially blinded by funk. "Another One Bites the Dust" is a funk tour de force, while the lone hard rock song on *The Game* is its funk equal. And then there's the album's forgotten dark horse, "Don't Try Suicide."

Without *Hot Space* to compare it to, this strange dance club direction and the even less expected rockabilly/'50s angle seem like outliers, novelties even. But what I find really exciting about *The Game* is what happens on the rarely discussed tracks. In 1979, the Cars released their second smash album, *Candy-O*, produced by Roy Thomas Baker.

The Game was produced by Reinhold Mack, and we hear some of the essence of Mack's influence on Queen as he set upon what Roger Thomas Baker had done with the band previously. We sure don't hear what we thought Baker was all about on the Queen's first four albums.

Coincidentally, though, in 1978 and 1979, Baker had produced the first two smash-hit albums by a Boston new wave band called the Cars, so for argument's sake, let's call what we *do* hear on *The Game* more about the idea of fangless American new wave, perky but still guitar-driven, and especially evident in songs like "Rock It (Prime Jive)," "Need Your Loving Tonight," and "Coming Soon" (of whose opening drums practically quote the Cars' "You're All I've Got Tonight"), each of them energetic and cheeky, two of them even quite heavy, but all of a manner Queen had never tried before. Roger's singing adds a bit of youthful edge, but it's really about Brian playing those simple rhythms, along with the low-budget keyboard stabs that evoke images of leather-jacketed Queen falling out of the truck onto the streets of Manhattan and hitting the clubs, rubbing shoulders with the Rolling Stones and David Bowie, all surprised to see each other there.

That's the dimension of *The Game* that is refreshing to me—not the funk or rockabilly. But then, having put us in this snap-happy place, Queen brilliantly offers the final third of the record to old-school fans, denying them any metal but still slaying them with "Play the Game," "Sail Away Sweet Sister," and closing masterwerk "Save Me." I like to think of these as the traditional Queen workhorses that carried the glitzier bells-and-whistles hit singles on their backs, helping make *The Game* not just commercially but creatively worthy of triple platinum in the US, and moving an estimated four million copies worldwide.

Whatever you embraced, whatever you dismissed—rockabilly, funk, new wave, or more trad Queen—the band sure packed a lot of living and lively debate into *The Game* as they took the '80s by the horns, realizing that artists take risks or die. As luck would have it, the riskiest moves paid off famously with songs of such superlative quality that any Queen fan, jaded or in high school, couldn't help but love them.

POPOFF: *The Game*—new decade, new era for Queen?

WRIGHT: It's a game-changer! [*laughs*]. And in many ways, it opens the floodgates to styles of Queen to come that I did not care for. If I'm not mistaken, there's synthesizer for the first time on a Queen album, as well as pop tunes like "Crazy Little Thing Called Love" and "Another One Bites the Dust"—Elvis on one hand and a disco beat on the other. So, I could see hardcore '70s Queen fans not liking *The*

Game. However, to me, it's that album that started a new direction—their Journey *Escape* or Foreigner *4*. I liked more what came before in each case, but for that one moment these bands melded the old with the new so well that they succeeded both creatively and commercially.

UNTERBERGER: I think that Queen—and this is unusual for a band at that time that was very much in the mainstream—were willing to take at least some chances that a lot of other groups in roughly their same field would not have. The two most famous songs on *The Game* are so unlike songs that they were the most famous for. Many people wouldn't even have recognized the band.

With "Another One Bites the Dust," there are interviews where the guys figure people are going to be pissed off, that they're going to hear the song, which is almost a version of rap, and they're gonna say, "I hate that music and I don't need to hear this." But at the same time, there were going to be millions of people who say, "That's Queen?! I would've never guessed. What else do they have?"

POPOFF: Reinhold, what was your experience working with the band for the first time?

MACK: Well, I wasn't too familiar with what the band did before. Obviously, I'd heard some of the big hits, but other than that, it was a new band for me and I just listened to what they were doing in the studio, on the studio floor, and I thought that's pretty darn good. So, we kept it like that, as opposed to the previous stuff, where everything was so super tight and tightly mic'd. Just by doing that, I think I changed it around quite a bit.

POPOFF: What was the Mack sound as you saw fit to apply to Queen?

MACK: I like it open. I hate to use this, but you get some air around it that you actually feel it and it's not just like somebody dropped a ball. You know, it's got some crack to it. As far as that snare sound goes, that is actually a very old technique I learned from the classical people. You don't mic the snare drum from an angle down toward it and one at the bottom. I just use one on the side—I aim it at the shell of the drum.

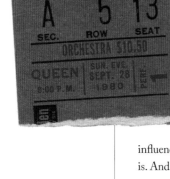

UNTERBERGER: The production, to me, is not so different or particularly radical. Especially on the songs that aren't the two hits. But there might be a slight sense of reaching out to listeners who aren't already Queen fans, not with the sound of "Crazy Little Thing Called Love," but certainly on "Another One Bites the Dust," which is bass-heavy and somehow more embraceable, not as arty or eccentric as previous productions.

WRIGHT: I agree that this is not that singular sounding—this is not the Mack of *Hot Space* or Billy Squier. Musicians, producers, guys like you and me, and the guy down the street—any time you're new at a job, you don't necessarily exert your influence and push as hard and tell them things that you think they should do, whatever the job is. And I would imagine with a band like Queen, you might be a little apprehensive the first time out to really push them too hard. So, I wonder if he did hold back. Queen already had a track record of success. *The Game* would put them in pop charts, but we're talking about a band that already had a decade of success. It does seem Mack restrained or Mack lite [*laughs*]. But at the same time, you have the introduction of synthesizers—you can hear the perspective changing.

MACK: Any project is itself; it has its own dynamic. Therefore, I just try to translate what I hear onto whatever medium it is, around the universe. I didn't get involved with the arrangements and moving choruses around. The band had done a few albums, they knew how to do it, they were very proficient musicians. So, these things were under control. And overall, I would say the happiest [*laughs*] time with the band was *The Game* because it was done completely without thinking about it, you know, just doing it.

POPOFF: Let's take a look at the opening track, "Play the Game," which isn't unlike "We Are the Champions" or "Somebody to Love."

UNTERBERGER: It's one of those anthemic Queen songs, like "Spread Your Wings," expressing this idea of you've got to do things your own way. And with a lot of Queen's core audience—which I think is fair to say at that time were adolescents—when you're really struggling to assert your identity, and often it's in opposition to what older people are saying, whether it's get a job or don't put on those silly clothes, it's something that has enormous appeal.

And now a lot of those original Queen fans are my age. I'm fifty-five and that's a record that helped form my identity as a youth. And for their kids—or in some cases now, their grandkids—it still has that appeal. It doesn't sound so dated. Different generations can still pull that messaging out of the song.

And as lead-off track, it's kind of a mood-setter. As big as the two hits were, you don't want to start off with "Crazy Little Thing Called Love" and have people think it's going to be a rockabilly record. It also feels like a song that could be the first song a live performance. And, actually, it was a fair hit in the UK.

WRIGHT: "Play the Game," for starters, the opening flourish, which they did with multiple tracks of Oberheim OB-X, kicks off the band's first use of synthesizers. They whoosh in with that sort of sound sculpture before the piano comes in. "Play the Game" is also a good way to usher in the album because it's a steppingstone between the old and the new Queen. It's a song of classic Queen sensibility—there are loads of vocal harmonizing and orchestration, plus Freddie singing the whole thing—but it's also on an album with "Another One Bites the Dust."

POPOFF: Well, let's look at that one. First off, Reinhold, I'm curious, was everybody on board with the idea?

MACK: Oh, nobody was really interested in that at all. It was, Deaky, John Deacon, who had the idea, and he played it to me and said, "What do you think of this riff?" And I said, "Oh, that's pretty cool. How do you want to put it down? Do you want to ask the others?" And he says, "Ah no, I'm not sure, you know, I've got nothing else. I've just got that riff." So, I said, "Let me figure out something."

So, I made this tape loop of this drumbeat, and John started playing, putting his bass on, and we sort of counted it out. It was basically just John and me in the studio, and I figured, if I started doing guitars or some keyboard stuff, just as a guide, I might run into deep diplomatic waters. So, whenever changes come, I just used a piano note, which I played backward and mangled a little bit through, what was it, a Marshall time delay? And inserted that at the right spot so it made some sense.

Certainly, some coolness started, and Freddie heard it and he went, "Yeah, now, have you got a line? What type of vocals do you imagine?" And John said, "I haven't really got much, but

The Game tour at the Fabulous Forum in Inglewood, California, July 11, 1980. The album helped form the identity of many a young listener.

something like 'another one bites the dust.'" And Freddie, being into the disco scene, boogieing, "Yeah, this matches, let's just do this." And we built a couple of things around it and that was it.

POPOFF: A truly shocking song coming out of Queen, no?

WRIGHT: Of course, and not one of my favorites. But I remember going, well, at least they got a friggin' hit. It's like, there's no way this is not going to be huge. But for me, it's the Van Hagar syndrome. I was such a David Lee Roth fan, I despised Van Hagar. But now that I'm a little older, I'm like, Van Hagar's pretty good, you know? There's some interesting stuff that I blinded myself out of.

That's how I saw "Another One Bites the Dust" at first: "Come on, this can't be the band that I love." I had a guy yapping at me once at a gig saying how much he hated "Come Sail Away," by Styx. I let him go through his rant, but I said, "Okay, there was a time when you were driving to work, and there was no one in the car with you, and the DJ puts on this song, and you cranked it to ten and you were singing, 'I'm sailing way!'" You know, you can't help it. And to me, that's "Another One Bites the Dust."

UNTERBERGER: It gets compared to heavy funk from the time, like Chic or acts like that, but there's also similarity to nascent rap. The first rap song most people ever heard was "Rapper's Delight," and if you listen to that backing track and then play the backing track to "Another One Bites the Dust," it's not a copy, but there are similarities. And the way that the chorus is sung, it's done as a slogan. It's not classic rap, even classic early rap, but it's obviously not sung in an operatic fashion like early Queen either.

And if you're looking at Queen's career as a whole, especially when they're being reassessed decades later, that song was a great boon to John Deacon's legacy in the group

Photo from *The Game's* cover shoot. Suddenly Freddie didn't look like a foppish aristocrat from the Middle Ages frolicking about the stage.

because he is not known as a songwriter like Freddie Mercury and Brian May were. But this is one of the most well-known songs of the era, a smash hit, and it was really his idea to go in that direction, at least on this track.

As for the Munich influence, Musicland was where some of the late-'70s disco smashes were recorded. And that sound would have been familiar in the United States through Donna Summer.

POPOFF: But a bunch of bands tried their hand at disco, and earlier than this, a case in point being the Rolling Stones with "Miss You."

WRIGHT: I think "Miss You" was better than "Another One Bites the Dust," which was better than "I Was Made for Loving You" by Kiss. There was ELO, Blondie with "Heart of Glass" and "Rapture." "Another One Bites the Dust" has some cool guitar parts and cool music going on, but I would say this is Queen's "Do Ya Think I'm Sexy" [*laughs*].

POPOFF: I always say "Dragon Attack" is the sister track to "Another One Bites the Dust," yet it's also *The Game*'s heaviest song.

WRIGHT: My favorite on the record. From the first time I heard it to now, I don't get tired of it. If "Another One Bites the Dust" was cool, it would be "Dragon Attack." It's similarly repetitive, where the guitar line is the bass line too. But Freddie was on fire on that song. When he gets raw and he's singing about dirty shit but he's making it not dirty at the same time, I just love it. And the lyrics to that are downright X-rated in a way. As opposed to songs that reflect the relationship side of Freddie, "Dragon Attack" was the get down, make love side of Freddie [*laughs*]—although, of course, Brian May wrote it.

I also like the solo section, where Roger is just wailing away on those tinny toms. He has said that that's a particularly hard song to play; it's hard on his right wrist for some reason. To me, "Dragon Attack" fits the category of hard rock Queen. Even though it's not arranged or produced particularly heavy, I could hear that right after "Sheer Heart Attack" and it wouldn't be overly jarring. But I don't want to see Adam Lambert singing it [*laughs*]. We gotta be cool at our age about replacement singers, and I could see him singing many Queen songs, but I don't want to see him singing "Dragon Attack."

MACK: I always thought they tended a bit more toward pop. They're not really a heavy rock band, which probably goes without saying. Because, you know, the chord changes, and the way the harmonies go and everything, you can't really describe Queen as your verse-bridge-chorus-chorus-chorus-bridge-solo type of standard rock. I never felt that they were your typical heavy rock thing.

POPOFF: On a different tack, what do you think of this cover art?

WRIGHT: It worried me. Because I'm sure back in those days you did what I did. If you liked a band and they put an album out, you didn't wait to hear all the songs—man, you went out

The rockabilly-flavored "Crazy Little Thing Called Love" b/w "Spread Your Wings," Japan, 1979. A vigilant Reinhold Mack captured an informal run-through of the song in an LA studio, resulting in the new album's first single.

and bought it. Even though *The Game* may have been the first I bought, I had older sisters who had Queen albums, so I was well aware of the early stuff.

So, I decided to buy this record. And the only song I'd heard was "Crazy Little Thing Called Love," because it came out months ahead of the album. So, when I saw the cover, I thought the whole thing was gonna be rockabilly! And I don't know if they were greasing it up because of that movie, *Grease*, but that thought crossed my mind.

I liked the contrast between the black leather though and the silver. For an American, that's an Oakland Raiders thing. But Freddie can't pull off tough guy—come on, he looks like a nerd. Maybe they were trying to be cool, but it didn't turn out too cool [*laughs*].

UNTERBERGER: There were some albums from that time where people who weren't new wave suddenly seemed like they were trying to jump on that bandwagon, say Billy Joel with *Glass Houses* and Linda Ronstadt with *Mad Love*, more in image than the actual music. With Queen's look, the biggest shock was suddenly Freddie doesn't look like an aristocrat pouncing around from the Middle Ages. Suddenly he looks kind of macho, which is something he would keep to the end of his touring days.

POPOFF: Well, let's address "Crazy Little Thing Called Love." Reinhold, can you provide some background?

MACK: The album started in bits and pieces. The first thing we did was "Crazy Little Thing," and that wasn't planned. I was in LA and got a call that the band was in the studio. So eventually, I just figured I'd go there. And nobody really was into doing anything, because they'd just come off a tour in Japan and wanted to store their equipment for a couple of weeks.

And I asked the road crew if I could just put together a really simple setup—drums, bass, keyboards, and guitar—so in case somebody wanted to do something, I was ready. What happened was Freddie came in, he had this idea, and thought he could just try it out. No need to get sounds or do this and that. And they just went through the motions of learning it, and I was on my toes and recorded it.

And after they'd done, really, just one take, I said, "Here, you want to listen to it?" And Freddie said, "No, we didn't get sounds or anything, so let's not do that." And I said, "You know, I got sounds [*laughs*], and you could spend three or four minutes of your life just checking it out, see how it comes across." And then it was, "Oh, this is really happening, come on, let's do this, let's finish that." And that's how it happened.

And then somebody at Elektra, the former label there, people heard it and put it out and it was number one, *bang*. And this still wasn't like album time. I think it was on nine charts, and then we thought we'd better build an album around that [*laughs*].

POPOFF: How interested were these guys in what you were doing as a producer? Who out of the band rolled up their sleeves and had a hand in the engineering and the producing?

MACK: Well, usually guitars were left to the guitar player and bass to the bass player. Everybody to his own; nobody would really say anything or interfere. It was just, like, with Brian, maybe, what do you think? It could be a bit brighter or could we use a different guitar? With "Crazy Little Thing," there was this huge writeup in *Melody Maker* where Brian moaned about me forcing him to use a Fender guitar and a Fender amp for the solo part on "Crazy Little Thing Called Love." I just said, "Look, what this thing sounds like, it sounds like it needs this but you

don't want to play." And he says, "No, I can get it on this guitar," his beloved fireplace, or Red Special, as he calls it. And I said, "Sure you can, but this is authentic and let's just stick to that." And so it was "Okay, moan, moan, moan, let me just do it." And that was that.

POPOFF: How did it work on the album's more traditional Queen tracks? Songs like "Save Me" and "Sail Away Sweet Sister"?

MACK: That was more sort of just regular work and doing overdubbing and these vocals. There's a very nice writeup in Brian May's *Queen in 3-D* book where he talks about how I worked, or how I do work. It's interesting and made me laugh so hard. I never really saw it from that angle. His main quote was that he was into doing things a certain way, getting the drums right, getting the guitars right, getting each individual bit right, the lead vocals, the backing vocals.

And since I'd been working with the Electric Light Orchestra before, there were never enough tracks, never enough space, so I was used to putting harmony guitars or vocal harmonies on tracks where they didn't belong, where nothing was happening at that time. For instance, the lead guitar wasn't playing, so I would use that track for vocals and so on. So, it was pretty confusing for the onlooker to understand what I was doing.

And he asked, "Can you actually hear everything?" And I said, "No, probably not" [*laughs*]. Because this is actually true. In the general scheme, everything was right and everybody liked it,

The Game Tour, 1980. Thanks to his bass line, "Another One Bites the Dust" was a great boon to John Deacon's legacy in the band. As the disco-ball '70s gave way to the neon '80s, Queen evolved, too—note the primary colors, ties, and sporty kicks.

but it wasn't perfectly done because I didn't have two twenty-four tracks. I just dealt with what I had. Usually my main objective is to keep the technical crap out of the artists' way. I'm never, "Oh, let me try to set this up" or "Now we've got to check this" and make people wait when they're dying to do something real quick.

And Freddie, he was like my soulmate. Whenever he wanted to do something, I'd say, "Okay, do it," *bang*, there it is. And toward the end of our work together, over the years, I would do a mix and I'd call him and say, "I think I've done it." And all he'd say is, "Is it good?" And I'd go, "Oh, yeah, it's not too bad." And he said, "That's all I need to hear." So that was pretty cool.

POPOFF: Excellent. Let's finish up with some of these deep album tracks. What do you make of "Don't Try Suicide"?

WRIGHT: I like the song and I think Freddie was a genius. Freddie is singing a song about suicide and you can dance around the room. It's a horrible topic, but he addresses it while your toes are tapping. It's a simple song and it wasn't a hit. I imagine it got most of its play from those turning over "Another One Bites the Dust," because I remember from my single, that was on the flip side. It reveals one of the band's many alter egos. They don't prog out and it's not heavy in the least. But you know it's Queen. Still, it's different and strange, and it's them taking that left turn.

UNTERBERGER: "Don't Try Suicide" is one of the stronger non-hit tracks, and it's actually got a little bit of a Stray Cats rockabilly feel. Of course, Queen would not be influenced by the Stray Cats, who were rising to prominence by that time, but there's that snaky jazz rockabilly feel, almost spy music. Maybe it's a little new wave–influenced. They're addressing an extremely controversial subject.

It's a strange song, because you listen to it in passing and you think, well, they're doing a public service announcement to teenagers—don't attempt suicide. How do we get them to not think it's kind of cool to commit suicide? But when you look at the lyrics, it's not that dogmatic. It's kind of like, well, don't do it because if you're thinking about it and you're trying to get attention, nobody cares anyway. There's some ambivalence. It's more disturbing lyrically than you would think.

A collection of Polish and Soviet flexi discs from 1979 and 1980.

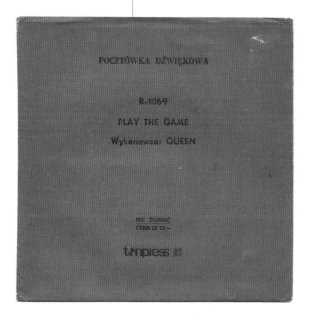

POPOFF: Finally, we've got "Save Me." Putting this last, I wonder if the band was trying to leave us with a sense of reassurance.

UNTERBERGER: Yes, possibly, because "Save Me" seems like the song that would've been the most reassuring to longtime Queen fans, especially those attracted by the power ballads. But at the same time, I don't think it's a calculation. "Okay, we're taking some chances with some of the songs on this record, but we've got to have something for the old fans." It's something that came naturally to them, since their career.

It might've been a surprise to them, but also to the label and people in the business that "Save Me" was not a big hit. And that the other two songs, which were not their style, were the huge hits. The record business is pretty conservative in their projections, and I think if you had played the album in its entirety to people in the business, they would've said, "Well, you've got to go with 'Save Me' because that's what people want from Queen." And they did use that in Britain, but in the United States, the other two songs were massive.

MACK: Traditional Queen song with a standard melody. With a song like "Save Me," the band would play as a three-piece, sometimes as a four-piece with the piano, depending, and then Brian would go, "Okay, this is a good take," then we'd double the guitar. Then I basically would add a voice, which then was doubled, and since there were never enough tracks, I'd let him do one and then when he was doing the other one, I copied the first one into the second one. So, I was saving one generation of tape, and that's probably what made it sound better. And then, you know, first voice, second, third, sometimes fourth and fifth, depending on how huge it should be.

WRIGHT: What an album ender. Classic Queen with that huge setup that builds to the crescendo of the chorus. That just begs you to scream out "Save me!" with Freddie. It also features Brian May all over the place. He's playing piano, guitar, synthesizer, acoustic. It's the closest thing on the record to a musical masterpiece. Without Freddie's voice, as an instrumental, the song would still have loads of emotion and power.

POPOFF: One last thing: Do you hear some new wave influence on this album or is that just me?

WRIGHT: I'd buy that. One of my favorites, and maybe the happiest song on the album, is "Need Your Loving Tonight." That's very Cars, and Roy Thomas Baker had just produced the Cars, coincidentally. Maybe somebody in the Queen camp was keeping an eye on what their old producer was doing.

Also "Rock It (Prime Jive)," sung by Roger, for the most part. Can you imagine Freddie singing this? He couldn't have done it. This song is tailor-made for Roger. It's my favorite Roger vocal. But it's got a Cars-like synth line, for sure. I'm shocked to look back in history and see that this wasn't released as a single and made into an FM staple. But it's a bit old-time rock 'n' roll too, isn't it? If "Crazy Little Thing Called Love" is kind of a nerdy guy trying to be Danny Zuko in *Grease*, "Prime Jive" *is* Danny Zuko, you know? [*laughs*] It's the cool version of "Crazy Little Thing Called Love."

But new wave? I don't know. I mean, the middle finger of the Pistols was a prostate check for Queen [*laughs*], but more in that it was an annoyance, not something they took to heart on *News of the World* or *Jazz*. As you say, there are hints of it here, although that would be American skinny-tie new wave and definitely not punk.

You get so many emotions on *The Game*. Yeah, a little bit of new wave in the songs we talked about but also in "Coming Soon." But there's also the pomp of "Play the Game" and "Sail Away Sweet Sister" into the sinister badass-ness of "Dragon Attack" to disco to the '50s sound of "Crazy Little Thing" to the heavy message of "Don't Try Suicide." You're almost tired out by the time you get to "Sail Away Sweet Sister"—the classic that time forgot—and "Save Me." One thing I can say about *The Game* is that across all of this there was a pop sensibility. And the result of that is that it set me up to be really excited about what they were going to do next.

OPPOSITE: *The Game* tour, the NEC, Birmingham, England, December 5, 1980.

RELEASED DECEMBER 8, 1980

9 FLASH GORDON

WITH REINHOLD MACK, DANIEL NESTER, AND NINA NOIR

SIDE 1

1. **Flash's Theme** 3:22
   (MAY)

2. **In the Space Capsule
   (The Love Theme)** 2:21
   (TAYLOR)

3. **Ming's Theme (In the Court
   of Ming the Merciless)** 2:53
   (MERCURY)

4. **The Ring
   (Hypnotic Seduction of Dale)** 1:15
   (MERCURY)

5. **Football Fight** 1:29
   (MERCURY)

6. **In the Death Cell
   (Love Theme Reprise)** 2:26
   (TAYLOR)

7. **Execution of Flash** 1:05
   (DEACON)

8. **The Kiss
   (Aura Resurrects Flash)** 2:11
   (MERCURY)

SIDE 2

1. **Arboria
   (Planet of the Tree Men)** 1:41
   (DEACON)

2. **Escape from the Swamp** 1:37
   (TAYLOR)

3. **Flash to the Rescue** 2:47
   (MAY)

4. **Vultan's Theme
   (Attack of the Hawk Men)** 1:15
   (MERCURY)

5. **Battle Theme** 2:20
   (MAY)

6. **The Wedding March** :56
   (MAY)

7. **Marriage of Dale and Ming
   (and Flash Approaching)** 2:04
   (MAY, TAYLOR)

8. **Crash Dive on Mingo City** :46
   (MAY)

9. **Flash's Theme Reprise
   (Victory Celebrations)** 1:39
   (MAY)

10. **The Hero** 3:31
    (MAY)

ORIGINAL SOUNDTRACK MUSIC BY QUEEN

PERSONNEL:

FREDDIE MERCURY – *vocals, piano, synthesizer;*
BRIAN MAY – *guitar, vocals, piano, synthesizer, guitar orchestration;*
JOHN DEACON – *bass, guitar synthesizer;*
ROGER TAYLOR – *drums, tympani, vocals, guitar*

GUEST PERSONNEL:

HOWARD BLAKE – *additional orchestral arrangements; assorted voice actors*

Recorded at TOWNHOUSE STUDIOS, *London;* THE MUSIC CENTRE, *Wembley, London;*
ADVISION STUDIOS, *London; and* UTOPIA STUDIOS, *London, UK*
Produced by QUEEN

OPPOSITE: Groenoordhallen in Leiden, Netherlands, November 27, 1980, a few days before the release of the *Flash Gordon* soundtrack.

OVERLEAF: According to Reinhold Mack, Freddie was not a fan of tedious soundtrack work. Just rockin'. . .

Obviously not of the same ilk as the rest of the Queen catalog, *Flash Gordon*, due to its substance, as far as these things go, nonetheless warrants short examination and some level of inclusion as a "real" record in the canon.

As is often the case with soundtracks, there's no gratuitous popping in of various bands here, nor is there popping in of recent Queen hits. In fact, there's really very little that is not from Queen in terms of effects or typical classical orchestration.

What we get with *Flash Gordon* is an entirely interesting, mostly instrumental album that offers fans a time-jumping opportunity to ponder how pre-Mack Queen of *News of the World* or *Jazz* might treat some of the more provocative modern experiments on later albums like *The Works* and *The Miracle*. In other words, the instrumental soundscapes and sculptures on *Flash Gordon*—for example, "Football Fight," "Battle Theme" and even the lone "cover," "The Wedding March"—are both forward-thinking and full up with the embarrassment of creative riches evident during the band's hallowed and fecund 1970s run.

On top of a flood of varied and provocative musical calling cards (each kept brief so the program moves along like *Sheer Heart Attack* and *Jazz*), there are two absolute corkers, full songs with vocals: the badly titled "Flash's Theme" and "The Hero." The first was successfully milked as a single and both were added to the live set, thrilling the deep fan who would come to appreciate the fleeting magic of "The Hero" on stage in all its Taylor-surged and May-electrocuted heavy metal glory.

Out in the market, the record lived up to its limited potential, charting high around the world, reaching gold in the UK, selling as a value-added seven-inch, wholly on the strength of a single that rode the monster wave generated by *The Game*. And as a feedback loop, "Flash's Theme" no doubt gave *The Game* additional legs, almost to the point where Queen's 1981 might have been enough to save them from their 1982 . . . so that they could muddle their way through 1983 en route to a much more comfortable 1984.

POPOFF: What are the circumstances surrounding the making of the *Flash Gordon* soundtrack?

NESTER: They did it on the quick. And the thing I've learned over the years is that they did it not so much in tandem with *The Game*, but before *The Game*. If you're a super-duper Queen fan and you follow all the liner notes and see that no synths were being used all along, up until *The Game*, it was really during the recording of *Flash Gordon* that they started using the Oberheim OB-X.

And they did that sort of piecemeal. They eventually switched over to recording for the next proper studio album, *The Game*. So even though *The Game* came out before *Flash Gordon*, they'd actually laid down the tracks and switched over to using the synthesizer because it's faster. Each of them had their own little assignments, little song cues for *Flash Gordon*.

POPOFF: Reinhold, what do you recall about working on the project, and what were the challenges, working in tandem with a film?

MACK: What happened was, they were asked to do this film score. And, you know, Deaky, John Deacon, did most of the keyboard stuff, but they had just started it. And at some point, I don't know who called me, but it was, "Do you fancy coming down to"—I think it was Advision Studios—"and checking this out?" So, I went down and said, "What have you got?" And it was all these bits and pieces, and I said, "Yeah, I don't know." First, I need paper and pencil to try to make head and tails out of it.

And then we went to Townhouse Studios and we had just about every conceivable tape machine—the thirty-five-millimeter scopic three-channel and the nineteen-millimeter seven-channel film machines—because a lot of that stuff was, you know, just on weird film equipment.

A Japanese promo copy of "Flash's Theme" b/w "Football Fight." The single is a straightforward song with unabashed Queen power.

So, I had to transfer all that and make something out of it. Then together with Brian, strangely enough, we developed the single, with all the stuff I thought at the time was pretty modern, because of the dialog of the film within the music, and just built that.

And then I think I went to De Lane Lea and mixed the film track, which again was totally creepy because in England, they had all this union stuff, where I wasn't allowed to do it, but if I did it, all the union guys had to leave the room in order not to see me doing it. Essentially, I was the poor guy struggling with all that equipment. And the film mixing boards are a bit bigger than most boards, so I was trying to put that into some sort of perspective, which I kind of succeeded.

I mean, it was very similar to *Highlander*, where we were also asked to do that score. Doing music scores for movies is tedious. You've really got to love doing that. And, obviously, Freddie didn't love it. He likes the recording and making the tracks or song and that's about it. To show you what Freddie is like, since we were working quite a bit in Montreux at the studio there that Queen bought, and the engineer David Richards worked there and wanted the go-ahead for spending money on equipment and whatnot, and he asked Freddie, "What do you want me to do with the studio?" And Freddie said, "Oh my God, dear, just push it into the lake" [*laughs*]. So yeah, no patience, no interest in technology. He just liked doing his thing and having a good time.

POPOFF: Well, at least Freddie's well represented on a couple of tracks here, namely "The Hero" and "Flash's Theme," the single.

NESTER: Yes, those are the two proper songs. "Flash's Theme" is great because it has that falsetto, "Just a man with a man's courage," all that sort of stuff. It's a simple, straightforward song, but it has that unabashed Queen power. This album is one of the last for a long time, maybe until like *Innuendo*, that has those big, multilayered vocal choruses and guitars. It's interesting to hear basically the sonic palette of *The Game* but with multilayered Roy Thomas Baker–like production. "Flash's Theme" definitely is one like that, and "The Hero" for sure.

And then you've got these weird little song pieces, like "Crash Dive on Mingo City." "Football Fight" sounds like a soundtrack to a porn movie. But it was kind of neat when the reissue came out and they had an earlier non-synth version of it that sounded even more like an adult film soundtrack [*laughs*]. Then there are some beautiful things like "The Kiss" and "The Ring (Hypnotic Seduction of Dale)." You've got some really high falsetto from Freddie— really, really beautiful stuff.

It's an interesting album because they're doing this in the spirit of a side project. And they're switching to synthesizers as they move along in the studio. So, for me it's far more interesting than I originally thought; at the time, it just felt like a holdoff between *The Game* and Greatest Hits. Pretty interesting stuff.

POPOFF: Nina, what are the highlights on this record for you?

NOIR: "The Hero," definitely, because that one's like the big epic moment in the movie, right? It was more like a traditional song that you hear in a movie like that, but it still has a lot of weirdness to it. Although, granted, with the vocals it's more palatable than some of the other tracks on that album.

In our tribute band, Killer Queens, we perform "Flash's Theme," but we just do a portion of it because it's kind of repetitive and boring, especially without the spoken dialog. We did a Queen-inspired wedding that was *Flash*-themed, and we had to do "The Wedding March." And that song is intense; it goes all over the place. There are all these weird chords and it's got kind of a minor, eerie feeling to it. That album is by far the strangest collection of Queen music you will ever hear. And I think a lot of people don't really pick up on the fact that it's a Queen album.

POPOFF: "Battle Theme" is also somewhat of a gem.

Roger at Nippon Budokan, Tokyo, February 1981. "Battle Theme" may have featured the band's last fully rocking, noncomputerized drums for quite some time.

NESTER: Yeah, there's where you get the signature multilayered Brian May stuff, and that's with live acoustic drums. To me, the drum track sounds more John Bonham than you'll ever hear Roger Taylor sound until maybe *Innuendo*. They're probably the last fully rocking, noncomputerized drums for a long, long time. So, it's really interesting if you sort of historic-ize the album. They are done with certain things by 1981. Unfortunately, there's not a lot of proper songs, rather little sketches. That's the nature of the soundtrack beast, I suppose.

POPOFF: What kind of movie is *Flash Gordon* and how well was it received?

NOIR: When I first saw the movie, I was so taken aback by it. I was like, what is this?! I suppose it would be classified as science fiction, but it borders on B-grade comedy horror. It's like *Star Wars* but with a lower budget. And it became a cult classic because of how bizarre it is. I think that Queen really wanted to start writing for film, so that was their way of getting in. Then they went on to do *Highlander*, which, with "Princes of the Universe" and all that was just fantastic. But, you know, they had to start somewhere.

MACK: Different movie I know, but "Princes of the Universe" is actually very interesting. That entire beginning, I made the drums, not as a tape loop, but I think that was a Linn drum machine. And the guitar, there's the bending down of the note. For that, Stefan, my assistant, played just the *eedly-eedly-eedly* and I ran the harmonizer down one octave. Freddie heard it and said, "This is so huge, this is massive," and then they started to pick up on that. It worked okay for the movie, but for the album, I should have really put more work into it. That's why I'm only half on that album, *A Kind of Magic*. But that album as a whole, I can only quote Freddie, playing the title track and saying, "Just listen to this crap. Now it's a hit. And we tried so hard to make something decent."

POPOFF: Funny. But at least working on that film generated a bunch of fully formed songs, right? Not to mention a movie that was taken a little more seriously.

NESTER: Yes, for sure. I mean, you've really gotta think about the movie *Flash Gordon* and the soundtrack separately. The movie was considered a total flop. And there are lots of reasons for that. One of which is the producers hated the lead guy, Sam Jones. They thought it was the beginning of a franchise à la *Superman*. But really, it was regarded as a low-budget movie. But the thing that got missed—as would happen with a lot of things—is that it was kind of a campy, Adam West *Batman* type of thing when the industry was moving more into the super-serious, Christopher Reeve *Superman* type of franchises. So, it was behind its time and ahead of its time—at the same time.

POPOFF: Do you remember people talking about the record?

NESTER: The record came out after *The Game*, Queen's most successful album yet. For a couple of months—as Brian May likes to say—they were the biggest band in the world. And this is the album that comes out when they're the biggest band in the world [*laughs*]. Their follow-up to "Another One Bites the Dust" and "Crazy Little Thing Called Love"—songs heard around the world—is a soundtrack to a campy sci-fi movie.

But they could do anything they wanted at that point. Some people don't even count it as a proper Queen album, but there's a whole cult of fans for the soundtrack; it's like an audio play because it interlaces movie dialog. And there are hipster types who think of *Flash Gordon* as the best Queen album ever. I don't know if I would go that far, but it definitely has some interesting things on it. It's far more interesting than just the theme song.

OPPOSITE: *Flash Gordon*—the film—was widely considered a flop. Though Sam Jones played the lead, most of the movie's posters featured Max von Sydow's character, Ming The Merciless, as the main character.

RELEASED MAY 21, 1982

SIDE 1

1. **Staying Power** 4:10
(MERCURY)

2. **Dancer** 3:47
(MAY)

3. **Back Chat** 4:33
(DEACON)

4. **Body Language** 4:32
(MERCURY)

5. **Action This Day** 3:32
(TAYLOR)

SIDE 2

1. **Put Out the Fire** 3:18
(MAY)

2. **Life Is Real
(Song for Lennon)** 3:31
(MERCURY)

3. **Calling All Girls** 3:52
(TAYLOR)

4. **Las Palabras de Amor
(The Words of Love)** 4:29
(MAY)

5. **Cool Cat** 3:48
(DEACON, MERCURY)

6. **Under Pressure** 4:03
(QUEEN, BOWIE)

PERSONNEL:

FREDDIE MERCURY – *vocals, keyboards,
drum machine, synthesizer bass;*
BRIAN MAY – *guitar, vocals keyboards,
drum machine, synthesizer bass;*
JOHN DEACON – *bass, guitar, drum
machine, synthesizer;*
ROGER TAYLOR – *drums, percussion,
vocals, guitar, synthesizer*

GUEST PERSONNEL:

DAVID BOWIE – *vocals;*
ARIF MARDIN – *horn arrangement;*
REINHOLD MACK – *synthesizer bass;*
DINO SOLERA – *saxophone*
Recorded at MOUNTAIN STUDIOS,
Montreux, Switzerland, and
MUSICLAND, *Munich*
Produced by QUEEN *and* MACK;
"Under Pressure" produced by QUEEN *and*
DAVID BOWIE

**OPPOSITE: North American leg of the *Hot Space*
tour, September 1982. *Hot Space* featured hints of
new wave, R&B, and even '60s girl group sounds.**

10 HOT SPACE

WITH JIM JENKINS, REINHOLD MACK, DANIEL NESTER, AND DARIUS RUCKER

Whether the bravest band in the world or the stupidest, Queen broke some sort of record with *Hot Space*. For if these things can be measured, *The Game* to *Hot Space* has got to represent one of the biggest record-to-record direction changes in rock history.

Not so much disco as it is various flavors of clubby dance, including a bit of new wave with "Action This Day," sensual R&B with "Cool Cat," and a sort of '60s girl group feel with "Calling All Girls," *Hot Space* is further shocking in its use of synthesizers and drum machines. Sure, Queen had used synths before, and but to replace Roger with robots . . . that was a new travesty.

What's more, even on the record's cursory nods to traditional Queen—the ballads "Life Is Real (Song for Lennon)" and "Las Palabras de Amor (The Words of Love)," and swampy hard rocker "Put Out the Fire"—the band adopted a new sonic palette, which helped send even the Queen we thought we knew into a hot space, needles in the red, woofers fried.

On board for the second time is producer Reinhold Mack, and this is the first time where Mack's signature sound emerges for Queen, with the

"Body Language" b/w "Life Is Real," Spain, 1982. The second single from *Hot Space* reflected Freddie's desire to infuse the band's new material with the energy he was experiencing in discotheques.

producer cranking the mids and turning drums into an exciting sort of slap and whack. Hints are foreshadowed on some of the new wavey songs on *The Game*, but it's all laid bare here on "Put Out the Fire." Mack would soon to take this sound to Billy Squier with great success, and even to the likes of Black Sabbath circa *Dehumanizer*.

Despite the bracing, provocative freshness of *Hot Space*, this was not a happy time in the Queen ranks. Already prone to torrid fights over the creative process, the guys within retreated further into fortified camps. Freddie, now out and proud and almost manically immersing himself in gay culture (in Berlin no less), was egged on to take control of the record's direction by his personal manager Paul Prenter, who strove to control communication between his coddled charge and the rest of the band.

Roger and Brian boiled over Freddie's new vision for Queen but went along. May's "Dancer" is a nice compromise, given its Mack-smacked hard rock chorus. "Action This Day" represents a similar synthesis. Brian is omnipresent over an angular Devo-like rhythm, while Roger defends the song by singing it with Freddie. It's both a techno version of "Fight from the Inside" and a literal fight from the inside.

Like Roger in "Action This Day," Brian pipes up and lets us know he was at the sessions through his duet with Freddie on the swellegant "Las Palabras de Amor," which despite the sweeping vistas of its choruses, is best remembered for Brian's solo guitar.

As for John Deacon, well, he's a bass player, and one can always find funk fun as keeper of the fat strings in such sparse and danceable songs. Remember, we're coming off the smash success of the bass-driven "Another One Bites the Dust," which is morphed into the likes of "Staying Power" and "Body Language," the latter unfathomably issued as a single. As for John's actual writing, there's "Back Chat," arranged in sync with the rest of the album but melodically rich and a little post-punk, and "Cool Cat," on which Deacon plays most everything, including finger-popping bass, while Freddie conducts his entire vocal in falsetto. "Back Chat" features Deacon pretty much building the whole song, as the guys could barely stand each other's company during this drug-and-drink time of disillusion in Deutschland.

Stuck like a scene stealer of a bonus track at the end of the album (which it should have opened) was the band's beloved collaboration with David Bowie. Recorded at Montreux amid the protracted and sullen sessions for *Hot Space*, "Under Pressure" was issued as a single six months before the album's low-key launch. It pretty much steamrolled the full-length as band and Bowie lifted spirits across 4:08 of swirling pop magic turned hard rock crescendo after crescendo. Credited to the whole band and Bowie, "Under Pressure" hit No. 1 in the UK and Canada but reached only No. 29 in the US. That, however, doesn't represent the song's significance: not only has it become one of the band's enduring classic rock staples, it was played live at every Queen show until the band ceased touring in 1986.

"Under Pressure" saved *Hot Space* from complete commercial disaster. "Body Language" charted despite itself, but four additional singles released across various territories were never taken to heart. "Under Pressure," part of the album but in some ways not (especially at the time), was surely instrumental in taking the record gold in the United States and a pretty impressive triple platinum in the United Kingdom. Still, *Hot Space* remains the most controversial and hotly debated record in the Queen catalog, although, given some middling material still to come, not the most universally reviled.

POPOFF: What changes does the band make for *Hot Space*? It's two years since *The Game*, and the guys are experiencing a lot of success.

NESTER: Well, the change is there are two camps now. One camp is John Deacon and Freddie Mercury, who want to capitalize on the musical, financial, and commercial success of "Another One Bites the Dust," and then there's Roger and Brian, who are the rock camp. So, the sequence of how this album's recorded was basically Side B first and then Side A. They record stuff like "Put Out the Fire" and, I think, "Calling All Girls" first, in Montreux, in the studio that they now own that Bowie and everybody—REO Speedwagon, Deep Purple, Bowie—all recorded in. They bought it so they could sit there and compose music and write songs in the studio.

And then a couple months later, they go to Musicland in Munich. They've already switched to Reinhold Mack for *The Game*, but they bring Mack into Musicland, the studio that's owned by, or least founded by, Giorgio Moroder. Now, Giorgio Moroder is arguably the inventor of disco, or electronic disco for sure, the guy behind "I Feel Love" by Donna Summer. Basically, they're in disco and synth central, socially and musically.

And Freddie is going to gay bars in Munich, and there are two camps there too: the hetero camp and the gay camp. And Freddie, if he wasn't out before, he's out and about now. He's single and he wants to mingle [*laughs*]. He's going out and listening to disco and he wants to get that energy going with the new Queen material. That's where songs like "Staying Power" and "Body Language" come from. Those high BPMs with electronic drums. Really spare stuff. If you pair "Staying Power" and "Body Language" with "I Feel Love" by Donna Summer, stuff starts making sense. At least musically speaking. Does it make sense for Queen? As a rock band? That's a whole other question.

JENKINS: Brian and Roger were the rockers, most definitely. But Freddie could rock out, even in the beginning. I think it was harder for Brian and Roger to realize what they could do, particularly introducing synthesizers, which was probably a big thing for them because they hadn't worked with synthesizers before. Roger was quite open to the idea of synthesizers and probably Freddie and John went along with it. But I think it was harder for Mack to get Brian to accept this new way of recording.

POPOFF: Reinhold, what dynamic did you see inside the studio?

MACK: Everything was different. Because the band were at a point where they weren't quite sure whether it was better to split up or do something completely different or even turn up in the studio. It was mostly one person at a time, which made it kind of hard to record a band. So, a lot of my technique of making loops and making stuff up where nothing was, you know, just to fill, turned into a pretty tough chore. You had to make drumbeats and get a bass groove on. I programmed synthesizers there, and next day somebody else would come in, "Let me hear what you did," and, "Oh, I'm not so sure about this or that, but let me try to put guitar on."

And since it wasn't heavy on guitars, Brian didn't really fancy it, and then he left again, and then Deaky left again. It was very scattered and for me excessively difficult to hold together. You can't really crack the whip and tell people, "Come on, pull yourself together, let's do something." That doesn't work with that band at all. I just had to make do with what there was.

Freddie liked it a lot, because it was danceable and he was into that sort of thing, at least at that time. Deaky liked it because it was groove-heavy, and Roger liked it to some extent. So yeah, you know, it gradually came forward. It took about nine months or something.

POPOFF: What is the sonic palette or complexion of *Hot Space*?

NESTER: I think Mack is bringing a new sound to *The Game* for sure, different drum sounds, more sparseness when it comes to guitar work, keeping things simple. At that point, Queen were kind of going nuts. They were in these different camps, they were partying all night, I think Mack's job at that point was to wait at the desk until one of them showed up and also facilitate the synths and the drum machines and all that tech stuff that was really new to them. I don't think he did that much with like, super rearrangements, like maybe Roy Thomas Baker did. I think of him as being a much more revolutionary producer for *The Game* than for *Hot Space*.

POPOFF: Flash back to the record hitting the shelves in May 1982.

RUCKER: I was in high school and people were surprised. They had put out this huge, successful record with *The Game*, but then again that was surprising too. The stage had been set for *Hot Space* with "Another One Bites the Dust." And then the other surprise was "Crazy Little Thing Called Love," which helped put Queen at another level. They have this big funk anthem and this little rockabilly song. That was showing their depth.

And then with Hot Space, they put out this synth-pop thing, and no one knew what to think. It was one of those things where people were like, "Do I like this or not?" [*laughs*] But I loved it. I'd always been a Queen fan so I was conditioned for surprises.

POPOFF: What are a few of the more interesting tracks on the record?

NESTER: Not to jump to the end, but I think of "Las Palabras de Amor" and pair it with "Teo Torriatte" from *A Day at the Races*. This is their quite lovely homage to their international audiences. They had just toured South America and Mexico, these huge soccer stadiums, and this is one of Brian's totally sincere homages to their fans.

It's really well written, but it has that muddy, plodding aspect that doesn't make it rise above. And I think of that as a function of its production values. There's the riddle of the muffled production values with *Hot Space*. I can't get over it. I listened to it again on vinyl a couple days ago, and I'm like, what's going on here? It has a lot to do with the drums having so much of an echoey aspect to them. The guitar is definitely not mic'd the way Brian May would have them mic'd. But at

the same time, he has this great song that has a sort of flamenco solo on it—great stuff.

POPOFF: And how about at the Freddie Mercury/R&B end of the room?

NESTER: One of my favorites there is "Cool Cat." If you listen to *Hot Space* as a casual Queen fan, you have to let *Hot Space* be *Hot Space* [*laughs*]. What *Hot Space* wants to do is be a pop disco album. When you think of songs like "Dancer" or "Staying Power" or "Body Language" or "Cool Cat," those are the songs that excel at the sonic palette Mack and Freddie Mercury lay down.

"Cool Cat" has like two or three things happening. I don't even think Brian is playing on that. I think that's John Deacon. It's one of the best vocal performances I've ever heard Freddie do. They never played it live. But in an alternate universe, Bowie's voice would still be on there— he did some backing vocals that he wanted removed—and it would've maybe been a hit. I often think of a bizarro world where *Hot Space* was a hit and nobody minded that it was sort of disco. At the time, quite a few rock bands put out sort of disco songs and they met their commercial Waterloo, right?

POPOFF: Of course, *Hot Space* wasn't a success, was it?

MACK: No. You know, with them, if you look at the entire history of the albums, they always had like a huge hit and then the next one was kind of so-so and then the next one was huge again. You go *News of the World* and then you get *Jazz*, and then you get *The Game* and then *Hot Space* and it just follows the pattern.

POPOFF: Jim, general impressions of *Hot Space*?

JENKINS: *Hot Space* makes me feel good. I love "Back Chat," "Staying Power," "Dancer." It was a different approach, and it made them sound fresh. It was released at the beginning of summer, and it just felt right for me. And of course, the David Bowie collaboration. I just think *Hot Space* is great. I like the fact it wasn't really my type of music, but those opening tracks are terrific. I hear "Back Chat" now, which is probably my favorite track on the album, and it makes me feel happy.

POPOFF: There's very little Brian May to be heard.

RUCKER: That was the big surprise for me. And back in the day, for us as kids, guitar was everything. Brian May was one of those cats who we all wanted to be because he was so original. A lot of guitar players are regurgitating, reinventing the wheel, playing variations on what they've already heard. Brian May was coming up with all this stuff and it was just great. All those heavy metal players who were playing these great riffs . . . Brian was playing better riffs. And it was original stuff. Him and Freddie were changing the world of music, really [*laughs*].

And now they come out with a synth-pop record that doesn't have a lot of guitars. No one was expecting it, especially after the success they just had. I liked it, but a lot of people turned away from them because it didn't have a lot of Brian, who to a lot of people was as important as Freddie in that band.

POPOFF: What about one where Brian really takes control, namely "Put Out the Fire"?

NESTER: I love "Put Out the Fire." A lot of Queen fans say they liked the songs, but the production sounds muffled, like they put a pillow on the drums. It doesn't sound like a true rock song. And I think a lot of it is the '80s production values. They discover drum machines and electronic drums, I should say, like pads, triggered drums, that sort of stuff, and that technology sort of takes me out of the songs when I listen to them these days.

With "Life Is Real (Song for Lennon)," the thing that I think of is twelve-year-old me listening to this album, listening to "Put Out the Fire" as the gun control song and then going right into the Lennon song. It's kind of "on the nose," as one interviewer said. And it certainly works as far as the sequence goes.

I think, again, the production values seem to get in the way, but it's a great lyric. And it has little pastiche-y stuff going on, like the tandem piano thing that sounds very Beatles-esque.

POPOFF: "Life Is Real (Song for Lennon)" sounds like it could be a Brian May song, but it gets a sole Freddie credit. Which brings up a point: What do you make of this strange circumstance where most Queen songs are credited to one writer?

MACK: Simply so that the monies get paid out evenly. In the end, I think, they started crediting it to "Queen." But generally, it was, yeah, four songs for Freddie, four songs for Brian, two or one each for Deacon and Taylor. Just to add to it, in the case of *Hot Space*, and most of the albums, really, they didn't have anything done at all [*laughs*] coming into the studio. They just sort of made it up while they were there. They didn't have anything—ideas, yes, but not rehearsed or anything.

POPOFF: Four writers, but three distinct vocalists.

MACK: Yes, and well, Freddie was superb. I mean, he usually did one take and that was it. During my time, he'd kind of look through the window and say, "You didn't seem to be too excited about that one. Let me do another." And I said, "No, no, that's fine, that's just me." I always had this doubtful look on my face [*laughs*]. So, he did another one and, you know, that was it. On maybe some of the highest notes, he tried three or four times to get it, but that's it. But he could sing those and they'd be fine.

And with Brian and Roger, when it came to the harmonies, it was the perfect match. Brian is a little bit below and Roger is in the upper spheres—or stratospheres. It just worked

OPPOSITE: Brian rocks a Flying V in 1982. The guitarist had complained that he didn't care for the R&B direction on "Back Chat."

perfectly. And as individual singers, Roger is good. Brian, too, there's no question, but Freddie was just the front man, so why change it?

"Staying Power," obviously it's a shame that this track was put together in the studio. Because later, on tour, they played that slightly differently and it would've been killer if the band was at that stage as opposed to you know, making this layered sandwich. I mean, it's not bad, but imagine if they would've played it a couple of times live—that would've been so much better because of the energy it had live.

I do like most of those tracks. I think it's a really good album, but it's like half a year before its time. If you think how Olivia Newton John started to make these fitness and exercise-type videos, it would've fit that craze perfectly. And the title *Hot Space* was a perfect fit to that as well, as was "Body Language." This is all before this whole aerobics era came to fruition. Freddie was way ahead of his time.

NESTER: I will go to my grave saying I really like "Staying Power" [*laughs*]. It's the most synthy, drummy thing, but there's a lot of great songwriting on this album. It's just the sonic quality of it that I think throws people off. And Reinhold is right: you listen to live versions of "Staying Power" and it sounds like "Immigrant Song." I mean, it's crazy how it could've sounded. But I still like the simplicity of it. And the horns. There are actually horn charts on that song that surprised me then and surprise me now.

And again, as much as Brian May complained about how he wasn't into the R&B direction, that guitar stuff on "Back Chat" is among my favorite Brian May guitar soloing ever. Queen often says this wasn't the right album at the right time. Because then you had *Thriller* come out with an Eddie Van Halen solo on basically an R&B track. But that's sort of like, hindsight is 20/20.

By 1982, Queen was a band that fans and rock listeners could count on to deliver. "Under Pressure" was an immediate classic from *Hot Space* (and its only big hit).

POPOFF: I've been saving the best for last. *Hot Space* would have been a wasteland of deep tracks if not for "Under Pressure." What is the significance of that song in the Queen canon?

RUCKER: "Under Pressure" is an all-time classic. I'll never forget the first time seeing that video on MTV and just freaking out, even though they weren't in it. I'm a huge Bowie guy, and you hear Queen doing a song with Bowie . . . I thought it was one of their best songs. The production is awesome, the way they trade vocals, but beyond that, the song is so meaningful. It was important at the time and so serious. And that part at the end, when Freddie is singing, "Why can't we give love one more chance?" is still one of my favorite moments in rock history.

Just the memories of this record. Queen was one of those bands that we all listened to in high school. You were happy when a new Queen song came out because it was always solid. They had great songs, and "Under Pressure" was clearly a classic and the only big hit off that record.

JENKINS: Bowie was staying in Montreux. He banged along to the studio to see Queen, who were recording. And they went out for dinner, had a few drinks, went back into the studio rather late and started jamming, just seeing how they were singing together, Freddie and David. Of course, a battle commenced, who could sing the strongest?

And they just started writing, and literally within a day, there's "Under Pressure." Which is quite amazing. You've got two rock giants working together. That's how it happened—very simple story. It wasn't planned, it was impromptu, and it was quite an amazing piece of work and a worldwide hit. It's a pity they didn't make a video; probably went in their own directions and never had the time. But the song is terrific. That's how that was born, very simple.

NESTER: Queen are one of the top five biggest bands in the world at that point. Bowie is not, and perhaps in a lull in between his identities. They just get together and drink a whole lotta wine and do a whole lot of other stuff. Brian May hit some minor headlines in 2017 when he said, "Oh yeah, we had tapes of us doing 'All the Young Dudes.'" Any Queen fan would love to hear that.

But they decide to do a song, and the process of like four people who are always arguing now becomes five. So, John Deacon comes up with a bass riff, and according to Queen lore, they go for dinner and he forgets it. But somebody remembers it for him, possibly David, who also possibly changes it substantially. And they worked from that.

And this is kind of a funny story. Freddie says, "Let's go in the booth and just do a vocal thing and we won't listen to each other and then we'll see what comes of that." I thought it was David Bowie's idea, sort of a Brian Eno, let's-do-this-avant-garde thing, but it was Freddie who suggested it. And then when Freddie went to do the playback with Bowie, he's amazed that their vocals are interlacing so well. But Bowie cheated and listened to Freddie in the studio and sang back to those vocals.

And then it turns a little catty, in postproduction, where it goes to New York to the Power Station to finish up the song. I don't think they ended up hating each other, but there were grand musical compromises to get that thing out. Brian May has often said, both in the studio and the postproduction, he really laid back and didn't really assert himself. He's just playing like twelve-string guitar on that track, with a little Red Special at the end. It's not a guitar extravaganza by any means. It's pretty much like two divas in the studio singing their asses off.

POPOFF: Do you know what more each of them would've wanted out of the track if they got their way?

NESTER: That's the question. Even before Bowie died, Brian would say he had different ideas but laid back to keep the peace. It's like, whoa, what did you want to do? Did you want it to sound like "Brighton Rock" or something? There are different vocal things that happened. You'll hear on the *Greatest Hits* version "people in the streets" repeated a couple times more, and Roger is more in the mix on the, "Love's such an old-fashioned word." He's higher up in the mix in some versions. So, there are different mixes. And then there's the sort of cash-in *Greatest Hits III* "Rah Mix."

POPOFF: What is the magic of that song? Why was it so big?

NESTER: I think of it as an arena new wave song. It's got the hallmarks of new wave, like sparseness and different finger snaps and all that stuff, but really, it's just a kickass rock song. And it's really unabashedly emotional. It's probably the most emo song in Queen's oeuvre, at least in the '80s. And what a weird song tacked onto the end of *Hot Space*, almost like, "Oh yeah, we did this song as well."

Funny thing, apropos of nothing, John Deacon in interviews would say, "What's great about synthesizer bass is that it frees me up to do other things like play guitar." And I always thought that was the most bizarre statement. John, you're in a band with arguably one of the top-twenty guitarists in the world. You think this is your opportunity to play more guitar?! [*laughs*]

Beginning with the *Hot Space* tour, there's another keyboard player, a fifth person on stage. That person is doing the sort of percolating keyboards, and there's John Deacon with what looks to be a friggin' Fender Squire, playing little scratch funk stuff. It's always been bizarre to me. I've never thought of John as a super instrumentalist. Roger is really the secret weapon as far as that goes. He can put together an entire demo, and there are songs in the Queen catalog where it's pretty much just Roger.

POPOFF: Funny. To close, with the pain of the stark slap in the face now subsiding after almost forty years, how do you view *Hot Space*'s place in the catalog?

JENKINS: Mack took them in a different direction. He brought them into the '80s in terms of studio ability. They had been keen on multilayered harmonies, both vocal and instrumental, and I think Mack lessened the use of that technique. He made them think differently in the studio and he made them sound very fresh. Across *The Game* into *Hot Space* and then *The Works*, he brought out the different sides of their characters. Bottom line, he made them construct things with a simplicity they wouldn't have considered for themselves in the '70s.

If they hadn't recorded *Hot Space*, I don't think we'd be talking about *Made in Heaven* or *The Works*. I really feel that they had to go through a change to be that band that is still discussed today. It's the same with the Beatles and Led Zeppelin. In thirty years, will you be talking to someone about the One Direction of the day? I want to say no. But someone will be ringing someone up and talking about Queen in thirty years.

RUCKER: I figure they were changing so drastically because they didn't want to stay stagnant. Things can get boring. I don't think they changed to get bigger. I think they just changed to stay a great band. That was one of the wonderful things about them. They just kept evolving into something different when they wanted to.

MACK: There was no interest from those guys in what the label thinks. It's like, we do it and you get to hear it when it's done and that's that. There's no letting them hear it along the way. The only thing I could have fathomed with *Hot Space* was that the entire album would be ditched by the band saying, "Okay, we don't release that."

POPOFF: Really? There was the real possibility that they might've just walked away from the entire thing?

MACK: Well, some people, definitely. Not everybody, but I'd say fifty percent [*laughs*].

NESTER: What those guys think of *Hot Space* is a bit revisionist. You have to differentiate between what they were saying at the time and later. Brian and Roger controlled the narrative from 1991 on, really. If you're an amateur Queen-ologist like I am, you have to think of the interviews in the context of the time, both during and after *Hot Space*, and then what they say twenty years later. What they said then was tail-between-their-legs type stuff. But Roger said something really direct in the last documentary. Freddie especially wanted *Hot Space* to sound like it was music that could be played at a gay disco and Roger didn't want that. But Roger wouldn't have said that in 1982 or 1983. It would be just like, "Well, what we want now is a more traditional Queen sound, so that's why when we did *The Works*, we called it *The Works*."

But, sure, with *Hot Space* I think Queen went back to the disco buffet one too many times [*laughs*]. They went to the trough, they got a little greedy. Still I think *Hot Space* is maligned in Queen circles a little unfairly. I don't know if I did a super job defending it, but then again, how do you defend the indefensible? [*laughs*]

OVERLEAF: The Netherlands, April 1982. According to producer Reinhold Mack, the band was completely unconcerned with the label's reaction to *Hot Space*.

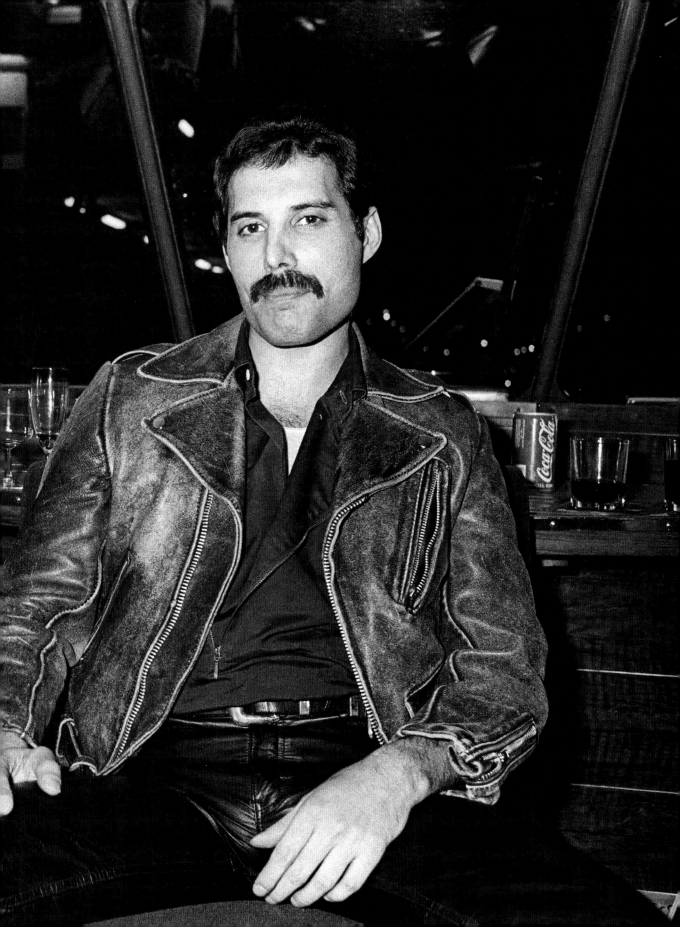

RELEASED FEBRUARY 27, 1984

11 THE WORKS

WITH JIM JENKINS, IAN MOSLEY, AND DANIEL NESTER

SIDE 1

1. **Radio Ga Ga** 5:45
(TAYLOR)

2. **Tear It Up** 3:24
(MAY)

3. **It's a Hard Life** 4:03
(MERCURY)

4. **Man on the Prowl** 3:25
(MERCURY)

SIDE 2

1. **Machines
(Or Back to Humans)** 5:01
(MAY, TAYLOR)

2. **I Want to Break Free** 3:15
(DEACON)

3. **Keep Passing the
Open Windows** 5:15
(MERCURY)

4. **Hammer to Fall** 4:21
(MAY)

5. **Is This the World
We Created . . . ?** 2:10
(MERCURY, MAY)

PERSONNEL:

FREDDIE MERCURY– *vocals, keyboards,
sampler;*

BRIAN MAY– *guitar, vocals;*

JOHN DEACON– *bass, guitar, synthesizer;*

ROGER TAYLOR– *drums, percussion,
drum machine, vocorder, synthesizer, vocals*

GUEST PERSONNEL:

FRED MANDEL– *piano, synthesizer,
synthesizer arrangement, programming;*

REINHOLD MACK– *Fairlight
programming*

Recorded at THE RECORD PLANT,
Los Angeles, and MUSICLAND, *Munich*

OPPOSITE: Promo photo for *The Works*. **After
the wobble that was** *Hot Space*, **Queen made
somewhat of a return to formula.**

After the wobble that was *Hot Space*, Queen allowed their next album to be swallowed up by formula. But when each ticked box is represented by a strong song that is almost a percolating ecosystem run by renewables, formula is fine.

There's a sense of recharged batteries or new beginnings to *The Works*, including a new record deal with EMI. The band had taken a break from one another, scotching a proposed South American tour to embark on solo projects. Recording took place at the familiar Musicland Studios in Munich, but also at The Record Plant in Los Angeles—the first time the band recorded in America. Finally, *The Works* represented the first time the band took full advantage of MTV's rising influence, producing bold videos for "It's a Hard Life," "Radio Ga Ga," and "I Want to Break Free," the first a hilarious portrayal of public perception of a typical Queen party.

A pile of recorded material wasn't used, much of it linked to Freddie's solo career, although the bulk of it could have been issued as a doppelganger to *Made in Heaven*. Far and away, the gem of the lot was "I Go Crazy," a spirited heavy rocker featuring the immortal line, "I don't wanna go see Queen no more, no more." The song was used as the B-side to the experimental synth-rock

QUEEN

I WANT TO BREAK FREE

"It's a Hard Life" b/w "Is This the World We Created . . .?" UK, 1984. Some pegged "It's a Hard Life" as the album's "Bohemian Rhapsody," owing to the snippet of opera at the beginning. In retrospect, this was false; nothing compares to "Bohemian Rhapsody" for sheer sonic joy.

anthem "Radio Ga Ga" and represents, arguably, the final vestige of the fast 'n' loose Queen last heard on *Jazz*.

In a turn of events that could not be predicted and is a rare occurrence in most rock careers, *The Works* saw a second life that has bolstered its reputation over time as the '80s *Queen* record was allowed to live alongside *The Game*. Through marquee outdoor dates at Wembley Stadium and Live Aid, and the band's second live album, *Live Magic*, Freddie and band, through power of performance, willed "Radio Ga Ga," "I Want to Break Free," and "Hammer to Fall" into classic status, Freddie shouting the songs into homes 'round the world. Little else from the record survived past due date, but three evergreen anthems from any record is enough to paint a smile on ya.

The Works was a global phenomenon, unremarkably stalling at gold in the United States but selling an astounding 650,000 copies in the band's UK homeland and another half million in Germany, notching platinum in Canada and elsewhere in Europe. Conjecture perhaps, but part of the success, again, might be attributed to the record coming alive on stage, a trio of hits stealing the show to the point where the band's last tour was as much in support of *The Works* as it was *A Kind of Magic*.

POPOFF: To start, what causes Queen to shift priorities again and make a record like *The Works* after *Hot Space*?

NESTER: I think we're looking at a band with its tail between its legs and kind of giving the people what they think they want. People have come up with parallels. "Tear It Up" is this record's "We Will Rock You." "Man on the Prowl" is their new "Crazy Little Thing." "I Want to Break Free" is kind of like "Who Needs You."

So, there are attempts to relive past glories. People think of "It's a Hard Life" as this one's "Bohemian Rhapsody," more so because of like the opera at the beginning. But "Man on the Prowl" is pretty obvious. It's kind of depressing for me to think of it that way, to tell you the truth. It does feel like a band that is playing it safe, and to my mind, it's the first time ever in Queen's history where you could say that.

MOSLEY: It wasn't a surprise when they changed radically from record to record. They didn't care whether songs were long or short, same as Marillion in a way. And that was very attractive with Queen, that they chopped and changed in their arrangements. They always had great melodies. Even if it was a basic backing track, Freddie Mercury always blew everything out of the water.

But even going back to '73, '74, when I was doing prog with Darryl Way's Wolf, everyone I knew said what a great band they were, although it did seem that people were split—you either hated them or you loved them. I always thought they were a great band. And it was all sort of confirmed to me when we did a German tour with them in 1986.

POPOFF: Were Queen viewed as a prog band back in 1974 by people like you who were clearly in the prog community?

MOSLEY: No, that was left to the likes of Genesis, Crimson, Pink Floyd, and Yes, of course. I always thought of Queen as more of a rock band. I never really think of even progressive rock bands as progressive rock bands unless the lyrics are all about fairies and goblins. Queen were a good rock band that didn't seem to have any barriers holding them back. And they were very high-energy as well.

But they were also misunderstood. Especially in America; they couldn't make out Freddie Mercury at all. Just their image—were they a glam band? It revolved around Freddie, didn't it? The way he dressed, the way he looked, the way he wore black nail varnish. They had this aristocratic vibe. In those early days, from what I gathered, they were working and touring really hard and were completely broke. But by this point, the mid-'80s, they were beyond all that and just massive.

POPOFF: For the record, back to 1984, why did they call the album *The Works*?

NESTER: It's attributed to Roger: "We're gonna give them the works." We're gonna give them, you know, all the stuff that we do that people forgot we can do. But again, not to judge a book by its cover, but if you put *Hot Space* and *The Works* side-by-side, you're seeing a band that is taking big chances with *Hot Space* if you ask me. And then you look at *The Works*, they hire like an old-timey black-and-white movie photographer, George Hurrell, to take their photo, and they're in sneakers. I mean, it's a great band photo, don't get me wrong, but it's a metaphor for everything about the album—sonically, songwriting- and packaging-wise, it's not taking any chances [*laughs*].

Palais Omnisports de Bercy, Paris, September 18, 1984. *The Works* stalled at gold in the US but sold an astounding 650,000 copies in the UK homeland and another half million in Germany.

JENKINS: The adjustment was to go back to what Queen were known for. *Hot Space* had sent them on a different track. *The Works* let people see that they were still Queen. I think it was more of a band effort as well. *Hot Space* is great album, but in America it didn't go down as well. I think with *The Works*, it was back on track. But the sad thing was that they never went back to tour America, so America never got to witness the stage setup for *The Works* tour, which was based on *Metropolis*, the Fritz Lang movie. The stage set was amazing, with one of the best lighting rigs they ever used.

POPOFF: The album opens with what would be a commercial triumph: "Radio Ga Ga." Is it also a creative triumph?

NESTER: I'd say "Radio Ga Ga" is the bright spot because it's the least tail-between-its-legs song on the album. It's got the synthesizer bass part, or co-bass part, and there are more cool things going on than meets the ear. It has electronic drums, but it also has the cool multilayered harmonies in the chorus and the lyrics are kind of clever. It has a message. And it's also the first hit single by Roger Taylor. "Calling All Girls" was a Roger Taylor–penned song and a single, but not a hit. So, it was a boost for Roger financially and ego-wise. Because at this point, he's got one solo album, *Fun in Space*, that is in the stores and another in the can, *Strange Frontier*, that came out a few months after *The Works*. There's a whole growing canon from him; he's not the George Harrison of Queen, but he's close [*laughs*].

JENKINS: I remember the first time I heard "Radio Ga Ga." The video was based on *Metropolis* and they needed extras and asked the fan club to come along to Shepperton Studios. When they played the song to us so we could hear it, I thought, well, this is quite

Givin' 'em "the works" during a legendary three-night run at London's Wembley Arena, September 1984.

poppy and a little bit different. I felt it didn't really represent the album. It was more of an extension of *Hot Space*.

But when you're making a video, they play it so many times, and the more they played it, I thought, this is really catchy, it's starting to get into me. Of course, the power of the video didn't hurt either. The handclapping sequence we were told to do, when the video was shown on TV over here in the UK, it really got to the audience, which could be seen a year later at the Live Aid concert. So, I think it's still a damn good pop song—it sounds fresh in 2017 even though it was recorded in 1983.

POPOFF: And what do you make of the lyric?

JENKINS: It's celebrating how good listening to the radio was and is and could be, so it's the past, the present, and the future. The radio is a great form of media for putting out music. You get a record played in the States and it gets out to millions of people and can become a smash hit. The song is about the importance of radio, the power of radio.

POPOFF: It's funny Roger writes "Radio Ga Ga," but he doesn't sing it or anything on the album, and neither does Brian.

NESTER: No, and they are all lead singers, no question, but oddly not here. I always thought of Roger Taylor as a Rod Stewart–sounding lead vocalist. Brian is sort of for the emo songs; he does his best on the ballads. I was gonna say he's a nice break from Freddie Mercury, but that's kind of rough [*laughs*].

But Roger, it's interesting, because he's the highest parts on "Bohemian Rhapsody" and the early glam-sounding stuff. If you listen to the old Sweet albums, there's always the super, super high thing, and Roger does those kind of parts, but for Queen. But then on lead, he's not doing that. I'm a fan of Roger's voice for sure.

And on later tours, he would do "Under Pressure" with Adam Lambert. To show the importance of Roger, he's really credited in the Queen camp as the guy who was making it happen, taking it across the finish line. He was the guy who was friends with Bowie and who really helped broker everybody signing off on the final version. There are like scenes of, is Bowie gonna show up first or is Freddie going to show up first at Power Station to finish this song? Just ridiculous egos. And Roger is the guy who figured it out.

But, no, you're right: no Roger on *The Works* and no Brian. Strange.

POPOFF: Ian, what is your take on Roger and what he brings to the band?

MOSLEY: Fantastic, and underrated, because he's so musical. The thing that stood out for me was when they did the tribute concert for Freddie at Wembley Stadium and they had lots of guest artists come up. George Michael, Annie Lennox, loads of different top-notch artists.

The video for "I Want to Break Free" tanked in the US. Dressing in drag was more culturally acceptable in the UK.

What I noticed about Roger was that he was more or less the musical director. In between when he had a drum break, he'd be standing up conducting people in and counting people in. He's a fabulous musician. He's got a very good technique, but he doesn't use it a lot. Only when it's necessary.

But what I really admire about Roger and Brian both is that they're carrying on because they love playing music. And if it means that they're playing Queen tracks live with Adam Lambert and people get to hear them, I think that's just wonderful. They love music and they're not doing it for the money. Roger, after we did the tour with them in '86, Marillion were doing a gig in Zürich and I was walking down the street and suddenly I saw Roger walking toward me. I said, "Hello, Roger, what are you doing here?" This is only a few months after he'd been playing to ninety thousand people in a stadium. He said, "Oh, I'm playing a little club up the road, to about three hundred people." With his own band. And so that's just brilliant [*laughs*]. Again, it's because he loves music. He loves playing, and he loves performing.

POPOFF: "I Want to Break Free"—why was that such a great success as a single?

JENKINS: I think the video helped in Europe [*laughs*]. Roger Taylor's wife at the time suggested that the band get into drag. The video is so entertaining. People in the UK and Europe seemed to get the message. Guys dressing up in drag was more popular over here than your side. In America, it totally bombed. I don't think people liked the fact that they were dressing up in women's clothes.

But it was a parody of a British soap opera called *Coronation Street*. And it was a fantastic song about wanting to break free from daily routine. It's written by John Deacon and it's such a strong song. And very commercial, very, very successful in the UK. It's the single that lasted longer in the charts than any of the other songs that they had, which is quite amazing. John was great for writing straight-ahead pop music.

But my favorite is probably "Keep Passing the Open Windows." It's one of the pop-type songs that Freddie would come up with now and again. He'd gone to Montreal to meet the director Tony Richardson about a movie that was being made, *The Hotel New Hampshire*, and Queen were asked to write a song for it. Freddie wrote "Keep Passing the Open Windows" and it never got used for the film but luckily went on *The Works*.

NESTER: Not a fan of that one. There are a lot of soundtrack attempts in the Queen catalog. Jim Beach, their manager—or, really, the business guy—dipped his toes into movie producing. So, there's a film adaptation of John Irving's novel, *The Hotel New Hampshire*. I've tried to watch it a couple times to no avail. I view the song as a precursor to "Breakthru" on *The Miracle*, with the sort of chuggy-chug bass line. It's probably one of the most Broadway-sounding songs in the Queen catalog—and I don't mean that in a good way.

POPOFF: Opening side two is "Machines," rarely remembered, more of a sound sculpture than a song.

NESTER: "Machines" is sort of like an excuse for Brian May to play some guitar. Queen

John wrote "I Want to Break Free," which became successful in part on the strength of its accompanying video.

has always been a closet sci-fi band. Sure, they did *Flash Gordon*, and really, *The Highlander* soundtrack, but they always had like a whole sci-fi/nerd thing. And sonically, whenever you have the vocoder, that's a big Reinhold Mack thing. He's the guy who did that with ELO, so there's a part where the machine is talking back with a vocoder.

On the subject of synthesizers and electronic drums, by the time you get to *The Miracle*, everybody in the band can put together a whole demo. They had all figured out how to work drum machines. And the drum machines are the things on the final products, which is, oh my God, really?! That's the way we're gonna go?! [*laughs*] But back at *The Works*, they're still doing full-band stuff.

JENKINS: I love "Machines," but you're right—it's funny, it's one I tend to forget about. It's a collaboration between Brian and Roger. It's got a modern, synthesized feel, but when you listen to it you can hear that it's pure Queen. You can hear old-style Queen with new-style Queen in the one song. It was used as the B-side to "I Want to Break Free." In America, you got the instrumental version.

I love collaborations, because you don't know what direction it's going to go, but that was a really good one. Quite futuristic, but you've also got the rock songs as balance. "Tear It Up," by Brian, typical guitar-based song, which was fantastic live. "Hammer to Fall," another rock song—I thought America would've lapped up those two songs. Then of course "Man on the Prowl" is a little bit like "Crazy Little Thing," a rockabilly.

POPOFF: At the end of the album we get "Is This the World We Created . . . ?" An afterthought?

NESTER: I'd say so, or it feels like that the way it's sequenced here. It was kind of a quickie song. They wanted to end the record on a quiet note. But as a fan, I remember thinking, "This is crazy! This is a Mercury/May co-write!" I never thought I'd see the day. But other than that, I think of it as a minor song in their catalog. But after the big "Give it to me one more time" ending to "Hammer to Fall," it really does the job it's set out to do, which is a quiet outro, a peaceful ending to the whole album.

POPOFF: What do you think of the idea that even though "Radio Ga Ga" and "I Want to Break Free" were the conventional hits from *The Works*—selling as singles and selling through radio and video—it's really "Hammer to Fall" that supported the side, that sort of transcends the times and doesn't date like "Radio Ga Ga"?

JENKINS: We got strong Queen hallmarks on "Hammer to Fall." Set against *Hot Space*, it was Queen as we knew Queen. It was such a big song, and live it worked extremely well. It's working today for Queen and Adam Lambert, so there's something about the song. It's very, very popular. It made people realize that Queen were a rock band. When "Hammer to Fall" exploded, people went, oh my God, that's the Queen we love.

It took you back to Queen. You pick up an album and it has on it a name and you expect it to sound like the group. And when you picked up *The Works* and you listened to it, you could see Queen through those first songs. And when "Hammer to Fall" came on, almost at the very end, it just blew you back. It was like "This is Queen." It was old-style Queen brought into the '80s, if you understand what I'm trying to say.

POPOFF: But pointedly there's something different than the old Queen. Since I was a teenager and heard the likes of "It's Late" and then "Put Out the Fire" as new releases, and very much so both "Tear It Up" and "Hammer to Fall," I've never been able to shake the idea that Brian was suddenly stacking up chords on these heavy songs, like Bad Company or Kiss. Are the heavier songs now made up of dependable "Louie Louie" chords?

JENKINS: I know exactly what you're saying, and that has to be Mack. That is the influence that Reinhold had on the band. He made them approach the songs so differently in the studio. They were used to Roy Thomas Baker and multitracking— the vocals, the instruments, everything was multitracked. And I think Mack taught them, no, don't do that, keep it basic and let's see what we get out of it.

Now with *Hot Space*, because of the way the album was going with the dance-oriented songs, Brian wanted to rock it out. I think Brian's contributions of "Put Out the Fire" and "Las Palabras de Amor" let people know that, yes, it is Queen you're listening to. But I think it was good that they had found themselves changing direction because it stopped them being stale. But to your point, I really feel that Mack cut down on the excess and simplified things. It was simple, but still very, very clever.

POPOFF: And Daniel, how about you? What did you view as the purpose of a song like "Hammer to Fall"?

NESTER: Well, I think for people like me who were fourteen and had their hormones chugging through them, and who had bought *Hot Space* like a loyal fan, we regarded "Hammer to Fall" as a return to form. And it really, really was. It didn't chart. None of these things cracked the Top 40 in the States except "Radio Ga Ga." But for those who bought the album like I did, that was like, wow, this is how a rock band version of Queen would sound in 1984. And so that is in my top twenty or thirty Queen songs for sure.

Brian pulls the shirtsleeves back for "Hammer to Fall" b/w "Tear It Up," US, 1984. Set against *Hot Space*, it was a return to the Queen fans knew.

POPOFF: Do you think its shelf life has been extended by the Live Aid version, or in general, the favorable reception of the song over the course of the band's last couple of touring cycles?

NESTER: Yeah, I think so, but MTV cut away during "Hammer to Fall." I was at Live Aid in Philly when I was like sixteen, and I saw that whole set, and of course I'm sitting there going like "Queen are great—yay!" And they're just showing it on the screens from London. And that was one of the few sets they showed on the TV screens. But nobody knew what that song was.

POPOFF: I'm thinking more the Wembley stand, perhaps.

NESTER: Yeah, okay, for sure! But still I think the "Hammer to Fall" at Live Aid was the star-making song in terms of that last golden period for the band, that slingshot of fame they enjoyed in '85 and '86. Freddie's dancing with the camera guy and everything and it was really the perfect Queen moment, where there's no lights, no pyro, and they're just standing there in jeans and T-shirts. For anybody who was a classic rock-ist like I was, you're like, wow, this is Queen just kicking ass and taking names.

MOSLEY: Sure, I mean, it seemed to have been quiet on the Queen front until Live Aid. To me, that's when they became even bigger, almost suddenly, and completely global. I went to Live Aid, and I was watching the bands from up in the clouds somewhere and I thought this

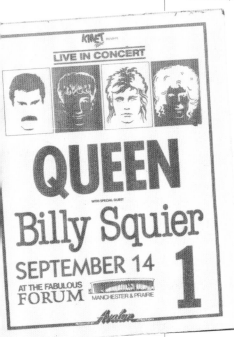

is ridiculous—everyone looks about half an inch tall. I actually left. I went home and I watched the rest of it on TV.

And when Queen came on, they just were so spot on. Freddie had the whole of that stadium in the palm of his hand. Going on without soundchecks in a festival situation like that, things go wrong, the sound is usually a bit iffy and you never know what you're going to get. And you wouldn't have known that there was any adversity. With no soundchecks, Queen was just perfect.

But yes, I think that's when people suddenly went, whoa, this band is something else. And then a few years later, there was *Wayne's World*, that scene in the car that opened up the eyes of another generation. If you tried to plan it, you couldn't. It seems like everything fell into place from the Live Aid thing, the *Wayne's World* thing, they just got bigger and bigger. But, yes, short answer, both "Hammer to Fall" and "Radio Ga Ga" grew in stature from what the band did with them live in 1985 and 1986, basically their swansong as a touring band.

POPOFF: "Hammer to Fall" builds and builds and then just explodes when you get to the "What the hell we fighting for?" line. That's the most intense magical recorded Queen moment of '80s, is it not?

NESTER: Yeah, and the lyric is kind of '80s Cold War stuff, so it was a perfect song to play in the mid-'80s. But I think a lot of people forget that with Live Aid, they were somewhat pushing their recent single. Even with that short set, a half-dozen songs or whatever, they did "Radio Ga Ga" and "Hammer to Fall." "Hammer to Fall" was the fourth and final single, and they really sold that song that day. So, yeah, I see what you mean, because for me, "Hammer to Fall" is really embedded with Live Aid. But it's interesting to see how over the years, even North America has agreed with that as well.

POPOFF: Jim, how about you? How much of what this record is about can we attribute to Mack and his ideas about production?

Wembley Arena,
September 6, 1984.

OVERLEAF: Bob Geldof
confers with Prince Charles,
while David Bowie chats
with Roger and Brian
during the Live Aid concert
at Wembley Stadium,
July 13, 1985. Queen
gave arguably the greatest
performance at either of
the historic concert's
two venues.

JENKINS: Mack took them into the '80s. That transition period, Mack helped them with that, did them a world of good. And yet listen again to *The Works*. You can hear it's Queen. It had to be Queen after the disappointing sales of *Hot Space*. People wanted Queen back. And, by God, we got them back on that album.

RELEASED JUNE 3, 1986

12 A KIND OF MAGIC

WITH RALPH CHAPMAN, STEPHEN DALTON, AND IAN MOSLEY

SIDE 1

1. **One Vision** 5:08
   (QUEEN)

2. **A Kind of Magic** 4:23
   (TAYLOR)

3. **One Year of Love** 4:26
   (DEACON)

4. **Pain Is So Close to Pleasure** 4:19
   (MERCURY, DEACON)

5. **Friends Will Be Friends** 4:07
   (MERCURY, DEACON)

SIDE 2

1. **Who Wants to Live Forever** 5:13
   (MAY)

2. **Gimme the Prize (Kurgan's Theme)** 4:32
   (MAY)

3. **Don't Lose Your Head** 4:35
   (TAYLOR)

4. **Princes of the Universe** 3:30
   (MERCURY)

PERSONNEL:

FREDDIE MERCURY – *vocals, keyboards;*
BRIAN MAY – *guitar, vocals, keyboards;*
JOHN DEACON – *bass, guitar, keyboards;*
ROGER TAYLOR – *drums, vocals, keyboards*

GUEST PERSONNEL:

SPIKE EDNEY – *keyboards, UMI and BBC B computer keyboards;*
JOAN ARMATRADING – *incidental vocals;*
STEVE GREGORY – *saxophone;*
NATIONAL PHILHARMONIC ORCHESTRA – *strings*
Recorded at MOUNTAIN STUDIOS, *Montreux, Switzerland;* MUSICLAND, *Munich;* TOWNHOUSE STUDIOS, *London; and* ABBEY ROAD STUDIOS, *London*
Produced by QUEEN, MACK, *and* DAVID RICHARDS

OPPOSITE: Montreux, Switzerland, May 11, 1986. *A Kind of Magic* isn't the most beloved of Queen albums, considered by many to be representative of all the things that could go wrong for bands making records in the mid-'80s.

Its legitimacy diminished by its association with the *Highlander* film (six of nine tracks appear there), *A Kind of Magic* is conversely emboldened by its branding. The color that begins with Live Aid is splashed onto the album cover, then onto Freddie and his yellow bomber jacket as the album is juiced with life in a celebration across Europe. The most historic dates were at Wembley in July, resulting in a '92 live album, and the band's last show ever, at Knebworth, August 9, 1986, which sucks up most of the oxygen on the *Live Magic* live album, a record that reduced the inconsequential studio album to a tour program with a bonus disc.

What I'm getting at is that 1986 was all about Queen live, with *Live Magic* issued five months after *A Kind of Magic*, and with the couple dozen shows promoting the record among some of the most memorable and massively attended concerts of the band's career. If one thinks of "One Vision" and even "Friends Will Be Friends," it's because of their impact live, with memories of their studio origins receding into a haze of dated '80s-ness.

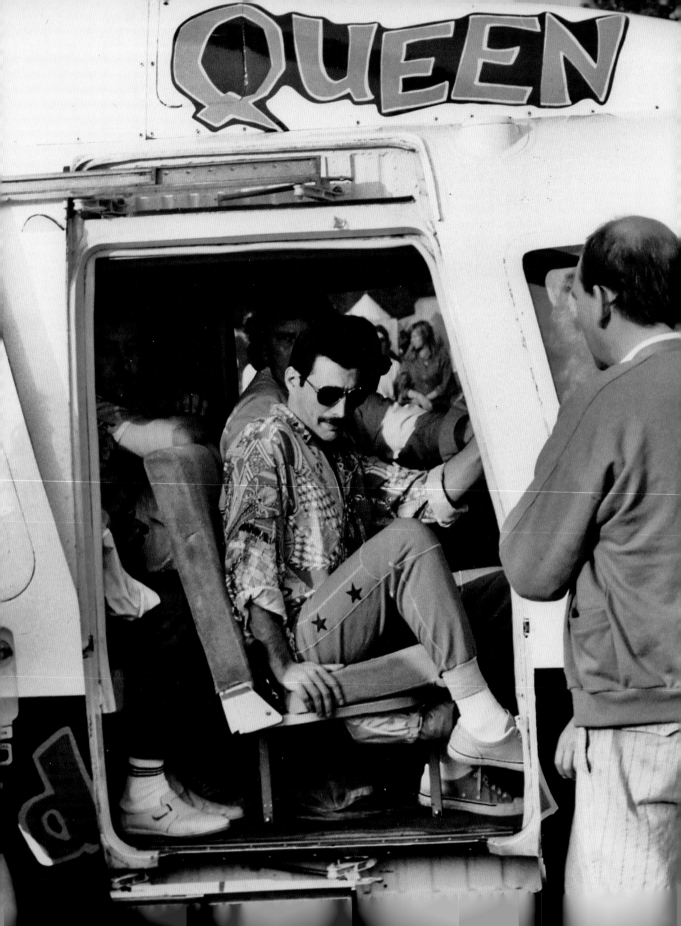

Back at the business end of the band, *A Kind of Magic* was a fragmented affair, right down to its production, which found a sort of airless Dave Richards digital knob-job butted up against Mack sounding as Mack-like as he ever would. "One Vision," "Gimme the Prize (Kurgan's Theme)," and "Princes of the Universe" comprised a suite (despite the first being for a different movie, *Iron Eagle*), all about the same speed, distinguished by smacked 'n' slapped percussive backbeats over which Brian made much noise. It's basically "Put Out the Fire" and "Tear It Up" all over again; nonetheless, the first is a damn sturdy song, while the latter two feature Freddie and Brian hitting listeners over the head with all they've got, no brains but much brawn.

Elsewhere, Queen felt their way to a level of connection with their European base despite the album wafting over the heads of anyone who might care in America. "Friends Will Be Friends," "Who Wants to Live Forever," and "A Kind of Magic," through a combination of single releases and sun-dappled live rendition, each helped push *A Kind of Magic* to astounding sales in Germany (750,000), France (200,000), and the UK (600,000). Each offered a particular form of pop button-pushing at least tenuously connected to Queen's rainbow of emotions from records past: the first drunk; the second ambitious, ostentatious, and classical; and the third modest, irresistible, and campy, like a lazing '80s take on their vaudeville canon.

The rest of the record—"One Year of Love," "Pain Is So Close to Pleasure," and "Don't Lose Your Head"—sound like *Hot Space* outtakes or Freddie solo songs, further adding to the album's fragmented nature and the nagging idea that *A Kind of Magic* is nothing more than a long and forlorn tour EP: a third of it with all the noise pollution, already sounding like samplings from an ongoing tour; another third bonus tracks left off an imagined better studio album; and the final third clinical, airless studio renditions of ballads that can't help but transmit some charm once brought to massive outdoor stages. Further to this EP vibe, the record offers only nine selections, almost all of them natural three-minute numbers stretched to four-and-a-half or five minutes, even if in many cases the amusing musical excursions, the origami-like exercises in arrangement, are the parts that should have been kept rather than the maudlin verses and choruses.

All told, this isn't anything piles of deep Queen fans haven't considered. *A Kind of Magic* isn't the most beloved of Queen albums, and it is considered by many to be representative of all the things that can go wrong for bands making records in the mid-'80s. But rather than dwelling on what the album wasn't, I'm perfectly happy to have its memory drowned out by the whirring blades of the Queen helicopter and the roaring European crowds that ignored any of the critical griping and just danced the album to a level of success that found Queen manic on a multicolored sugar high, soon to crash but for one last magic moment throwing a fabulous party.

POPOFF: Let's start with your first impressions upon hearing *A Kind of Magic* in the summer of 1986.

CHAPMAN: Well, to back up a bit, Queen had lost me on *Hot Space*. "Body Language" struck me as revolting. Pan forward, I had been watching "The NewMusic" TV program and "Radio Ga Ga" came on, and if you recall the video, they had scenes from *Metropolis* and it was futuristic. And I thought, Queen, I'd forgotten all about you, and I was immediately entranced with that song. I went downstairs and asked my dad for some money and I immediately went to Sam the Record Man and I got a cassette of *The Works*, which struck me as this extraordinary comeback.

Flash forward a year and Live Aid happens. Everyone knows that Queen was monstrous at Live Aid. They blew everyone away. You really got a sense that that was a continuation of the energy that happened on *The Works*, and the next record was going to be extraordinary.

Freddie arrives at the Knebworth Festival, August 9, 1986, for what would turn out to be the band's last show with their iconic front man.

OPPOSITE: The band's
rockin' side came back
to life on their 1986
tour. Freddie performs at
Groenoordhal, Leiden,
Netherlands, June 1986.

So [*laughs*] a year later, *A Kind of Magic* came out, and it was the same week as *Invisible Touch* and I was a diehard Genesis fanatic. And although Queen had sort of glam and proto-metal roots and Genesis was a prog band, they were basically the same vintage. So in the mid-'80s, I was loving kind of dinosaur bands, and so this was a great moment to have these two records come out almost simultaneously.

And I put on *Invisible Touch* first, and of course, the first song was "Invisible Touch" and I was crestfallen, to a point. It seemed, at the time, that song was disposable. But the album seemed to get better and better, so by the end, I was excited again.

Then I put on *A Kind of Magic* not knowing anything—this is pre-internet—and kind of the inverse happens. The first song is "One Vision." I had seen the film *Iron Eagle* that it comes from, and I thought, oh, that's an exciting Queen tune. It had this very dramatic synth intro—I guess it was MIDI cello, but it was very dramatic—right into this driving tune that had all the marks that I loved of Queen. It was riffs, a great vocal, and that wonderful style that Taylor had on the hi-hat. Plus, it was a true Mack production, very room-sounding, and a beautiful reverb on the snare that brought such energy. But then, like I say, the inverse happened.

"A Kind of Magic" single
b/w "A Dozen Red Roses
for My Darling," from the
film *Highlander*, 1986.
The second track and
second single drag down
momentum created by the
album's opener.

POPOFF: Before we move on to what happens, how about you, Stephen?

DALTON: The first thing to say about *A Kind of Magic* is that it's partially a film soundtrack from *Highlander*, which is pretty much the most '80s movie ever made. So, it has that kind of extended rock video soundtrack feel. And like a lot of soundtracks, it's probably unfair to judge this one against *The Works*, which, I think the band was much more invested in and wound up to be fairly packed with hits.

A Kind of Magic, obviously it's not a full soundtrack, but that element is woven into it. And like a lot of rock band soundtracks, it's a bit flabby, sort of characterless, because soundtrack music has a secondary purpose.

So, I don't think it's a classic Queen album, although it falls at an interesting point in their career after Live Aid boosted their profile enormously. It's also a couple years after they played Sun City in South Africa and I remember that they were seen as sellouts and politically on the wrong side by a lot of my peers. But it's definitely not their best album; they're coming out of their imperial phase when they make this record.

POPOFF: Where does *A Kind of Magic* go after this loud hello titled "One Vision"?

CHAPMAN: The next track is "A Kind of Magic," which wasn't Mack. Interestingly enough, it was a David Richards production. Momentum ground to a halt. It seemed weak, pop craft for the sake of pop craft. Interesting that it's Roger Taylor, because there was something about the synth that sat under the vocal. The way it ascended and descended reminded me of "Radio Ga Ga," in the verses. And I started to get irritated. Despite the similarity, it didn't have any of the import and majesty, lyrically, of "Radio Ga Ga," which was about the death of radio and connected very much to my childhood and my approach to consuming music.

And the video was them dressed as bums and there was animation similar to Roger Chiasson's cover art. That artwork comes alive in that video, but it just looked like what Genesis did in the "That's All" video three years before. And the song just seemed like a flimsy

"Friends Will Be Friends (Extended Version)" b/w "Friends Will Be Friends" and "Gimme the Prize (Kurgan's Theme)," 1986. Lyrically, "Friends Will Be" is very much Freddie being anthemic, but musically it seems flat.

piece of pop. Not to mention as the band's first title track, you expected something major.

Right after that was John Deacon's "One Year of Love," which brought me back to my memories of *Hot Space*. John was into Motown and soul. But the real problem is the vocal—it was so overwrought. I wasn't smart enough to know back then that maybe this isn't in Freddie's key, but he oversings it. It was forcing me to feel something as opposed to allowing me to feel something. Plus, there was a ghastly sax solo, which had me realizing that Queen was very much moving on or was a band that was constantly progressing. But as with *Hot Space*, it felt like a progression that held no interest for me.

DALTON: "A Kind of Magic" is duff. It drags. I love Queen when they're melodramatic and full of emotion. Whether from Brian's blazing guitar or Freddie's operatic vocals, it was often powerful and moving. But then around this time, they started to get staid and bloodless and clinical, and I think "A Kind of Magic" is one of those songs. It's polished family entertainment, and you don't really want that from a big bombastic rock band.

MOSLEY: Well, I can confirm that "A Kind of Magic" was one that went over great live. It grabbed me instantly and grabbed the audience instantly as well. Everybody would be singing along with it straightaway. The dominant things in Queen were usually Freddie's vocals and Brian May's guitar sound and his solos, but by *A Kind of Magic*, it was more about vocals. Plus, it seemed to me that lyrically the songs got more personal and that their melodies just got better. We played a half dozen shows with them on that tour, and whenever they played a stadium with these new songs, they'd suddenly have these overblown melodies that just grabbed you and seemed to get bigger and bigger. Also the arrangements were more precise—there was less wasted space.

POPOFF: Let's shift gears and look at some of the heavy material. What are your thoughts on "Gimme the Prize"?

CHAPMAN: Dreadful. In interviews the guys said that they weren't doing music expressedly for a soundtrack, it was still a Queen album. They were gonna make it so it would survive as a Queen record. But on a subconscious level, the lyrics put emotional distance between the material and me because it was for a soundtrack. But "Gimme the Prize" is the only song that really screams out it's from a movie. It's so overlaid with dialog from the film, it almost sounds like Queen having a duet with the film. So cheesy.

"A Kind of Magic" was for the film, but then they Queen-ified it. The fact that they didn't exercise that kind of editorial control on "Gimme the Prize" baffled me. It would be different if it had been a proper soundtrack with interludes and segues and dialog sprinkled throughout. But this, I felt I was having the wool pulled over my eyes. Or they were a spent force and they were trying to infuse drama into a song that sounded like a potboiler rewrite of something they had already done before. And seven songs in, you're already tired of the record. If they were trying to distance themselves from the idea that this was a soundtrack dressed up as a Queen album, why mire that track with pieces from the film?

DALTON: "One Vision" is a great song. That's the spirit of Live Aid all over again. I mean, I hated it at the time, because I was young and opinionated. But listening to it now, it's got that swashbuckling, rambunctious, classic Queen feel, like any big Brian May guitar anthem. And it stands up, I think, more than thirty years later, maybe not as a first-rank Queen anthem but at least a second-rank Queen anthem.

But "Gimme the Prize," I think they're churning it out by that point. They seem to be doing a bad pastiche of AC/DC or Zeppelin and I'd rather they did a bad pastiche of Queen. They're relying on power and surface drama instead of actual songwriting. When they sound like any other rock band, then they don't sound like Queen.

POPOFF: But the band's rockier numbers really came alive on that stadium tour. Queen found a way to make this record a huge hit in Europe exactly the same way that Live Aid gave *The Works* an extra kick in the pants.

MOSLEY: For sure. The set list they played in Germany in '86 was amazing. I remember "One Vision" as being stunning. It was if when they wrote it they just knew it was going to come across really well live. I was privileged, because I stood by the side of the stage at every concert and watched them, and when they came on, their first bar of music, it just completely blew me away, their sound. First, I thought this is a real true stadium band. They had the capabilities of making it feel intimate for a stadium audience. Second thing was that they are a proper real band. It's not just Freddie out front with backing musicians. They're one of the best bands I've ever seen live.

A Kind of Magic flopped despite a thirst for British bands in North America at the time. James Park, Newcastle, England, July 9, 1986.

POPOFF: Ralph, would you grant at least that "Who Wants to Live Forever" packs some emotional drama?

CHAPMAN: What I love about that song is it utilizes one of the secret weapons in Queen, which is Brian May as a vocalist. And it's a duet, which is always an effective tool, in my mind. And second, it has that beautiful Brian May/Michael Kamen score. However, it does sound like movie music, not like an organic part of the vision of a record. It sounds, again, like an outlier. And it was only there because that was Brian May; it was one of his pieces from the film.

MOSLEY: I just remember that track being epic live, and on the studio version, Freddie's voice is so great. And since Freddie died, I find it quite disturbing, really, because it affects me when I hear it. That's just me being sentimental. For me personally, what was a real shame is I really wished that we played that Wembley gig with them, because I always wanted to play the old Wembley Stadium before it was pulled down and rebuilt. I just wished that we could've stayed on the Queen tour to the end.

DALTON: With "Who Wants to Live Forever," the use of orchestra gets them around the slightly blah studio sheen. That one stands up okay; it helps the quite low ratio of good to bad stuff on there.

POPOFF: Back into the more obscure songs that they didn't play live on the tour, how about "Pain Is So Close to Pleasure"?

CHAPMAN: The first Mercury/Deacon tune. So, John is involved again, and there's Freddie sounding like he sounded on "Cool Cat," doing a falsetto. And again, it didn't speak to me. It sounded like something George Michael would do. And at that point, that was a pejorative. It sounded like everything else as opposed to Queen. I thought this is a total departure. The drums are now drum programming. What was so much the character of Queen, Roger's style of playing, was gone. And that wasn't unprecedented. Because "Radio Ga Ga" is very much drum programming, but it was a sonic outlier on *The Works*. This seemed to be setting the tone that, from the percussion perspective, this was going to be a largely faceless electronic record.

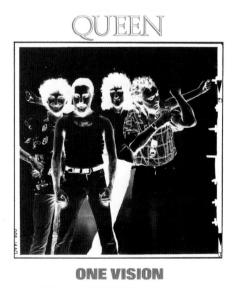

"One Vision" b/w "Blurred Vision," Australia, 1985. With its dramatic synth intro, this single was first heard a year earlier in the film *Iron Eagle*, starring Lou Gossett Jr.

ONE VISION

DALTON: This one's got that sort of feather-light jukebox Americana feel to it, like a plastic, ersatz version of doo-wop and R&B, but so watered down and so deracinated, really, so characterless, so sort of decaffeinated, that it's almost unlistenable. And I don't mind those pastiche-y, Broadway, retro kitsch things that Queen did, but it's gotta be done well, and I think that's one of their most characterless songs in that style.

Let's see, "Don't Lose Your Head" is kind of a thin, disco rock sketch. I do like when Queen detour from hard rock into funk and disco and electronic. That's when you get some of their more interesting experiments. But by this point, I think they're parodying themselves.

I know this one was played on the tour, but I like "Friends Will Be Friends," which has a lot of Freddie's emotionalism in it, which is one of their big selling points. That doesn't get deadened by the sort of soundtrack-y technology side of the album.

Another factor, this is their first digitally recorded album. You're in the middle of a revolution in studio technology and they're using things like the Yamaha DX7. They're famous for having a "no synthesizers" rule in the '70s, and now they're embracing technology. But it's at that time when technology was so fresh that hardly anybody could operate it properly. Talk to famous producers from that period like Trevor Horn and even they couldn't handle these enormous new technological developments.

I think a lot of the records from that early- to mid-'80s period—not just Queen, everybody—they've got a clinical, slightly constricted, slightly airless, bloodless feel, and I think part of that is the technology coming through at the time, which people had yet to master. The technology added a deadening sheen on top of a lot of those records.

CHAPMAN: Sure, but also this record was dogged in my mind by its sequencing as much as anything. If you look at side one, once you got past "One Vision" into "A Kind of Magic," which is a midtempo pop song, and then you get into the faux-soul of "One Year of Love." It's this full-blown MOR excursion with strings, and these almost Temptations-style, Freddie Mercury backing vocals.

But with the odd exception, like "Princes of the Universe" and "One Vision," for the most part, they were sliding into a faceless, plastic pop area. We have three songs in a row that were just kind of laying there. And then "Friends Will Be Friends"—with the exception of the guitar break we're into the same kind of thing, which is programmed drums. I think Roger uses some Simmons pads. But it was really boring; there was nothing visceral about it, although in "Friends Will Be Friends" Mercury is mining lyrical territory that he had with "Keep Passing the Open Windows" and "Don't Try Suicide." It's very much Freddie being anthemic, but musically, it just seemed by rote.

POPOFF: Any thoughts on this album cover?

DALTON: It's possibly the worst album sleeve in Queen's career. Possibly at the time it looked current, but now it looks like something for a sort of *SpongeBob SquarePants* kiddie TV cartoon. The typeface is too zany, it looks horrible. Which, again, you can tell when artists are having their fallow periods if you just check their album covers. The worst album covers almost always go along with the worst albums [*laughs*]. It looks like it was handed off to some corporate flunky and dashed off in a weekend with a deadline looming.

POPOFF: Not that it would have mattered, given the songs enclosed.

CHAPMAN: No, and it's fascinating to me, if you think about when *A Kind of Magic* was released, in the summer of '86, it wasn't like the North American marketplace didn't have a thirst for established British bands. The year before, Dire Straits' *Brothers in Arms* went nine times platinum. Peter Gabriel's *So*, which came out a month before, five times platinum. Genesis *Invisible Touch*, six times platinum.

And *A Kind of Magic* failed. In short, it was an ill-conceived record, poorly sequenced, with baffling decisions. Mixed in with the idea of an equanimity of writers that didn't actually serve the band but served themselves. It had short-term gains but long-term failure.

One more thing I want to say about "One Vision," which speaks to the odd choices they make and how I may have developed a real cynicism about them. "One Vision," which is reportedly inspired by the words of Martin Luther King Jr., is very much the kind of utopian fantasy that Lennon espoused in "Imagine." Lennon, I don't think, would have ever licensed the song to a film like *Iron Eagle*, which was this jingoistic American war movie. It was bizarre.

And then when I heard "Gimme the Prize," the prize seemed like success more than art.

One can only speculate: If they would've toured in America, would the record have sold? I don't know. People would've gone to the shows, but largely on the strength of their back catalog. Yeah, maybe "A Kind of Magic" would have got a boost from a single's point of view. I don't know the ins and outs of how Capitol came to promote *A Kind of Magic*, but the videos got played and *Highlander* was a big movie. So, there has to be something else. *A Kind of Magic* had pretty mixed reviews. There was the message that got out that whatever you saw at Live Aid was not going to be on this record.

So *A Kind of Magic* only got to No. 46 and barely got to gold. I just thought the world hates Queen now. What I didn't realize is *A Kind of Magic* was a huge record in Europe. I had no idea. I should've known because *Live Magic* had come out and there's the picture of the helicopter over what looks like a crowd of three hundred thousand people. So, they were obviously massive in Europe and this record was registering there.

POPOFF: Ian, any closing thoughts on this record or on being there to witness the tour for it?

MOSLEY: Well, this happened with Marillion too, but usually your latest album is a kind of reaction to the album before it. If you've had a massive album, with the next album you start with a blank canvas and it's hard work. It gets harder and harder on the writing front. Sometimes that can tear bands apart. But I think if you survive, ultimately, if you're grownups about it, it'll bring the band together. I'd heard rumors that with Queen there were a few set-tos between band members.

But it's the same in any band, really. Occasionally, someone will say something, and maybe not be looking at the bigger picture, especially on the creative front. When you're writing, if you're a guitarist, you want to play some serious guitar, but it might not be the right thing to do. But the thing is, the Queen guys were all so individually talented, they were going make a good album. And as we've seen, a clutch of these songs proved themselves live and the album did good business across Europe.

A lot of it is down to Freddie. He's just a one-off—so much charisma. There's an aura around him when he walks onstage. Even when you walked past him in the backstage, you go, wow, that's Freddie. But also, the whole band. As I said, standing by the side of the stage, you could feel the chemistry. Looking across, it was just like, yes, this is a real, true band, just them against the world.

RELEASED MAY 22, 1989

13 THE MIRACLE

WITH RALPH CHAPMAN, PATRICK MYERS, AND DANIEL NESTER

SIDE 1

1. **Party** 2:24
(QUEEN)

2. **Khashoggi's Ship** 2:47
(QUEEN)

3. **The Miracle** 5:02
(MERCURY, DEACON)

4. **I Want It All** 4:40
(MAY)

5. **The Invisible Man** 3:56
(TAYLOR)

SIDE 2

1. **Breakthru** 4:07
(MERCURY, TAYLOR)

2. **Rain Must Fall** 4:20
(MERCURY, DEACON)

3. **Scandal** 4:42
(MAY)

4. **My Baby Does Me** 3:22
(MERCURY, DEACON)

5. **Was It All Worth It** 5:45
(MERCURY)

PERSONNEL:

FREDDIE MERCURY – *vocals, keyboards, drum machine;*
BRIAN MAY – *guitar, vocals, keyboards;*
JOHN DEACON – *bass, guitar, keyboards;*
ROGER TAYLOR – *drums, percussion, drum machine, vocals, keyboards*

GUEST PERSONNEL:

DAVID RICHARDS – *keyboards, sampler*
Recorded at MOUNTAIN STUDIOS, *Montreux, Switzerland;*
TOWNHOUSE STUDIOS, *London; and*
OLYMPIC STUDIOS, *London*
Produced by QUEEN *and* DAVID RICHARDS

OPPOSITE: Onstage at London's Wembley Stadium, July 1986. Speaking about AIDS back in this period, Freddie noted that he had tested in the clear, though he would become more circumspect over the years.

By the time *The Miracle* was staring out from shelves in the spring of 1989, Freddie had already had some friends die of AIDS. Talking about it back in 1986, he had said that he'd been tested and was in the clear, but as time went on, he had become more circumspect on the subject. By 1989, insiders were taking note that Freddie was not making the scene anymore, with Mercury himself admitting that AIDS had spooked him. Further, the band was not touring but off doing side projects, Roger with the Cross, Brian with British comedy group Bad News and new girlfriend Anita Dobson, and Freddie with Montserrat Caballé. John was traveling the world. Notably, Brian was experiencing black depressions brought on by the demise of his marriage to Chrissy Mullen, as well as the death of his beloved father, Harold, to whom he was very close.

When the album dropped, it was almost by surprise. Unfortunately, few were begging for it. Concern over Freddie picked up, but in what looked like

the preemptive move of a band fully prepared not to tour it, there were five production videos, with Freddie more alive in each one than in the last.

"Invisible Man" and "Scandal" seemed weak choices for singles tracks, but "Breakthu" was a smart, propulsive song of interesting production that oscillated between electronic drums and real drums, something dearly lacking on much of this record. In fact, if one could describe one trait to this record, it would be its overt use of electronic rhythms and synthesizer as ear candy. This is the Queen record with the most gratuitous use of synthesizer, but also the most sophisticated and detailed use, almost like the more successful experiments on Judas Priest's *Turbo* album, where you think, "They could covert me to this."

The other songs chosen for video and single attention lean toward tradition. "The Miracle" manages to be jaunty and frivolous while avoiding a maudlin and predictable. "I Want It All" had the effect, like Michael Douglas in *Wall Street*, of making greed good, an appropriate message over the song's thrusting but not all that imaginative heavy metal chord patterns. Sticking with the heavy for a moment, "Was It All Worth It" contains more frost and fire, Brian freeing himself up a bit, extrapolating, finding that heavy metal creativity last heard on *Jazz*.

The opening two-track suite, "Party" and "Khashoggi's Ship," served a similar purpose as "I Want It All," reinforcing the band's image as dripping in riches, decadent, out of touch. Sonically, the ostentatious electronic jamming of circuits reinforced how busy, busy Queen were at staying pricey and above the rabble. I can't stress this enough: in 1989 there was a narrative that hair metal had gotten too rich for its britches and that the earthy mud rock being made in the rain up in Seattle would wash it all away. And here was Queen rubbing our noses in it and underscoring their desire to hobnob by elsewhere drumming up flashy club-kid tracks to keep Khashoggi and the hoi polloi dancing all night.

It's fun for the deep Queen fan to make their own *Miracle* using some of the extraneous but finished songs from the sessions. I could do without the lazy rockabilly of "Stealin'," but "Hijack My Heart" and especially "Hang On in There" would definitely make my cut in place of, say, the ridiculously synth-drunk "Rain Must Fall" or the stealth funk of "My Baby Does Me."

With Queen having not played on North American soil for seven years and not touring this record either, the album came and went with barely a stir, additionally unsurprising given the

Roger Taylor's band, The Cross, b/w "Rough Justice," Germany, 1988. With Queen not touring, its various members were off doing side-projects.

mania of the multiplatinum hard rock coming out of California at the time. As it turned out, despite the potential death knell of no live performance, the album was a brisk seller in the UK, Germany, parts of Europe, and Australia, driven by the success of "Breakthru" and "I Want It All," which became an anti-apartheid anthem in South Africa—ironic given the band's ill-advised run of shows in Sun City back in 1985. Ultimately, the record is said to have sold five million copies around the world, despite stalling at gold in the United States, thus framing *The Miracle* as another album that reminds us how global Queen had become—and perhaps how tastes and trends differ around the world.

POPOFF: What should we know about *The Miracle* to understand it better?

NESTER: A couple of things. It's the first of two, maybe three, albums, if you count *Made in Heaven*, of the band knowing that Freddie's days are numbered. This is the first album where they go with the full-band writing credit. This is the first album where they're all writing songs together and they're trying to get as much done as they can. Sonically speaking, there are some good parts and there are some bad parts, some dodgy parts. This is the first Dave Richards co-production. Mack is gone.

As well, there are a few B-sides. Like they don't even know how to pick their own material at this point and I don't think they're even that worried about it. "I Want It All" is a gimme, sort of the "Hammer to Fall," the Brian May rocker that can't go wrong, and they at least have the smarts to have that be the lead single. At this point, they don't really care if they're gonna make it in the States. They're not going to tour behind this. They're saying that Freddie doesn't want to tour.

So, there's a lot of different things going on and it's a really strange album. It was a strange album to try to interpret and parse back in 1989. It definitely wasn't with the times at all, sonically speaking. It was a European-sounding Queen album, just like *A Kind of Magic* before it. But then you have these awesome B-sides, like "Hang on in There," which was the B-side to "I Want It All."

CHAPMAN: With Queen, I had gotten into this despairing pattern in the '80s where when you were in the middle of it, it seemed like shit upon shit. You look back now and think there were so many great records in the '80s, but at the time you were constantly holding onto your old guard for dear life, hoping they were going to do something that matched previous glories.

Knowing that I had hated *A Kind of Magic*, I still remember being in Sam the Record Man and pulling *The Miracle* off the wall, along with Paul McCartney's *Flowers in the Dirt*, with the hope that McCartney was going to continue what he did on *Press to Play* and that Queen were gonna shock me back to life with something like *The Works*. I got home, and unfortunately with *The Miracle*, it was the same thing I felt with the previous album. I had that sense of, there's nothing unique about this anymore. There was no breath in those arrangements, those recordings. There's no room; everything was so jammed.

One of the great things about the best Queen records is you could hear the personalities of each instrumentalist, and what's more, they each had this wonderful approach. You could hear all these elements congeal into this magnificent sound because the recording techniques were more austere, they were dealing with maybe a sixteen- or a twenty-four track. And on *The Miracle*, it's a wall, it's an assault.

MYERS: *The Miracle*, I think, is the journey toward *Innuendo*. That sounds obvious to say, but for me, you can hear a renaissance. With Queen, you can hear somewhat when the band are not functioning as a four-piece but as two groups of two. John and Freddie used to write quite a lot around the *A Kind of Magic* period. They were still doing it in *Innuendo*, but you can begin to hear it sort of coalescing as a four-piece again. I mean, they decide to share the songwriting credits even though those songs were primarily originating from one or the other of them. But you can hear the songwriting beginning to develop into something that became, I think, massively interesting.

It's never been one of my favorite albums, but it's got some amazing tracks. I love the experimentation of "Party" and "Khashoggi's Ship." I sometimes wonder, when you're sharing credits, if the lyrics by committee are the best way. It worked well with "One Vision," but I don't think it always works well. But sure, tracks like "I Want It All" and "Scandal," I think Brian's tracks are extraordinary. John Deacon's tracks sometimes take me a while to warm up to, but now I absolutely adore "Rain Must Fall." Like I say, not one of my favorite albums, but I take it as a signpost toward *Innuendo*, which is one of my all-time favorite albums.

POPOFF: Speaking of "Party" and "Khashoggi's Ship," I've never been able to shake this view that—along with "I Want It All"—they made Queen sound like rich snobs. I equated "I Want It All" with frat boy rock.

NESTER: I'm okay with those songs because I think of them as decadent songs like "Dead on Time" from *Jazz*. Queen weren't of the people [*laughs*]. They were of the people musically, but they were pretty unabashedly this cocky band. I don't know if they should've been the leadoff tracks—"I Want It All" should've been the leadoff track, then we'd be having maybe a different conversation about "Party" and "Khashoggi's Ship."

CHAPMAN: I hear what you're saying. I didn't get frat boy, but I got a sense of decadence, like royalty or fake royalty. "I Want It All" was inspired by something that Anita Dobson, Brian May's new lover, had uttered at one of the shows. May tells the anecdote of her being at Wembley and she saw a certain amount of applause when people recognized her because she was such a big personality. But she apparently looked at the huge crowd and said, "I want it all and I want it now." So that sense of, I want success, I want wealth, I want, I want.

So even though the song has root with Brian and Anita, I almost saw it as some sort of expression of Freddie and his fabulous lifestyle. I'd listen to these interviews and the sense was "I just wanna party, I just want to have the most amazing time in the most amazing places." Just consumption, consumption, consumption.

I think you're onto something. There was no soul. "Party," "Khashoggi's Ship," "I Want It All"—I thought this is a party band. You remember the stories of Mercury loving to go to the discotheques and partying and watching him in every single interview where he's saying something provocative and he's

Japanese promo copy of "I Want It All." Purportedly, the song was inspired by something uttered by Anita Dobson, Brian's new lover.

always got a cigarette. The whole image of Queen's shifted for me. Even if they were rocking out, it felt false. And uninteresting. It may not have been *A Kind of Magic*, but it was now traversing a different area that I didn't care about, more bombast than heart. I was immediately let down.

MYERS: In terms of lyrics, "I Want It All" is a real ballsy "get out of my way, I want to grab the world" song. A kid coming up from the streets not taking any shit from anyone. Brian's future wife, Anita, was in the middle of a career that was going great guns and she came out with that phrase at one point and it appealed to him. That sort of earnest and simple, but quite naked, ambition. Sometimes that's a powerful thing. You don't always want to knock that.

It's a very British thing to look down on that attitude. "Oh, no, no, no. False modesty is the way forward here." But here it's "Saw that, I want it, I'm gonna take it." And I like it. I think it's a really powerful song. I love the fact that they did the double-time thing, which I enjoyed to great effect on things like "It's Late." These were all little signposts that, even though the song itself I didn't think was particularly original for Queen, signaled good things were on the way.

POPOFF: That was the first single from the record, followed the next month by "Breakthru." Cool drums, sort of this oscillation between electronic and acoustic.

NESTER: Yes, you'd have to take it measure by measure, practically. And as much as I would I look for heavy guitar stuff in these Queen songs for a return to form, it opens with full-on multilayered vocals for a different sort of return to past glories. Listening to these later Queen songs, they're really challenging, man [*laughs*]. Because they've fallen off their high horse. They're trying to keep up with the times. This is like Kiss without makeup or Black Sabbath with Glenn Hughes—they're limping along.

And there are some flashes of brilliance, but they just don't know when the flashes happen. I mean, it kills me. "Hang on in There" should've been a single and it was nothing more than a B-side. It's a great, great song with this cool outro jam. It's like, wow, this is what Queen could've sounded like if they didn't get in their own way.

CHAPMAN: I agree. I listened to some of those B-sides and there was one tune, "Stealin'," that was this kind of hokey Freddie Mercury tune. And I thought, why didn't you put that on the record?! It would've popped the bubble of bombast in a way they used to be able to do. Like there's "Death on Two Legs" and then "Lazing on a Sunday Afternoon" comes right after that. The ability to do that is one of the many reasons I dug Queen so much. They were very Beatles-like in that ability to traverse genres effortlessly and make it work.

MYERS: Melodically, "Breakthru" reminded me of Don Henley's "The Boys of Summer." What I find interesting is that the videos from that album seemed very much geared toward a younger market. You've got them racing ahead on a train, you've got "The Invisible Man" playing computer games, and suddenly they all come out and appear. I was fifteen or sixteen when that came out, and it felt like, oh, they're aiming for an audience that is younger than me. Even though I was pleased to hear "I Want It All" as this strong, melodic rock track, the rest of the album didn't jump out at me. I could hear stuff in it that was interesting, but it sounded like a band in the process of change.

CHAPMAN: "Breakthru" was the only track I liked instantly. And in fact, this was the only Queen album I never rebought on CD. At one point, I'd bought this Harman Kardon CD burner, and one of the first things I did was take my record and do a needle drop of "Breakthru" because it was such an outlier. It seemed like this brief window—for whatever reason—into the old Queen. There was a relative austerity to that arrangement, although people can disagree. And there's John Deacon's beautiful, propulsive bass solo that gives way to Brian May's gorgeous guitar passage. Maybe it was one of the stronger riffs. Maybe there was a yearning quality to it. That song had humanity.

"Breakthru" reminded me of "Machines," which is another one that is heavily techno but had an understanding to it musically that made it work—that song was about technology meeting humanity. On "Breakthru," there wasn't a glossy Fred Mandel synth solo, there was that driving bass solo. And where the bass actually sounded like a bass.

But that's one of Roger's, and I was a huge Roger fan and paying very close attention to him on these albums as well as his solo material. Funny story, in the summer of '87, I visited Townhouse Studios where Queen had recorded. I just bluffed my way in, saying I'm a musician from Canada, I want to see the facilities. And the person on the phone said, "Well, you can't go in the mixing room because U2 are there. But Queen are recording, and they're on lunch right now, so if you can get down here, I can show you around." So, I got down there and there was Freddie's piano and there was John's bass, and I have a picture of me beside the piano.

And as I was leaving, I bumped into Roger Taylor. I was so excited. I said, "Oh, Mr. Taylor." He just stared at me. I said, "I'm a huge admirer of your work." He said, "Are you some kind of American?" I said, "Actually, no, I'm Canadian." He stared at me. And I said, "I love *Fun in Space.*" Which was his first solo record. And he said, "Oh, nobody bought that record." And I said, "Well, I did, and 'Let's Get Crazy' is such a fantastic song." And he just said, "You are an American." And he walked across the road and got in his silver Aston Martin and tore off.

POPOFF: Man! So middle of '87, they would've been recording some of the early tracks for *The Miracle*, right?

CHAPMAN: That's what I wondered about, because you do any sort of research and they started in early '88. But they were there. I mean, I didn't see the other three that day, but I saw a Roger. And the assistant engineer, a fellow named Keith said, "Yeah, that's Freddie's piano." And I got to

Clear vinyl version of "The Invisible Man 12" Version" b/w "Single Version" and "Hijack My Heart," 1989. Videos for the new album's singles seemed geared for a younger market.

go in the Stone Room, which wasn't set up with drums. That's the drum room at Townhouse, where "In the Air Tonight" had been recorded—pretty much the most iconic drum room ever built.

POPOFF: What did you think of the cover art?

CHAPMAN: To me, it was inspired by the fact that they were no longer going to credit songs individually. They were acknowledging, finally, that Queen was this large, monstrous single beast. I thought it was reflecting that business decision. It also reminded me of, there's a bar scene in the *Battlestar Galactica* movie with this woman performer who has three sets of eyes and three mouths. It was freakish.

I also thought it was amusing that the album was called *The Miracle*, and the picture's obviously a miracle. But it's also a comment that it was a miracle that the band had stayed together as long as it had. And it was a miracle that we found a band that had these four disparate minds that could write and play so many instruments. For those reasons, I thought it was a clever cover, although it wasn't particularly visually appealing—it's kind of gross. I know Iron Maiden's artist Derek Riggs thought that the band took the idea from the painting he did for "The Clairvoyant" single.

POPOFF: "Scandal" was issued as a single, backed with "My Life Has Been Saved." Didn't trouble the charts in the US, although it got to No. 25 in Britain.

NESTER: "Scandal" has a guitar motif as the hook, so that's really interesting for me. Then there's "The Miracle," which is kind of a big synthy song. Brian May seems to be a fan of it, but for me, the production, the synths, get in the way.

You could imagine that Queen thought *The Miracle* was going to be the last album, and I'm kind of glad it wasn't. It ends with "Was It All Worth It," and there are some theories out there among the Queen-errati, that that was their "The Show Must Go On." They thought Freddie wouldn't make it through and this was their swansong. Even though the song is okay, I'm so glad that they lasted to do *Innuendo*, which is a terrific album.

But Freddie, if you look at the videos from *The Miracle*, he has a beard to sort of fill out his face. He's losing weight. He's definitely sick. This is a weird period where, depending on who you talk to or read, he might not have let the band in on him having AIDS or being HIV-positive. He's showing up, according to some accounts, to the video shoot of "Breakthru," for example, and not like telling anybody that he's sick.

POPOFF: Personally, I think the title track is pretty good—solid melodically, lots of ear candy.

"Scandal (12" Version)" b/w "7" Version" and "My Life Has Been Saved," 1989. One of the album's forgotten gems.

MYERS: Yeah, it's never grabbed me. I agree that it could've fit on *Made in Heaven*. I like it inasmuch as, given the situation that Freddie was in, he wrote something so positive. I like the cross-fade at the end, which gives it an anthemic overtone, with the "when we can all be friends" passage. There was the jaunty piano which they said was sort of emulating "Killer Queen," but it seemed miles to me from that as a track.

As a sentiment, I thought it was okay, but the lyrics had a lot more weight in the following album. And I think they lent themselves to stronger songwriting than this. But there was so much in this album that was moving in that direction. I found it encouraging, but for some reason I could never fully and emotionally invest in *The Miracle*.

POPOFF: Ralph, any closing thoughts on the album?

CHAPMAN: Well, the irony of *The Miracle* is that, in many ways, even despite the electronics, it sounds like a stadium rock record—and yet they knew going in that they wouldn't be able to tour. Actually, in the interviews at the time, they basically lie and say, "Yeah, we're hoping to tour." What's the expression Brian May uses? "We've just got to work out some details." But they were lying. They knew Freddie would never be able to tour that album.

POPOFF: Why do you think it sounds like a stadium rock record?

CHAPMAN: In the sense that it's got loudness, guitars, some of what Brian promised at the time, a human element. Plus the party rock decadence we were talking about with "Party" and "Khashoggi's Ship" and "I Want It All." Those songs seem like they would do well in a live setting, although maybe not "Party." They would transcend their shallowness, or my misunderstood belief of their shallowness, because they were largely band-driven. Where something like "Rain Must Fall" or "My Baby Does Me" couldn't have been done live, "I Want It All" strikes me as something that would easily work, and of course we get a tantalizing glimpse because the video is a staged performance of it.

POPOFF: Patrick, any final things to point out with this record that distinguish it?

MYERS: It's interesting how they wound up with so many extras. Apparently, they had loads of little bits that they weren't sure what to do with. But because they were writing by committee, they were just bringing everything they had and they'd just sort through it. The big single, "Breakthru," the bulk of the song was written by Roger and the beginning was written by Freddie. It was a process of cutting and pasting whatever seemed to work.

POPOFF: They're basically making *The Miracle* and *Innuendo* under the exact same circumstances, right?

MYERS: Well yeah, it's a continuation. They just carried on. I think they turned up to a couple of awards ceremonies and they did a Mike Reed Radio One interview, and that was the beginning and end of the marketing they did as a band for *The Miracle* and then went straight back in the studio. So, the work rate was great. But I think at the time it was really to support Freddie, because if Freddie didn't have this, there would be nothing to do other than his treatments and hiding from the press. Work is important in anyone's life, particularly when you're staring mortality in the face. You want to throw yourself into the work. Here's something you can do, here's something that will live beyond you.

When they did *The Miracle*, they hadn't actually been in the studio together for the best part of two years. And so much had changed. Brian's marriage had ended. I think his father was dying. Freddie was clearly dying. And to get back into the studio and find a way to make all that work—it's amazing. They effectively become a band reborn on *Innuendo*. And I think part of that process is getting those original tracks out on *The Miracle*.

NESTER: Ultimately, here's how I think of this album. Anything after and including *Hot Space*, if you're a rock guy, you're trying to find the pockets of rock Queen in the songs, because by now, synthesizers and electronic drums are a huge part of the equation. I think of electronic drums on *The Miracle* as being the whole album, practically. "Invisible Man" and "Rain Must Fall" and "Scandal"—all that stuff is electronic drums.

But lately, in my old age, I've started to think that's not really the point of listening to these albums. You're not trying to listen to the killer guitar solo in "Invisible Man" to the exclusion of the rest of the song. That's not the point of listening to music. Even though back in the '80s, I remember buying like a fucking Don Johnson album just so I could listen to a Dweezil Zappa solo. And that was how I would listen to Queen albums back then. Or how I would try to sell a new Queen album to my rock fan friends. I'd be like, "Listen, man, they're back!" But really, that's really not the point. They were Queen. They weren't like a rock band. They were the greatest band in the whole fucking world. They could do whatever the hell they wanted to! [*laughs*]

RELEASED FEBRUARY 5, 1991

14 INNUENDO

WITH CHRIS CAFFERY, STEPHEN DALTON, AND JOHN NORUM

1. **Innuendo** 6:29
(MERCURY, TAYLOR)

2. **I'm Going Slightly Mad** 4:22
(MERCURY)

3. **Headlong** 4:39
(MAY)

4. **I Can't Live with You** 4:35
(MAY)

5. **Don't Try So Hard** 3:39
(MERCURY)

6. **Ride the Wild Wind** 4:41
(TAYLOR)

7. **All God's People** 4:19
(MERCURY, MORAN)

8. **These Are the Days
of Our Lives** 4:12
(TAYLOR)

9. **Delilah** 3:32
(MERCURY)

10. **The Hitman** 4:52
(MERCURY, MAY, DEACON)

11. **Bijou** 3:37
(MERCURY MAY)

12. **The Show Must Go On** 4:34
(MAY)

PERSONNEL:

FREDDIE MERCURY – *vocals, keyboards;*
BRIAN MAY – *guitar, vocals, keyboards;*
JOHN DEACON – *bass, keyboards;*
ROGER TAYLOR – *drums, percussion, vocals,
keyboards*

GUEST PERSONNEL:

STEVE HOWE – *Spanish guitar;*
MIKE MORAN – *keyboards*
Recorded at MOUNTAIN STUDIOS,
Montreux, Switzerland, and
METROPOLIS STUDIOS, *London,*
Produced by QUEEN
and DAVID RICHARDS

OPPOSITE: Onstage at New York City's Madison Square Garden, February 1977. *Innuendo* represented the boys determined to send Freddie off with twenty years capped right.

Alas, we arrive at the last record Queen would make with Freddie still with us. Proof in the pudding, it's as if the boys were determined to send Freddie off satisfied with twenty years capped right.

However, *Innuendo* is also a record that conceivably comforted and even coddled Freddie, for it can be described as merely a highly professional, more organic and guitar-charged (albeit politely so) version of the melange of musics the band had put on *The Game*, *The Works*, and *The Miracle*.

In that respect, it should be viewed as a product of the '80s, not the '90s, when bands of Queen's stature and heritage were reacting to grunge by stripping back, variously trying raw or murk or dark or, in some cases, simply going back to what they did in the '70s, which effortlessly tended to cover at least some of those bases.

Instead, what Queen did on *Innuendo* was what hair metal bands did in 1991 and 1992: turn in their "We're trying really, really hard" album, whereon, dismayed over Pearl Jam and Nirvana, they vowed to erect the most competitive, perfectly recorded, smartly written, mature album they could possibly muster—but not leave their hair home.

QUEEN

INNUENDO
(EXPLOSIVE VERSION)

Everything except the title track feels like an early song that had now been going to the gym as well as the library. Putting it over the top is a soar-away bonus addition—for the rocker quota was already filled with "Headlong" and "The Hitman"—in the opening title track. The only time Queen ever went with Middle Eastern modalities was back at "Mustapha," where that was the whole idea. Here, they do that *plus* plow straight ahead all doomy. Instantly we notice that Brian May has put aside his arch axe tonality for a straight injection of high-powered arena rock guitar born and bred by big shot producers in Hollyrock, USA. And that would stay consistent throughout the album—where there is metal here, it is recorded "correctly."

"I Can't Live with You" is also somewhat in this realm of boot-strapping bonus, joyously reviving meteor showers of vocal harmonies and Brian's drill-bit solo guitar sound, all atop what is the record's fourth hard rocker, with "The Show Must Go On" offering a somewhat unheard of (back in the '80s, anyway) fifth. Offering matchups to expected styles, yet as superior versions, "I'm Going Slightly Mad" might be the band's best synth-pop song since "Radio Ga Ga," and "Don't Try So Hard" is a classic Queen ballad for the ages, torrid melody, tragic lyrics, and a *tour de force* vocal.

Elsewhere, the songs succeed mostly on the basis of their production and the exquisite detailing to finish them off. The melody of "These Are the Days of Our Lives" wilts with a dusty Sunday afternoon ennui that induces sleep—and as far as "The Hitman" goes, I appreciate greatly that strafing snare-swept passage but find the song stodgy and the lyrics chafing against the rest of the record. But count me a fan of "Delilah" (channeling the vaudevillian without re-creating it), "Bijou," and of course the fatal majesty of "The Show Must Go On."

Despite all manner of single being presented at points around the globe, most failed to gain traction, with "The Show Must Go On" slowly rising to its current near-mythical status through a series of formal releases and unprompted radio play beginning at the time of Freddie's death nine months after *Innuendo*'s release. Almost prophetically, the world's love affair with the song kicked off with its UK launch as a single on October 14, 1991, a month before Freddie's death, and in conjunction with the release of *Greatest Hits II*. Years later, "The Show Must Go On" represents Freddie's inspiring goodbye letter, more visceral and memorable than anything on *Made in Heaven*.

POPOFF: Would you agree that one big difference with *Innuendo* is the production, especially compared to *The Miracle*?

NORUM: Absolutely, it sounds enormous [*laughs*]—big drums, big guitar sounds, everything sounds really big and fat. I compare it to Zeppelin. It's quite wet, which I like. It has some good ambience on the drums, and some cool reverb and echo effects on the vocals, more so than the previous albums. Which reflects the trends of the time. I like bone-dry albums as well, that have no effects on them, but I prefer when it has reverb on the vocal and on the guitars and stuff like that, a little bit of room effect or ambient effect, especially on the drums.

CAFFERY: I think they purposely went with pristine production on *Innuendo*. If you look at the difference between, say, *Electric* and *Sonic Temple* from The Cult, I think that's where Queen went on that album, where everything was really modern and pristine. You really notice when bands put the time into serious production work.

POPOFF: Of course, another narrative surrounding this record is that Freddie was gravely ill by this point.

DALTON: Yes, you can't really talk about *Innuendo* without talking about Freddie's illness, because the record is absolutely made under the shadow of his looming mortality, which the band knew and he knew, and most other people who saw him at the time suspected, even though he repeatedly denied that he was ill. Now we look back at it through that filter, and it does color the music.

I think it's a better record than *The Miracle*, definitely. They seem to have escaped from that deadening studio sheen of the '80s albums. This is them coming into their own. It's the beginning of the '90s and they're not letting the technology master them—they are mastering the technology.

But the circumstances of Freddie staring death in the face, you feel it in songs like "These Are the Days of Our Lives" and "The Show Must Go On." There's that elegiac and heartbreaking kind of nostalgia. I think of *Innuendo* now in the same way as Bowie's *Blackstar* or Leonard Cohen's *You Want It Darker* or even Johnny Cash doing "Hurt," looking very fragile in that video. It does have that looming sense of doom about it. Obviously, it was done in a Queen way, so it's more flamboyant and glamorous, and perhaps more flippant, but there is that undertone of looming mortality.

NORUM: Yeah, those songs are great, and of course there was the video for "Those Are the Days" and "I'm Going Slightly Mad," which, well, it's a bit sad when you see the videos. Freddie looks so sick, so skinny. He knew he was dying, but he was still trying to make the best out of the situation. It's quite emotional to watch those videos.

POPOFF: Could you point out a few highlights on the album, some key tracks?

CAFFERY: Gosh, there are so many, but "I'm Going Slightly Mad" is interesting melodically, because of the video, and because it's so funny. I know he wrote that song with a friend, Peter Straker. "I think I'm a banana tree?" [*laughs*] It's so great. And I just love the delivery of the octaves that the vocals were put in. That song is one of my favorites, plus "I Can't Live with You." There was a mood on this record where everything kind of struck me.

And then there's "Bijou," where they were writing what they called the inside-out song. It's fascinating. Freddie Mercury's singing those guitar melodies for Brian May to play, which become the verses, and then Freddie shows up for the guitar solo break about a minute and a half in and that's how that song was written. And it's funny, but some of my favorite emotional David Gilmour–type Brian May playing on all the albums was that song. Amazing stuff.

DALTON: "I'm Going Slightly Mad" is obviously a Freddie creation. It was his Noel Coward homage. You probably don't need to be a Brit to appreciate it, but just the wordplay is very nice with all the ridiculous terms for being mentally unbalanced, like "knitting with only one needle" and "not my usual top billing." It's a very, very charming song. And I think it's rendered slightly macabre by the video because clearly they couldn't hide the fact that he was wasting away. But I think they shot those videos in color and then transferred them to black and white to try and disguise how skeletal and pale Freddie was looking. So it has that dark undertow, even though it's a perfectly joyful, late-Freddie song.

People have said that maybe he's alluding to the effects of AIDS. It could be read like that, but Freddie just wanted to entertain people. I think one reason he kept the diagnosis secret is he always wanted to give off a glamorous façade. I'm not sure whether he's directly addressing AIDS there, but we can't help see it through that filter nowadays.

NORUM: A favorite for me is "The Show Must Go On." It seems like they are saying, even though it's written by Brian May, well, when I'm not here on this planet anymore, the show should go on. Everybody knew he was dying. But coming from Freddie, what you hear is him telling the band, "I think the show should continue. I think you guys should continue doing what you do." I had a cover band together with Mikkey Dee, who used to be the drummer in Motörhead and now is in Scorpions, and we did "The Show Must Go On" and it was an amazing song to play live.

CAFFERY: Oh, I agree. "The Show Must Go On" is probably my favorite Queen song ever. When that song starts, I get incredibly huge chills through me. The very last Savatage tour we did, that record was our quote-unquote "five and dive" song, where the lights go out and you've got five minutes before the band comes on stage. Depending on what country we were in, the crowd would sing that song louder than the PA system. One time we were in Athens and we were playing a small basketball arena, and it was completely sold out. And it was one of the most amazing concert moments in my life. I remember saying to Johnny Middleton, I said everything I ever did working toward playing music was worth it just for that moment alone, waiting to play. I mean, that crowd was singing that song so loud. They sang everything in our show like that. That was the type of show where I could hear kids singing my guitar solos. But that song always seemed to get that reaction.

"The Show Must Go On" is haunting. It's basically talking about what's gonna happen once he does pass. The craziest thing about that one is the similarity to the "Days of Our Lives," where it's like they were talking about how great their whole thing was. It's not like they weren't living the best of times, but I think they knew when they were doing that record that was not the greatest time, because they knew the circumstances. There are not a lot of Queen records where the other guys in the band wrote lyrics that got to me like this record. "The Show Must Go On" and "Days of Our Lives" were written by May and Taylor, respectively, although I think Brian and Freddie may have written the first verse in "The Show Must Go On." But they just seem to be on the same wavelength with this record.

POPOFF: I'm programmed to be a fan of any and all heavy Queen songs, but I just can't warm to "Headlong" and "The Hitman." And "Headlong" was even the advance single in the US. Am I somehow missing the charm of these songs?

DALTON: No, I agree. "Headlong," I thought, was slightly tossed off, fake heavy rock, kind of like an AC/DC parody. That's not my favorite side of Queen. I think when they entirely let Brian May write a track, it becomes like a Brian May solo track, which misses some of the colors in the Queen rainbow. I mean, not just with Queen, but anything that smacks of "rock authenticity" is a turnoff for me. I like fakery and campery. For me, that's the lie that tells the truth. Whereas this kind of British, white, middle-class guys trying to be deep South bluesman [*laughs*] . . . I mean, I know that's not what they're trying to do, but anything that strives to connect to the authentic rock canon automatically raises my hackles. It's a fake form of realness to me. Sure, "The Hitman" I bracket with "Headlong." It's slathered on with a shovel, that kind of Brian May poodle rock stuff, which is just not my favorite type of Queen.

CAFFERY: An interesting thing about "The Hitman" is it's a metal song, but it was started by Freddie on keyboards. And "Headlong" was a straight rock song. When you got a Queen record, there would always be one or two of them, whether it was "Sheer Heart Attack" or "Stone Cold Crazy." It was almost like there was a formula to Queen albums. But they were always different—not any two of the rock songs were the same. And here, suddenly the "hoop diddy diddy" part comes in. Okay, it's Queen and they're putting in something no one else would do.

POPOFF: The title track, situated at the pole position, definitely makes an impression.

NORUM: It's a masterpiece. I love all the arrangements. It's incredible, all the different parts in there. It's timeless. When it comes on the radio even today, I crank it up and never get sick of it. It's still as exciting now as it was when it came out. I think it's because of Freddie's amazing vocal and the great melodies. One of their best ever. "Innuendo" and "Show Must Go On" are my two favorites on that album and they're similar in a way, with a kind of Zeppelin vibe, heavy and dark, although I like the pop songs as well.

DALTON: I think they're obviously referencing vintage Queen triumphalist rock with "Innuendo." I believe they wrote it as an homage to "Kashmir," right? It's got a nice Steve Howe flamenco guitar break in it. It's a slightly low-calorie version of Queen's virile and thrusting earlier self, but of course it's going to be when you consider how frail Freddie was when he made this record, I think a lot of that swagger is almost like a Wizard of Oz, wearing a mask as a distraction technique. But whatever their intentions were, I'd say they captured some of the old Queen swashbuckling grandeur.

POPOFF: Stephen, can you catch me up on a few we haven't talked about yet?

DALTON: Well, I would recommend "All God's People." That's got a roaring, gospel, bombastic feel to it, and the stacked vocal harmony thing, which they're good at. That was an outtake from Freddie's *Barcelona* record, so it's got that slightly operatic dimension, which appeals to me. "I Can't Live with You" is one a lot of people really like. To me it's a bit overly polished, a bit too much of a soft rocker. It's nicely crafted, but it doesn't grab me. I prefer Queen songs to slightly smack me about the face [*laughs*].

Now, "These Are the Days of Our Lives" I bracket with "Show Must Go On." Again, we have to see it through the filter of Freddie's death. But I think it stands up very well. That is one of the songs that I would compare to Bowie's *Blackstar*, really. It's got that summarizing feeling, but that kind of, "I'll never know the summers of youth again" feeling. Regardless of whether that was the intention, and regardless of whether Freddie even wrote the lyric, it's got that kind of feel to it now.

POPOFF: But I'll raise this point with you and I feel this way about *Made in Heaven* as well. *Blackstar* to me is like friggin' Van der Graaf Generator or Krautrock or the darkest creative corners of King Crimson, and "These Are the Days of Our Lives" is entirely housewifey, right? What is it with Queen, when in these later years, like half of *A Kind of Magic*, this song—the melodies, the arrangements—it's basically easy listening music, isn't it?

DALTON: Yeah, it might be a function of just becoming less hungry and more sort of tax exile–type rockers. I think a lot of the later albums basically sound like Switzerland: very neutral. Very polished, no grime, no poverty, nice views, quite expensive, but you wouldn't want to visit there. And I apologize to any Swiss people who might be reading this, but it's a very boring country.

POPOFF: I guess I haven't had you comment on the big closer, "The Show Must Go On." What role does this one play in your opinion?

DALTON: Well, again it fits into the Freddie dying narrative. It also taps into that defiant, triumphalist, muscular, pomp-rock tradition of Queen songs like "We Are the Champions" or "I Want It All." "Hammer to Fall," even. Considering how frail Freddie was, that's quite a good late example of that type of Queen song. And it's also a nice memorial to his spirit. Actually, Elton John performed it at the Freddie tribute concert. It has a kind of, "You must carry on the party without me, darlings," feeling about it, which I like. On another level, it's a great foreshadowing of Queen's business plan for the future. They're basically saying, we're going to milk the hell out of this career, with or without Freddie. The show must go on. The checks must keep rolling in.

POPOFF: Chris, any songs you wanted to chirp in on that we've not addressed yet?

CAFFERY: There's "Don't Try So Hard." That song was basically saying life is too short, be yourself, don't kill yourself trying to impress other people and your glory times will come. I definitely do believe that.

Also, it's funny that they say that Taylor did not want "Delilah" on the record. Because it was very well-known that Freddie didn't like "I'm in Love with My Car," and I can imagine a conversation where Freddie goes, "Well, I'll just write a song about my cat then!" And "Delilah" is not a great song. It's this goofy song straightup about his cat, and the cat peeing on Freddie's Chippendale furniture. But I can just hear Roger Taylor saying, "I don't want this on the record" and Freddie is like, "It's going on the album."

"Ride the Wild Wind," in the scheme of that album, is just more like an album track to me. It's one I would pass over. When I got this album, I owned a house with my brother and a friend, and we would stay up a lot and play pool. We had a bar in the house, and this record was one that would always make it to the late-night playlist. It kind of has that one groove in there which is kind of like Savatage's "Commissar" song. I love that it was number one in Poland! It's cool that the Polish people like it.

POPOFF: What are your views on the *Innuendo* cover art?

CAFFERY: Oddly, I'm working my new solo record, and I'm calling it *The Jester's Court*. And I think that's Freddie. He's the clown, the jester. He was that kind of entertainer, but an entertainer in such a different and colorful way. You don't have to necessarily make people laugh to make them smile. He always had that element to him, which was a little bit further over the edge than everybody else. Nobody would show up on stage in a pair of friggin' little white shorts and bare feet other than Freddie Mercury. He was that guy and I think that's perfect. I love the banana. So funny.

DALTON: It seems to harken back to their classic rock period. But maybe that's a deliberate allusion. If we're talking about them rediscovering some of their earlier heavy rock muscle, belatedly, maybe they are referencing that in the artwork. Then again, the band members might like that sort of Edward Lear surrealism. In that sense, it feels like a classic English piece of whimsy that could have been on a Caravan or Genesis album.

POPOFF: John, where does this record sit in the Queen canon for you?

NORUM: I don't think there's one bad song on there. It's the strongest Queen album, for my personal tastes anyway. A lot of people mention the old stuff from the '70s, but I think the last album they did with Freddie is the best one. Best songs, best production, best everything. It just has so much feel and emotion. Because of just knowing that was going to be Freddie's last album, I guess. He put so much effort and passion into his singing on that album. Which you can hear. And it was darker than some of the other albums. Not just because everyone knew he was sick and he was going to pass away, but you can just hear it in his voice. That's the little extra little thing in on that album.

DALTON: I think, given the difficult circumstances it was made under, it's probably as good as an album we could've expected from them at this point. It's not as lazy and characterless as *The Miracle*. It's not as good as *The Works*, which I think is probably a late classic, probably their last great record. But, yeah, it summarizes the whole synthesizer/studio polish period and throws back to their epic pomp-rock period. Self-consciously, perhaps, but I think in that sense it has a nice summing-up feel to it.

CAFFERY: I also want to pay tribute to Freddie's vocals on this album. His vocal performance was insane. You could tell he was probably dripping blood out of his lungs with the title track in particular. I know people who have died from that disease, who were vocalists. They were in the studio at the later stages of their lives and I watched that happen, when your body is taking a beating like that and you just hear that. But he was so great on that record. The tones and the lengths and the octaves and the pitches of everything.

He's just reaching and getting there too. He was literally pouring his life out. He was the one who said he was going to do this until the day that he dropped, and he never wanted people to know what it was that was going on with him. Because apparently, he didn't want to ever feel like people were feeling sorry for him, that he was capitalizing on this sickness in any way. Plus, I just think he was so a really proud and strong person.

It makes me sad because I feel like he died alone. Like he was dealing with that by himself. It seemed like he was a bit of a loner anyway; I just get that general vibe as far as people not really knowing a lot about him. But just to be in that position and know what's going to happen to you. Because at the time death was the only perceived ending.

It's really unfortunate that we had to lose him. But like I said, the thing that gets me is the fact that he must've been incredibly scared and lonely, but still, to the end, writing songs for everybody and doing what he did musically and creatively. That guy is a hero to me, man. Freddie was very special.

The band accept the BRIT Award for Outstanding Contribution to Music on February 18, 1990. It would be Freddie's last public appearance.

RELEASED NOVEMBER 6, 1995

1. **It's a Beautiful Day** 2:32
(MERCURY, DEACON)

2. **Made in Heaven** 5:25
(MERCURY)

3. **Let Me Live** 4:45
(QUEEN)

4. **Mother Love** 4:49
(MERCURY, MAY)

5. **My Life Has Been Saved** 3:15
(DEACON)

6. **I Was Born to Love You** 4:49
(MERCURY)

7. **Heaven for Everyone** 5:36
(TAYLOR)

8. **Too Much Love Will Kill You** 4:20
(MAY, MUSKER, LAMERS)

9. **You Don't Fool Me** 5:24
(QUEEN)

10. **A Winter's Tale** 3:49
(MERCURY)

11. **It's a Beautiful Day (Reprise)** 3:01
(MERCURY)

12. **Yeah** :04
(QUEEN)

13. **Untitled Hidden Track** 22:32
(MAY, TAYLOR, RICHARDS)

PERSONNEL:

FREDDIE MERCURY – *vocals, keyboards, drum machine;*

BRIAN MAY – *guitar, vocals, keyboards;*

JOHN DEACON – *bass, guitar, keyboards;*

ROGER TAYLOR – *drums, percussion, vocals, keyboards*

GUEST PERSONNEL:

REBECCA LEIGH-WHITE – *backing vocals;*

GARY MARTIN – *backing vocals;*

CATHERINE PORTER – *backing vocals;*

MIRIAM STOCKLEY – *backing vocals;*

DAVID RICHARDS – *keyboards*

Recorded at MOUNTAIN STUDIOS, *Montreux, Switzerland;*

METROPOLIS STUDIOS, *London; and*

ALLERTON HILL, *Cosford Mill, UK*

Produced by QUEEN; *co-produced by*

DAVID RICHARDS,

JUSTIN SHIRLEY-SMITH, *and*

JOSH MACRAE

OPPOSITE: Freddie is interviewed by a reporter from the *Daily Express* at his Shepherds Bush flat, London, 1969.

15 MADE IN HEAVEN

WITH JIM JENKINS AND PATRICK MYERS

Issued almost exactly four years after Freddie's death, Queen's last album is a work of such enigmatic quality that it is still hotly debated in fan circles, with opinions yawing madly on not only what the lyrics mean but as to what the very music itself is supposed to represent.

Whether one welcomes *Made in Heaven*'s disparate and inspiringly brave and uptempo denials of death, or welcomes the comfort and convention of the softly landing music written as the soundtrack, there's no denying that the two go together, and that the resulting bond creates an authentic album.

Indeed, there is a smooth reassurance to both the lyrics and music, taking the listener to a happy place and yet, subtly, chimera-like, a place shimmering between the buoyancy of a happy life and the blissful peace of a happy passing. This despite the record's improbable construction; if some do not wish to see the sausage being made, that is not only fine but arguably the approach that Queen asks of us.

And yet it must be dealt with, but in deference we can do so in broad stokes. *Made in Heaven* is derived roughly from three sources: (1) retelling songs that went toward Freddie's *Mr. Bad Guy* album; (2) fragments of songs and full songs from the '80s that went elsewhere or were set aside; and (3) most heartbreakingly, from new lyrics and, in some cases, music that Freddie was making on his deathbed, with the clear instruction to keep the music (and hopefully the joy) flowing after he was gone.

And what to make of "Made in Heaven"? What message falls out of this goodbye letter, penned a bit by Freddie and a lot by the band? As Freddie would have wished, the answer is that it's personal to each listener, and so from this end, the message that rises from the sounds within is, in aggregate, the idea that life is good and meant to be lived and then . . . we all leave the same way: with bliss, metaphysical simplicity, all earthy concerns gone, the journey entirely the same for all, death the great leveler.

It's a harsh way to put it, but as a celebration of life, and even as a suggestion of how one should live one's life and then responsibly arrange one's death, *Made in Heaven* is the same death as the granny down the street. This entirely melodically conventional collection of songs, top to tails, pretty much void of guitars and glossed with the least challenging of piano sounds, could be played at an elderly pensioner's funeral. The title on the sleeve appears crudely stamped, as if by the coroner; the cover photo depicts a lake and mountains and sunset. Freddie pipes up but not with rage: My life has been saved because, after all, I'm made in Heaven. A baby cries, a gospel choir sings, and a mother loves. At the end, there's a cozy winter's tale, a culturally universal trip down a long tunnel (while one's life flashes before their eyes, of course), and even a *statue* . . . this is heaven for *everyone*.

In this respect, it is essentially Pink Floyd's *The Endless River* but with expected reflections spelled out for us. Emphatically, though, this is *not* Roger Waters, who, with *Is This the Life We Really Want?*, mixes the tenderness of last and lost earthly love with the fire and responsibility of continued political rage despite being in his sunset years (reflected o'er as he looks under his Gulfstream, I might add). This is not David Bowie, who with *Blackstar* simultaneously ignored death and just worked, but also marveled at the trip, creating provocative music that captured the completely bizarre concept of dying, an artist to the end scratching out weird rhythms for a small audience. This is not Freddie Mercury saying, "I want you to take all my money and throw the wildest party you can, everyone in drag, cocaine everywhere, painted naked women in the elevators, darling."

As if in affirmation of the universally wished-upon gauzy comfort of Queen's vision of the ideal death, *Made in Heaven* sold in huge numbers around the world, except in America, oddly, although the record's gold certification there demonstrated that not everyone had moved on. But *Made in Heaven* went platinum in Japan and Canada; double platinum in France, Spain, and Austria; triple platinum in Germany; and an astounding five times platinum in the motherland, the United Kingdom, signifying sales in that territory of over one and a half million copies.

Made in Heaven was a success on so many levels. The album represents an extraordinary way for Queen to cap their remarkable story with dignity and, again perhaps most admirably, with an everyman universality that they had spent much of their career amusingly, knowingly, ironically, and, with a wink of the eye, suppressing.

POPOFF: How is the tone of *Made in Heaven* set up for us with the opening track, "It's a Beautiful Day"?

MYERS: With *Made in Heaven*, I think Queen did something really extraordinary. A lot of Freddie's lyrics, he would often disparage them and say, there's no meaning in it—I just write them. I leave them as wide-open canvases so people can put their own interpretations on them. That's certainly true; he would leave things in a general bracket in terms of heartache or having a good time so it would be widely applicable and reach a wide commercial audience. But having said that, the choices he makes reveal so much.

And what's extraordinary about the opening track, it really does frame the album quite amazingly. We've got to remember, when anyone first heard this album, there was a lot of anticipation and expectation. *Innuendo* was such a strong album, so meticulous and so beautifully produced, so you were willing this album to succeed in many ways, but wondering how on earth it could, because there wasn't a great deal of time between the releasing of *Innuendo* and Freddie passing on. How would this ever work as an album?

So, you start off with "It's a Beautiful Day." That's Freddie kind of making stuff up as he went along in the studio back in 1980. He starts off with "The sun is shining/I feel good/No one's going to stop me now." He's almost back into the same lyric as "Don't Stop Me Now." And you think, okay, this is great and his voice sounds rich like old Freddie. But with the slightly thinner tone—I was surprised when I heard it was 1980.

And then he moves into "Sometimes I feel so sad," but he still sounds fine, and then it's "so sad, so bad." And it's an extemporizing song. And then you suddenly start hearing that they'd left a lot of his breath in the recording. "So sad, so sad [*gasp*], but no one's going to stop me now." And his breath almost sounds labored.

And then suddenly it breaks off into this "It's hopeless, so hopeless" and you're left hanging there for a millisecond thinking, "God, has the party mask finally fallen away?" He's suddenly sounding not so great. He was sounding so strong, then he sounds breathless and suddenly he's whispering, "It's hopeless" into the microphone. It's an amazing piece of drama.

And then he turns it around again. He says, "It's hopeless, so hopeless" and you can almost hear him smile, "to even try" [*laughs*]. So, it's like he's taken the audience in, I don't know, three phrases, on a 360-degree journey. It's a beautifully superb move, to have started with "It's a Beautiful Day," because when he opens with that vocal, it's strong and strident and powerful and then you hear the frailty. It puts it all in context.

I think it was John Deacon who underscored it with the augmented chords, which give it an ethereal feel. Particularly when you frame the album as *Made in Heaven*. There's a light, shimmering touch to that album. Particularly when you wrap it up with David Richards' play-out track.

POPOFF: Interesting. Let's frame the circumstances here a bit more. How is this record getting made?

JENKINS: Well, *Innuendo* was Queen's last album with the four members of the band; they all worked on it together, even though Freddie was very ill. But you listen to the vocals, and they just blaze with the title track. It reminded me of old Queen from the early '70s. And then you had the power of "The Show Must Go On," with that heartbreaking lyric.

They finished recording the album and then Freddie wanted to do some more recording, and he started with "A Winter's Tale." Freddie lived for a while in Montreux. It's a beautiful place. It's mountains and a lake, slow pace, and he could walk around and not be hassled. He had this apartment overlooking the lake. And here he wrote about Montreux. So, there are smoking chimney tops and swans on the lake. If you ever go to Montreux, go in the winter, walk around and listen to "A Winter's Tale" because it comes alive.

So, you've got that song recorded, before he started to deteriorate. And then, you know, we lost him. The band lost him. And they decided to work with what he recorded. Because he wanted to do as much work as possible. Let's get down as much vocal as I can do, and then

when I'm gone you can work on it, put it together, and you know, you've got another Queen album. It must've been extremely tough for Brian, Roger, and John to sit in the studio and work on the songs that Freddie had recorded.

A song like "You Don't Fool Me" was all done in bits and that can't be easy. And of course, you didn't have Freddie's influence in the studio, but they said they felt his presence. When they were actually going about mixing songs, it was like, "Oh, I don't think Freddie would like it to go like that. He'd want it to go like this." And they redid a couple of songs that he included on his solo album, *Mr. Bad Guy*, sort of Queen-ified them. It must've been really tough, especially the last vocals they ever recorded, which was "Mother Love."

POPOFF: Let's examine that one, because that is a central song to this record.

MYERS: Totally crucial. You've got this thing about Freddie that was infusing a lot of his work, that it wasn't all about the Mardi Gras and the party. Throughout the '80s, there was a lot of saying that this life leaves you unhappy, this life isn't the life you want. "Hard Life" was exactly that, you know, "I don't want my freedom."

I believe Brian wrote the music to "Mother Love" and the lyrics are a co-write with Freddie. And with Freddie, there is a degree of presentation with a lot of his songs that willfully obscures things to a point. I don't think there's any of that in "Mother Love." It's almost Lennon-esque in its autobiographical nature. But songs that people associate with Freddie in his later years and assume he wrote, he often didn't. People, for some reason, think that he wrote "Who Wants to Live Forever." It was Brian. "Show Must Go On," again, was largely Brian. "Days of Our Lives" was Roger. They're written with Freddie in mind and to help him, because, you know, writing became harder and harder. This song was written with Brian, but to me it's Freddie's last authorial stamp.

I mean, the last song he fully wrote and recorded was "A Winter's Tale," but this song is, I think, a real straightforward work of art and an incredibly powerful sentiment. It's a very straightforward melody, nothing particularly distinctive, but lyrically it's extraordinary. Halfway through recording these two verses, his instincts told him, this needs a lift. The very last thing he recorded, more or less, was that thing that cuts in after verse one. They sort of recut it in two. The sort of middle eight happens early in that song with "I've walked too long

in this lonely lane," and "I've had enough of this same old game." He's referring to his own lyrics with "the game" and this, that, and the other.

It's a recurrent theme in Freddie's work. He's already virtually name-checked "Don't Stop Me Now." It's a mature reflection by the man with his dying song, with the last song he ever recorded, on what a soul needs, of where he is in life. The party is behind him. He doesn't want the passion, he doesn't want the drama that he courted in so many of his songs and in his own life.

POPOFF: Jim, what is your view of the purpose of "Mother Love" on this record?

JENKINS: The studio at Montreux, Mountain Studios, was different than a normal recording studio. The mixing desk was on one floor and the recording studio was on the floor above. So, they had installed cameras and screens so that Dave Richards, who was on the mixing desk, could see the band upstairs recording.

Well, Freddie was frail when he recorded "Mother Love." He couldn't get up the stairs to the studio, so he sat in a chair where the mixing desk was and sang his heart out. What you hear on the record was what he gave. If you go to Montreux today, the studio is now a museum. You can go into that recording studio and see where Freddie recorded "Mother Love." The spot where the chair was is marked, and you can actually play the song with just Freddie's vocal. You can take away all the instruments and listen to how he sang. I was there a couple months ago with a friend who is not a Queen fan, and he could not believe the power of Freddie's voice. It's haunting; it just brings tears to your eyes. And you think, my god, how did he do that? The man was ill. And his voice was perfect. But he didn't get to finish it because he just couldn't do any more work, so Brian finished the song.

POPOFF: And what do you make of the "Mother Love" lyric?

JENKINS: With the baby crying at the end, it's back to the womb. He was not well, and when you're not that well, when you're a kid, you wanted your mom, didn't you? Your mom would make you better, those loving arms around you—mother love. Brian was close to his mom and Freddie was close to his mom. Quite the song, powerful.

Quite strange, because it's situated near the beginning of the album, and when I play *Made in Heaven*—and I do play it quite a bit—I always feel drained after I listen to that song. After it, you still have to get through "My Life Has Been Saved." And then you get "I Was Born to Love You," which picks you back up; it's a gradual buildup. I love the Queen version of "I Was Born to Love You"—it just rocks. But by that point, "Mother Love" is behind you, you're back into the album and you go, "Oh yeah, I like this."

POPOFF: In a general sense, do you think the band is telling us not to feel too bad about Freddie?

MYERS: I wouldn't disagree with that. I think it's letting you see that, in spite of what was in front of him and what was unavoidable, you can face it with warmth and positivity and human spirit and honesty. The honesty of "Mother Love" is extraordinary. It would be a different album without "Mother Love." It's such a key moment, particularly because it wasn't curated by a band in sessions from god knows when. It wasn't reworked from his not-very-good-selling solo album. It was last will and testament time, that song. I think building an album around that song is extraordinary.

POPOFF: How about a brief tour of some of the other selections?

MYERS: Well, the curating does lead to some slightly odd moments with a title like "Too Much Love Will Kill You" and all this kind of stuff, and you think where is Freddie's stand in this? And "My Life Has Been Saved." But that's a typical John Deacon song. You've suddenly got this very breezy song [*laughs*]. "My Life Has Been Saved" was recorded in '88, '89 for *The Miracle* sessions and a version of it ended up being a B-side. It's one of those songs where they repeat the first verse by going, "So," in front of the lyrics, and then repeat the verse again [*laughs*]. Oh, come on, just write another verse! [*laughs*] But it was a B-side as far as they were concerned. I've warmed to the song, because I always warm to John Deacon's songs, because there's something straightforward and forward-looking about them. If anything feels a little undeveloped, it would be the guitar. But you can't complain about stuff like that on an album where Freddie isn't there. It's an extraordinary triumph over anything else.

POPOFF: How about the title track, which naturally becomes a centerpiece of the album?

MYERS: First off, I think it's one of the finest produced songs they ever did. It's glorious. It's one of Freddie's solo tunes that was kind of underproduced. I think he wanted to put an orchestra on and he did put on a piano doing a little semitone riff. Even when it was born, it sounded like it was begging, back in 1985, for Queen to do their version. It felt slightly under-realized on Freddie's solo album. You could feel that he had hopes for it, but I don't think it quite came off the same way that it does with Queen. It's quite easy to let those lyrics sort of wash over you because they can be viewed generally. But you do start to feel there is an agenda of legacy coming through. Also, I think Brian and Freddie dovetail so nicely in terms of guitar and voice.

POPOFF: And what's the story of "Heaven for Everyone"?

JENKINS: After *A Kind of Magic*, they were working on solo projects, having a little break from each other and doing their own things. Freddie started recording with Montserrat Caballé, and so when Roger put The Cross together, he probably thought, I've got this song, "Heaven for Everyone," but it's too good to just leave alone. And in the UK and Europe, he decided to use the Freddie vocal on the album, where for North America, Roger did the lead single himself. The first time I heard it, I was like, "What?! That's Freddie?!" A nice surprise.

Pink vinyl edition of "Too Much Love Will Kill You" b/w "We Will Rock You" and "We Are the Champions," 1996. Written by Brian, "Too Much Love . . ." was written prior to the sessions that produced *The Miracle*.

TOO MUCH LOVE WILL KILL YOU

But it was such a strong song and it has Queen written all over it, and the band decided to include it on *Made in Heaven*. In the UK and elsewhere, it was the first single lifted for the album. America got "Too Much Love Will Kill You" and then they got "Heaven for Everyone" later in the summer. It's one of these nice, easy-listening songs, much like "These Are the Days of Our Lives." Roger seemed to be able to write that type of tune, good for the radio.

POPOFF: How about "Too Much Love Will Kill You"? What's its pedigree?

JENKINS: Brian was going through some upheaval in his life. And he went to Los Angeles and stayed with a couple of friends and they ended up writing a song together. He took it to Queen as they started recording *The Miracle*. Freddie really liked the song and Queen indeed recorded "Too Much Love Will Kill You," intending it for the album.

But that's when they made the decision to credit all the songs to Queen. And then of course, Brian, had to say, "Um, I didn't write that one myself. I wrote it with two other people, namely Elizabeth Lamers and Frank Musker." So, it was like, we can't put it on the album because all tracks were to be written by Queen. So "Too Much Love Will Kill You" was taken off *The Miracle*. "All God's People" was not used either. That was supposed to be on *The Miracle* and that was written by Freddie and Mike Moran, left over from the *Barcelona* sessions.

POPOFF: And an important lyric, historically speaking, is "A Winter's Tale."

MYERS: Very postcard-y lyrics, notwithstanding that they are Freddie's last lyrics. I believe it's the last complete song he wrote and recorded and I think he did it in one take. He just walked in having written what he was doing, what he was feeling and what he was looking at. I wasn't sure when I first heard it because of the nature of the lyrics. I'm wary of list lyrics. And he drew us up a list of observations. And their video even echoes it. It's like they're writing on a postcard.

But as the last song he recorded, here's a man facing his own death. He's already looked at it down the barrel with "The Show Must Go On." He knew what he was doing when he recorded those lyrics. And "Mother Love," he's going to record later than this. But here he is, in the same way that when he recorded "The Miracle," he's choosing to look at the positive. He's choosing to look at stuff that he personally finds beautiful.

There's an amazing book, *The Singing Detective*, written by someone else who was also staring death in the face, a screenwriter named Dennis Potter. He was really big in England, and he had a little bit of lead time and knew it was coming. He said that you just don't have the focus of how beautiful the world is around you until you realize it's about to go. Then you get a real perspective.

And for someone who isn't in that position, it's easy to write off "A Winter's Tale" as sentimental. And it's valid if that's what you feel. But for me, I grew into the song realizing that this is the crystallization of someone who is at the very end of his life and to whom the beauty and simplicity of life is revealed. And what to most might be mundane, Freddie is describing with this sharpness of focus.

But he also makes a separation in those lyrics—that his world is different. He says my

world is spinning and spinning and spinning, am I dreaming? And he looks out and sees this world. It's almost like there's a glass sheet separating him from the world he's describing and the world he's in. It wouldn't ever be a song that I would jump to as one of my all-time favorite Queen songs, but in context of the album and the legacy of the man's work, I think it's remarkable.

POPOFF: I suppose it's fitting that we close with a look at the closing untitled ambient track. Although, there are in fact lyrics, are there not?

MYERS: Yes, well, "Are we running yet?" I think is the lyric, and then "Fab." You start off with "It's a Beautiful Day (Reprise)" which leads into this, which, I don't regard those tracks as particularly separate. For this version, the band is there, it's a galloping guitar, it's galloping drums, Freddie's riding it out.

But then I wasn't expecting ambient at the end of Queen's last album—at all! And yet in some way it's perfect. It was Dave Richards who put the whole thing together and then Queen realized, okay, now this works, we're going to go with this, and they added and helped out a little bit. It's very moving, but it isn't all uplifting and a golden escalator to heaven. It feels unwell at times, slightly delirious.

But then there's "Are we running?" and a moment where Freddie's laugh becomes sampled and then resampled and then it becomes a rhythmic engine. It moves into the *Thus Spoke Zarathustra*, sort of *2001* thing, building into the light-rushing-toward-the-tunnel climax. It's beautiful when you get that energy of his laugh and it's also so heartbreaking. When you first hear his voice, saying, "Are we running? Are we running?" and then his tiny little laugh becoming this engine, I just found it really moving contrasted against the way that "Mother Love" showed us that he had been this stadium god, you know, shouting and beckoning at the audience with a call and response and then the whole world singing it back to him.

In total, it feels like a sort of twenty-three-minute ambient play, with this laughter that becomes this rhythm that becomes this great big breaking out into transcendent experience. There's no other way to describe it. What's so sweet is it really seems like an offering to Fred. They're filling up every minute they had on that CD. There wasn't a spare second available to put anything else on.

And yes, it feels like Freddie signing off, and yes, it feels positive and spiritually uplifting. I think, ultimately, it's a fortuitous work of art that they crafted brilliantly. There are things that make me frown about the album; Freddie's voice is missing in a few harmonies and it breaks your heart. It sounds empty, not how you want it to sound, but you realize it can't. There are moments where you see that the dream is over.

But when Freddie says "Fab" at the end, it's like he's approving it. He's signing off to his band, saying thank you. And it's nice for us to hear him say "Fab." It's nice that he has the last word. It's so simple and heart-warming and it never fails to move me.

POPOFF: Jim, what emotions do you experience when you hear this closing piece?

JENKINS: Everyone has a different opinion on what that's about. For me, it's a journey. You're traveling and it builds and it builds, and then it ends. Is it the light you see ascending to heaven? If you're religiously inclined, maybe so. When it finishes, it's taken you to where you want to think it's taken you. Or it's taking Freddie. Is it Freddie's journey and you're sharing it with him? It's very strange and, in fact, I don't think they've talked about that track. And then when you finish it, it's where you think you go when you pass. Some people think you go to Heaven, some

ABOVE: Freddie Mercury
Tribute Concert for AIDS
Awareness, Wembley
Stadium, London,
April 20, 1992.

OPPOSITE: A regally attired
Freddie raises a crown during
a performance in 1986.

people think you go nowhere. We don't know, do we? Because nobody's ever come back to tell us.

And then "Fab." Very strange, isn't it? Yeah, I'd say he'd say he had a fab life. And he's become the legend that he wanted to be in life. The three guys in Queen know him better than anybody else, and they probably felt, yeah, he would say this is fab. Doing this album. Getting the songs out. He worked so hard to do those songs. They had to be released, didn't they? At some point. They had to be; otherwise, it would've been a waste. He worked hard in the studio to give them a recorded vocal. Fab. Well done, Fred.

Freddie obviously loved what Queen gave him. It gave him wealth, it gave him that fab life. But he did always think of fans, and that's an important message to get out. The fan club, they have an annual convention, and Freddie would give clothes for a charity auction. He loved people dressing up as him. And he loved people congregating together for him. He loved giving. And I think that's what life is all about, giving of yourself to people. Some of us are gifted. Some of us have a talent that is ridiculously crazy, and that was Freddie.

He did as much as he could in the time allocated to him. I think he was much more ill than people realized. And then it came to a time when he could do no more. We lost such a talented artist. I find it strange talking about him all these years on. It just proves how the man said, "I'm not going to be a star, I'm going to be a legend." And he did—he achieved that. He's always going to be around. Every few years there's a new generation and Queen get in there and youngsters seem to latch onto them. Freddie's got an immortality few people will ever have. And it's so like Freddie that the last thing we hear from him is "Fab." Which says so much, doesn't it?

ABOUT THE AUTHOR

MARTIN POPOFF At approximately 7,900 (with more than 7,000 appearing in his books), has unofficially written more record reviews than anybody in the history of music writing across all genres. Additionally, Martin has penned nearly eighty books on hard rock, heavy metal, classic rock, punk rock, and record collecting. He was editor in chief of the now-retired *Brave Words & Bloody Knuckles*, and has contributed to *Revolver*, *Guitar World*, *Goldmine*, *Record Collector*, bravewords.com, and lollipop.com. Martin has been a regular contractor to Banger Films, having worked on the award-winning documentary *Rush: Beyond the Lighted Stage*, the eleven-episode *Metal Evolution*, and the ten-episode *Rock Icons*, both for VH1 Classic. Martin currently resides in Toronto and can be reached at martinp@inforamp.net or martinpopoff.com.

ABOUT THE CONTRIBUTORS

CHRIS CAFFERY rose to fame as guitarist for East coast prog metal legends Savatage, appearing on four records with the band. Through that band's association with composer and conceptualist Paul O'Neil, Chris became a natural choice for guitarist in a new heavy metal Christmas idea O'Neil had dreamed up called Trans-Siberian Orchestra. With O'Neil's passing in 2017, Caffery became spokesman and de facto leader of the TSO empire. Chris has also recorded on several releases as a guest musician and toured as a solo artist and as guitarist for the legendary German metal vocalist Doro. Chris also appears regularly with eighteen-time Grammy Award winner Jimmy Sturr. Other ventures include personal and online guitar instruction, book writing, painting and sketching, photography, musical production, and public speaking.

RALPH CHAPMAN was writer and producer for a series on Canada's national broadcaster CBC telling the story of the network's legendary music and video archive. Previously, he served as writer and associate producer on the VH1 series *Rock Icons* and on the critically acclaimed eleven-part series *Metal Evolution*. Ralph was also part of the creative team behind the Juno Award–winning documentary, *Rush: Beyond the Lighted Stage*. Ralph continues to work with Iconoclassic Records as a project producer, notably overseeing the reissue of the Guess Who catalog. He continues to develop projects with Banger Films and with his own production company, Wesbrage Productions.

STEPHEN DALTON began his writing career at *New Musical Express* at the dawn of the 1990s. During his absurdly long tenure on the paper, he survived acid house, Madchester, grunge, Britpop, electroclash, New Grave, New Rave, and at least four 1980s synth-pop revivals. Since the late 1990s, he has been a regular contributor to *The Times*, *Uncut*, *Scotland on Sunday*, and various other publications. In 2008, he began writing about music and film for *The National*, a new English-language broadsheet based in Abu Dhabi. Over the years, he has met some of the most charmless egomaniacs and demanding divas in the music business. He has also interviewed countless personal heroes, including David Bowie, Debbie Harry, John Peel, Mick Jagger, Chuck D, J.G. Ballard, Jarvis Cocker, Neil Young, Radiohead, Depeche Mode, and Kraftwerk. He has never had a proper job and, frankly, it's now too late.

From humble farm roots in rural Minnesota, **DAVID ELLEFSON** conquered stages around the world as bassist of thrash-metal titans Megadeth. Revered for his unique, hard-hitting playing style, and dedication to his craft, Ellefson has woven a vast professional tapestry as a bassist, songwriter, producer, clinician, and author. As a member of Megadeth, he received ten Grammy nominations, was awarded countless gold and platinum records, and toured the world for the better part of three decades. In addition, David has lent his talents to several other recording and touring projects, including Soulfly, F5, Temple of Brutality, Altitudes and Attitude (with Frank Bello of Anthrax), and Metal Allegiance (with Mark Menghi, Mike Portnoy, and Alex Skolnick). Ellefson holds a degree in marketing and lectures on a variety of music- and business-related topics. He has also ventured into other forays as president of EMP Label Group (Ellefson Music Productions) and with his own coffee brand, Ellefson Coffee Co.

JIM JENKINS has been a fondly regarded Queen insider for decades, having assisted with official fan club events and written articles for the fan club magazine and Queen's official site. Jim has also served as the band's de facto discographer and written liner notes for official Queen videos and compilations. As a world-renowned Queen expert, Jim has been called upon for commentary by TV and radio outlets around the world. He is also co-author, with fan club president Jacky Gunn, of the official Queen biography, *As It Began* (1992).

HANSI KÜRSCH is lead vocalist for Germany's Blind Guardian, who have gained a reputation as heavy metal's answer to Queen (even calling one of their albums *A Night at the Opera*). In addition, Kürsch has provided guest vocals on more than thirty albums and is part of the duo Demons and Wizards along with Iced Earth guitarist Jon Schaffer.

Referenced in the lyrics of the Queen song "Dragon Attack," **REINHOLD MACK** (a.k.a. Mack) is a German record producer and engineer renowned for his work with Deep Purple, Electric Light Orchestra, Sweet, Black Sabbath, Billy Squier, and Queen. In 1981, *The Game* brought Mack and Queen a Grammy nomination for Producer of the Year. Mack's third son, John Frederick Mack, was named by Freddie Mercury and was a godson of both Mercury and John Deacon. Mack's other credits with the band included *Flash Gordon*, *Hot Space*, *The Works*, and *A Kind of Magic*.

For the past twenty-five years, **ROGER MANNING JR.** has infiltrated television sets, radio airwaves, films, and dance floors worldwide. Many are familiar with Roger through original group endeavors such as Jellyfish, Imperial Drag, the Moog Cookbook, and TV Eyes. After 1993's well-regarded *Spilt Milk* album, Jellyfish were lauded as alternative rock's second coming of Queen. A gearhead of vast electrical knowledge, Roger has assisted artists such as Beck and Air in the studio and in live performances. He has worked as a behind-the-scenes keyboardist, vocalist, arranger, and songwriter with hundreds of artists ranging from Johnny Cash to Paris Hilton, and on films such as *Lost in Translation* and *Team America*. Roger has appeared on records from Morrissey, Glen Campbell, Cheap Trick, and Roger Waters.

PAUL McCARTNEY is a Beatle, a Wing, a family man, an all-around good guy, and one of the most prolific and successful performers in rock. Perhaps most commendable—over and above his bass, piano, guitar, drumming, and singing talents as applied to many of the most beloved songs in the rock and pop canon—is his work for animal welfare, which put him in touch with Brian May, who is similarly concerned with myriad animal rights causes.

Since 1984, **IAN MOSLEY** has been the dependable presence on the drum riser for UK progressive rock legends Marillion. Previously, he spent the '70s playing with the likes of Darryl Way's Wolf, Curved Air, Gordon Giltrap, Trace, and Steve Hackett. Marillion, through eighteen studio albums and myriad other releases, have sold fifteen million albums worldwide.

PATRICK MYERS plays a hugely effervescent Freddie Mercury in the world's top Queen tribute act, Killer Queen. After Freddie passed in 1991, the then-students at London university staged their own homespun one-off concert for students who, like them, had never seen a Queen concert. They were offered a residency in the West End and international dates quickly followed. Patrick's training as an actor and subsequent vocal training have helped him explore Freddie's vocals and performance style. Killer Queen are to date the only tribute to Queen to have sold out the same arenas as Queen and have become regulars at extraordinary venues across the United States, including Red Rocks and Austin City Limits.

DANIEL NESTER is an essayist, freelance writer, poet, writing professor, podcaster, and Queen super fan. Among other books, he is the author of the memoir *Shader: 99 Notes on Car Washes, Making Out in Church, Grief, and Other Unlearnable Subjects*, as well as *God Save My Queen: A Tribute* and *God Save My Queen II: The Show Must Go On*, collections exploring his obsession with a certain band of pomp and circus pants. As a journalist and essayist, Daniel's writing has been widely anthologized as well as published in *American Poetry Review*, *Salon*, *The New York Times*, *Buzzfeed*, *The Atlantic* online, and the Poetry Foundation website. Daniel is an associate professor of English at The College of Saint Rose in Albany, New York.

NINA NOIR performs as Frederica Mercury in the all-female Los Angeles–based Queen tribute band Killer Queens. Additionally, Noir was selected by Geoff Tate for the Queensrÿche twenty-fifth-anniversary *Operation: Mindcrime* tour after recording on the band's *Frequency Unknown* album. In June 2011, Nina appeared on *America's Got Talent*, receiving high praise from Sharon Osbourne. She has been trained by some of the world's most elite vocal coaches. She is a songwriter and lends a hand directing others' projects with writing, recording, and rehearsing for live performances.

JOHN NORUM is lead guitarist for Swedish rock titans Europe, whose 1986 album, *The Final Countdown*, was certified triple-platinum in the United States and produced the band's own "We Are the Champions"–like anthem with its title track. Norum has also played with Dokken and Glenn Hughes, and issued seven solo albums.

DARIUS RUCKER is one of rock's most inspiring kings of the second act. As front man for Hootie & The Blowfish, Rucker was catapulted to success with the band's 1994 debut, *Cracked Rear View* (sixteen million happy customers served), and the single "Only Wanna Be with You."

After five albums with the band, Darius reinvented himself as a country artist and has released four consecutive albums to top the Billboard Country albums chart while earning a new legion of fans. In 2014, Rucker won his third Grammy Award, this one for his cover of Old Crow Medicine Show's "Wagon Wheel."

DEREK SHULMAN is best known to music aficionados as lead singer for well-regarded Scottish prog-rock act Gentle Giant, who issued eleven studio albums from 1970 to 1980. Post prog, Shulman enjoyed a long and illustrious career as a record executive, beginning at Polygram, where he rose to senior VP and signed Bon Jovi and Cinderella, among others. In 1988, he became president and CEO of Atco Records, where he signed Dream Theater, before becoming president of Roadrunner Records and overseeing signings like Slipknot and Nickelback.

DEE SNIDER. You know him as lead singer of Twisted Sister, whose third album, *Stay Hungry*, shook America in 1984 with songs like "We're Not Gonna Take It" and "I Wanna Rock." Since then, Dee has been involved in numerous charitable causes, including Dee Snider's Ride, Bikers for Babies, Gibson Girl Foundation, Jam for Autism, and Station Family Fund. Dee has also appeared in movies (*Deepwater*, *Frozen*, *Pee-wee's Big Adventure*, *Private Parts*, *Strangeland*, Warning: Parental Advisory, and the documentary *We Are Twisted Sister!*), the internet (*Dee Snider Radio* and *Take Back the Horns*), and in the literary world (*Shut Up and Give Me the Mic* and *Teenage Survival Guide*). Musically, besides Twisted Sister, Dee has fronted Bent Brother, SMFs, Van Helsing's Curse, and Widowmaker, and released three solo albums. There's also been radio (*Fangoria Radio*, *House of Hair*, and *Metal Nation*), television (*Celebrity Apprentice*, *Growing Up Twisted*, *Holliston*, *Motorcity*, *Rock & Roll Roast*, and *SpongeBob SquarePants*) and theater (*Dee Does Broadway*, *Puppets Shakespeare*, *Rock & Roll Christmas Tale*, *Rock of Ages*, and *Twisted Christmas*).

RICHIE UNTERBERGER has been writing about rock and popular music for more than twenty-five years. Of his eleven books, the most recent at the time of this writing was *Bob Marley and the Wailers: The Ultimate Illustrated History*. Richie's other titles have examined the music of Velvet Underground, the Beatles, the Who, and '60s folk rock. Unterberger has presented events featuring rare rock films at such venues as the main public libraries in San Francisco, Seattle, Portland, Oregon, and San Jose, and at the Andy Warhol Museum and the Library of Congress in Washington, DC. Since 2011, he's taught courses on the Beatles, the history of rock music, and San Francisco '60s rock for the College of Marin's community education program. Richie was among the journalists interviewed for film documentaries on the Byrds, Tim Buckley, Frank Zappa & the Mothers of Invention, the Doors, Neil Young, and New York underground rock in the '60s and '70s. Richie lives in San Francisco.

JED WRIGHT is the founder of highly respected internet institution Classic Rock Revisited, now nearing its twentieth anniversary as provider of top-notch interviews, reviews, and news. Jeb is also a guitarist and an author, having created an anthology of his interviews while also working on a memoir and fiction. Jeb is based in Arkansas City, Kansas—which made it likely that Jeb would wind up buddies with the guys in America's best answer to Queen: a big, bearded band called Kansas.

AUTHOR BIBLIOGRAPHY

Iron Maiden: Album by Album (2018)

Pink Floyd: Album by Album (2018)

The Clash: All the Albums, All the Songs (2018)

Judas Priest: Decade of Domination (2018)

Popoff Archive—6: American Power Metal (2018)

Popoff Archive—5: European Power Metal (2018)

Lights Out: Surviving the '70s with UFO (2018)

AC/DC: Album by Album (2017)

Led Zeppelin: All the Albums, All the Songs (2017); expanded edition (2018)

Tornado of Souls: Thrash's Titanic Clash (2017)

Caught in a Mosh: The Golden Era of Thrash (2017)

Metal Collector: Gathered Tales from Headbangers (2017)

Rush: Album by Album (2017)

Beer Drinkers and Hell Raisers: The Rise of Motörhead (2017)

Hit the Lights: The Birth of Thrash (2017)

Popoff Archive—4: Classic Rock (2017)

Popoff Archive—3: Hair Metal (2017)

Popoff Archive—2: Progressive Rock (2016)

Popoff Archive—1: Doom Metal (2016)

Rock the Nation: Montrose, Gamma, and Ronnie Redefined (2016)

Punk Tees: The Punk Revolution in 125 T-Shirts (2016)

Metal Heart: Aiming High with Accept (2016)

Ramones at 40 (2016)

Time and a Word: The Yes Story (2016)

Kickstart My Heart: A Mötley Crüe Day-by-Day (2015)

This Means War: The Sunset Years of the NWOBHM (2015)

Wheels of Steel: The Explosive Early Years of the NWOBHM (2015)

Swords and Tequila: Riot's Classic First Decade (2015)

Who Invented Heavy Metal? (2015)

Sail Away: Whitesnake's Fantastic Voyage (2015)

Live Magnetic Air: The Unlikely Saga of the Superlative Max Webster (2014)

Steal Away the Night: An Ozzy Osbourne Day-by-Day (2014)

The Big Book of Hair Metal (2014)

Sweating Bullets: The Deth and Rebirth of Megadeth (2014)

Smokin' Valves: A Headbanger's Guide to 900 NWOBHM Records (2014)

The Art of Metal (co-edit with Malcolm Dome, 2013)

2 Minutes to Midnight: An Iron Maiden Day-By-Day (2013)

Metallica: The Complete Illustrated History (2013); updated and reissued (2016)

Rush: The Illustrated History (2013); updated and reissued (2016)

Ye Olde Metal: 1979 (2013)

Scorpions: Top of the Bill (2013);
        updated and reissued as *Wind of Change: The Scorpions Story* (2016)

Epic Ted Nugent (2012)

Fade to Black: Hard Rock Cover Art of the Vinyl Age (2012)

It's Getting Dangerous: Thin Lizzy 81–12 (2012)

We Will Be Strong: Thin Lizzy 76–81 (2012)

Fighting My Way Back: Thin Lizzy 69–76 (2011)

The Deep Purple Royal Family: Chain of Events '80–'11 (2011)

The Deep Purple Royal Family: Chain of Events Through '79 (2011);
        reissued as *The Deep Purple Family Year by Year (to 1979)* (2016)

Black Sabbath FAQ (2011)

The Collector's Guide to Heavy Metal: Volume 4: The '00s
        (co-authored with David Perri, 2011)

Goldmine Standard Catalog of American Records 1948–1991, 7th ed. (2010)

Goldmine Record Album Price Guide, 6th ed. (2009)

Goldmine 45 RPM Price Guide, 7th ed. (2009)

A Castle Full of Rascals: Deep Purple '83–'09 (2009)

Worlds Away: Voivod and the Art of Michel Langevin (2009)

Ye Olde Metal: 1978 (2009)

Gettin' Tighter: Deep Purple '68–'76 (2008)

All Access: The Art of the Backstage Pass (2008)

Ye Olde Metal: 1977 (2008)

Ye Olde Metal: 1976 (2008)

Judas Priest: Heavy Metal Painkillers (2007)

Ye Olde Metal: 1973 to 1975 (2007)

The Collector's Guide to Heavy Metal: Vol. 3: The Nineties (2007)

Ye Olde Metal: 1968 to 1972 (2007)

Run for Cover: The Art of Derek Riggs (2006)

Black Sabbath: Doom Let Loose (2006)

Dio: Light Beyond the Black (2006)

The Collector's Guide to Heavy Metal: Vol. 2: The Eighties (2005)

Rainbow: English Castle Magic (2005)

UFO: Shoot Out the Lights (2005)

The New Wave of British Heavy Metal Singles (2005)

Blue Öyster Cult: Secrets Revealed! (2004); updated and reissued (2009);
    updated and reissued as *Agents of Fortune: The Blue Öyster Cult Story* (2016)

Contents Under Pressure: 30 Years of Rush at Home & Away (2004)

The Top 500 Heavy Metal Albums of All Time (2004)

The Collector's Guide to Heavy Metal: Vol. 1: The Seventies (2003)

The Top 500 Heavy Metal Songs of All Time (2003)

Southern Rock Review (2001)

Heavy Metal: 20th Century Rock and Roll (2000)

The Goldmine Price Guide to Heavy Metal Records (2000)

The Collector's Guide to Heavy Metal (1997)

Riff Kills Man! 25 Years of Recorded Hard Rock & Heavy Metal (1993)

See martinpopoff.com for complete details and ordering information.

IMAGE CREDITS

A=ALL; B = BOTH; L=LOWER; T=TOP

Alamy Stock Photos: p4, Pictorial Press Ltd.; pp34–35, PA Images; p46, Pictorial Press Ltd.; p50, tracksimages.com; p64, VintageCorner; p69, Trinity Mirror/Mirrorpix; p99, Keystone Pictures USA; p137, Pictorial Press Ltd.; p151, Pictorial Press Ltd.; p155, Pictorial Press Ltd.; and p177, Trinity Mirror/Mirrorpix.

Frank White Photo Agency: p56, Laurens Van Houten; pp66–67, Laurens Van Houten; p109, Laurens Van Houten; and p117, Frank White.

Getty Images: p2, Michael Putland/Hulton Archive; p8, Michael Putland/Hulton Archive; p10, Michael Putland/Hulton Archive; p12, Michael Ochs Archives; pp14–15, Michael Putland/Hulton Archive; pp17, Michael Putland/Hulton Archive; pp22¬–23, Shinko Music/Hulton Archive; p24, Redferns; p27, Ian Dickson/Redferns; p32, Ian Dickson/Redferns; p37, Michael Putland/Hulton Archive; pp40, Shinko Music/Hulton Archive; p41B, Joseph Branston/*Guitarist Magazine*; p44, Chris Walter/WireImage; pp53, Shinko Music/Hulton Archive; pp71, Shinko Music/Hulton Archive; pp73, Gary Merrin/Hulton Archive; p75, Jorgen Angel/Redferns; pp76–77, Gus Stewart/Redferns; p82L, Joseph Branston/*Guitarist Magazine*; pp83–85, Michael Ochs Archives; p87, Steve Jennings/WireImage; pp88, Michael Ochs Archives; p91, Erica Echenberg/Redferns; p92, Ed Perlstein/Redferns; p93, Steve Jennings/WireImage; p95, Michael Ochs Archives; p101, Georges De Keerle/Hulton Archive; p102, Michael Ochs Archives; pp106–107T, Michael Ochs Archives; p113, Ed Perlstein/Redferns; p115, Colin Davey/*Evening Standard*; p120, John Rodgers/Redferns; p123, Michael Ochs Archives; pp126–127, Mirrorpix; p129, Michael Ochs Archives; p133, Shinko Music/Hulton Archive; p143, Steve Jennings/WireImage; p144, Steve Jennings/WireImage; pp148–149, Rob Verhorst/Redferns; p153, Patrick AVENTURIER/Gamma-Rapho; p154, Nigel Wright/Mirrorpix; p157, Mike Maloney/Mirrorpix; p158T, Shelley Watson/Getty Images Entertainment; p161, Michael Putland/Hulton Archive; pp162–163, Dave Hogan/Hulton Royals Collection; p165, Suzie Gibbons/Redferns; p166, Dave Hogan/Hulton Archive; p169, Rob Verhorst/Redferns; p171, Mirrorpix; pp172–174A; p175, Suzie Gibbons/Redferns; p179, David M. Bennet/Hulton Archive; pp185–186B, Michael Putland/Hulton Archive; p189, Michael Putland/Hulton Archive; p193, Tom Wargacki/WireImage; p194, Mirrorpix; p197B, John Rodgers/Redferns; p199, Mark and Colleen Hayward/Hulton Archive; p200, Michael Putland/Hulton Archive; p203, Mark and Colleen Hayward/Hulton Archive; p204, George Wilkes Archive/Hulton Archive; p207, Lex van Rossen/MAI/Redferns; p208, Lex van Rossen/MAI/Redferns; p210, Mick Hutson/Redferns; and p211, Dave Hogan, Hulton Archive.

Mediapunch: p43, Ian Dickson; p49, Ian Dickson; and p119, ©Kevin Estrada.

Rich Galbraith: p26 and p28.

Robert Alford: p58; p61; p81; p110; and p130.

Voyageur Press Collection: pp6–7A; p8; p11; p13; p16B; pp18–19A; pp20–21; p24; p29; pp30¬–31; p34B; p36; pp38–39A; p45; p47; p51; p52; pp54–55A; p57B; p59; p60; pp62–63A; p65B; p68; p70; p72; p74; pp78–79A; p82T; p86; p89; p90; pp96–98; p100; p103A; pp104–105; p107A; p108; p111; p112; p114B; p116B; p118; p121B; p122A; pp124–125A; p128B; p131A; p132B; p135; p136; pp138–142A; p145–147A; p150; p152; p156; p158L; p159B; p160; p164; p167; p168; p170; p176; p178B; pp180–184A; p187; p188; pp190–192A; p197T; p198; p206B; p209; p212; and p215.

INDEX

Brimming with creative inspiration, how-to projects, and useful information to enrich your everyday life, Quarto Knows is a favorite destination for those pursuing their interests and passions. Visit our site and dig deeper with our books into your area of interest: Quarto Creates, Quarto Cooks, Quarto Homes, Quarto Lives, Quarto Drives, Quarto Explores, Quarto Gifts, or Quarto Kids.

First published in 2018 by Voyageur Press, an imprint of The Quarto Group, 401 Second Avenue North, Suite 310, Minneapolis, MN 55401 USA. T (612) 344-8100 F (612) 344-8692 www.QuartoKnows.com

Voyageur Press titles are also available at discount for retail, wholesale, promotional, and bulk purchase. For details, contact the Special Sales Manager by email at specialsales@quarto.com or by mail at The Quarto Group, Attn: Special Sales Manager, 401 Second Avenue North, Suite 310, Minneapolis, MN 55401 USA.

10 9 8 7 6 5 4 3 2 1

ISBN: 978-0-7603-6283-9

Digital edition published in 2018
ISBN: 978-0-7603-6284-6

Library of Congress Cataloging-in-Publication Data

Names: Popoff, Martin, 1963- author.
Title: Queen : album by album / by Martin Popoff.
Description: Minneapolis, Minnesota : Voyageur Press, 2018. | Includes bibliographical references.
Identifiers: LCCN 2018025527 | ISBN 9780760362839 (paper over board)
Subjects: LCSH: Queen (Musical group) | Rock music—England—History and criticism. | Rock musicians—England.
Classification: LCC ML421.Q44 P66 2018 | DDC 782.42166092/2--dc23
LC record available at https://lccn.loc.gov/2018025527

Acquiring Editor: Dennis Pernu
Project Manager: Jordan Wiklund
Creative Director: Laura Drew
Cover Designer: Laura Drew
Design and Layout: Beth Middleworth

Printed in China